TO HAVE . . . AND TO KILL

"I believe you," the doctor said, "but don't know *what* I'm believing. This is all so strange. I've never seen anything like it. I don't know if anyone else ever has either. Of course, I'll see what I can do but . . ."

They all heard it at the same time. All eyes turned toward the wall beside the bed. Esther heard it too and her eyes opened wide.

Into the plaster of the wall, an unseen hand started to carve large letters. They were about a foot high, uneven but deep. The plaster fell away in hundreds of fragments as the letters appeared one after another. No one spoke. No one tried to stop the invisible writer as he gouged the wall with his terrible message:

ESTHER COX, YOU ARE MINE TO KILL!

MINE TO KILL

David St. Clair

SEAL BOOKS
McClelland and Stewart-Bantam Limited
Toronto

MINE TO KILL

A Seal Book / March 1986

For information address: Bantam Books, Inc.

ISBN 0-7704-2094-X

Seal Books are published by McClelland and Stewart-Bantam Limited. Its trademark, consisting of the words "Seal Books" and the portrayal of a seal, is the property of McClelland and Stewart-Bantam Limited, 60 St. Clair Avenue East, Suite 601, Toronto, Ontario M4T 1N5 Canada. This trademark has been duly registered in the Trademarks Office of Canada. The trademark, consisting of the word "Bantam" and the portrayal of a rooster, is the property of and is used with the consent of Bantam Books, Inc., 666 Fifth Avenue, New York, New York 10103. This trademark has been duly registered in the Trademarks Office of Canada and elsewhere.

PRINTED IN CANADA

COVER PRINTED IN U.S.A.

U 0 9 8 7 6 5 4 3 2 1

For ZELL DRAZ . . .
one of the world's great ladies

With Thanks . . .

No author writes a book alone, and the following people were a tremendous help in this one:

Peter and Diane Latta, curators of the Cumberland County Museum, Amherst, Nova Scotia; Miss Beverly True of the Amherst Public Library; Marguerite Mackenzie at Reid's Book Store in Amherst; Don Carr and Ron Curtis in the Amherst Town Hall; and Walter Maltby, Department of Records in the Amherst Court House. And special thanks, in Amherst, to Isabel Campbell for scouring old newspapers, legal documents, and vital-statistics files.

Thanks to Mary Lou Atleson of Cuyahoga Falls, Ohio, for genealogical detective word; and to the Historical Society of Pennsylvania Library in Philadelphia and the research department of Central College, Pella, Iowa.

Thanks to *Fate* magazine editor Mary Margaret Fuller; to psychic investigator D. Scott Rogo of California; and to my friend-advisor-author Guy L. Playfair, of London, England.

In Warren, Ohio, many thanks to Erin Burnsworth and Mona Stevenson of the Warren Public Library. A very special thanks to Warren librarian Lois Stephens for uncovering a needle in the haystack. Thanks to Ruth St. Clair for putting up with me. And thanks to Mattie Marie Brainard for her typing, her criticism, her friendship, and who would make any ghost look pale with or without a sheet. . . .

And, of course, Patrick Janson-Smith and Marian Armstrong of Corgi Books in London; their decision made it happen.

Read This First

This is a true story. The facts have been researched, the names verified, the happenings vouched for.

Esther Cox really lived—and really went through the horrendous things related here. She is not the figment of a writer's imagination. No author could deliberately invent what happened to her.

Her case, of rare and malevolent spirit possession, was the talk of tiny Amherst, Nova Scotia, Canada, when it happened. Crowds came to stare at the house. People moved off the street when she passed by. The local newspapers reported the strange happenings as her fame—and local curiosity and repugnance—grew.

Several "experts" looked into the story long *after* the manifestations ceased and came to various conclusions as to why it couldn't possibly be true. That loud poundings on the housetop (that awoke the neighbors and brought them into the street in their nightclothes) were "hysteria" or "hypnosis." The same bugaboos were the cause, the latter-day experts said, of the sudden fires, flying hymnbooks, and the terrifying message on the bedroom wall. Yet, thirty years afterward, sixteen prominent Amherst citizens swore that what Walter Hubbell had published was true. The problem with experts is that they have to come up with something, something significant and different. Each of them.

The story of Esther Cox is considered Canada's number one case of possession and exorcism. What I have tried to do in this book, is to bring the facts and the research to the public before the entire episode is dismissed as "superstition" and "folklore."

Esther Cox really lived . . . and the frightening part is that what happened to her could happen to any one of us.

Without warning.

Now.

PART ONE

Wednesday, August 28, 1878

Esther ran the brush over her dark brown hair as she stared at the street below. Bob said he would be around after work, and even though the shoe factory hadn't yet blown its quitting-time whistle, Esther paced the bedroom floor and kept glancing out the window. She was in the children's room. She couldn't see the street from her bedroom.

Esther couldn't believe her good luck. Bob McNeal! Of all people. Of all the young men in Amherst, *he* had taken a fancy to *her*! All the girls in town agreed that Bob was the handsomest and most charming and most elegant of all the young unmarried men. He had deep blue eyes and jet black hair and a smile that made a girl immediately feel that she had been stuck with pins and needles. He had a small moustache and an athlete's body. Esther blushed every time she recalled his body. A nice girl didn't notice such things, she knew, but she couldn't help recall how fine and trim he had looked in his bathing costume at the shoe factory gathering last month.

And here she was, eighteen-year-old Esther Cox, a little plump, a little too much chest, tiny feet and hands, and dull brown hair. Bob had never seemed to notice these defects. Instead he commented on her grey-blue eyes, her clear complexion, and her fine teeth. Yes, she did have nice teeth, and that fine complexion glowed even more each time she recalled his flattering words.

And to think he was going to take her out for a ride this very afternoon. He was going to borrow a horse and buggy and it'd be just the two of them. She spent the day planning what was going into the supper picnic basket and had roasted a small chicken, made potato salad and a square chocolate cake. She would fill a heavy glass flask with hot tea just before it was time to leave.

This was Esther's first real outing with a young man. Her older sister, Jennie, usually caught all the beaux's attentions, not she. While Jennie was outgoing and laughed in public, Esther was quiet and stayed around the house helping her married sister, Olive, with the housework and with the raising of her two sons. People who saw Jennie and Esther together—and didn't know them—never took them for sisters. It wasn't that Jennie commanded all the attention deliberately, it was just something about her that made people's eyes fix on her. If they took a third or fourth glance, it might fall on Esther. She knew people referred to her as "Jennie Cox's plain sister" and it bothered her, but when Bob McNeal saw her and her sister on the street a week ago, it was to *her* that he paid his compliments and flashed his smile, not to Jennie.

She turned to the small mirror hanging on the wall over the chest of drawers and patted the high lace collar that brushed lightly under her chin. She had tatted the lace herself, during her free time over the weekend, so she could add it to her best black dress. Bob had never seen her in this dress. The time at the factory picnic she had been wearing light blue cotton and the time he met her on the street she had her gingham on, partially covered with her long black shawl. Esther had another dress and debated whether to wear it because while it was a lighter material it was cut so low a person could actually see the bones at the base of her neck. Her sister Olive (as well as Olive's husband, Daniel) thought that dress was far too daring for a first time out with a young man.

Daniel wasn't very pleased that Esther was going on this outing with McNeal. McNeal worked at the shoe factory, where Daniel was a supervisor, and there was something about the young man that Daniel didn't like. Whether it was his confident attitude about his good looks, or his conversational tone that made him sound as if he knew absolutely everything, he couldn't say. The young man had appeared from nowhere one early spring day, applied for a job, and been hired. He didn't have family in Amherst. Instead, he boarded out with an elderly couple in a house on the edge of town.

Edge of town. Daniel smiled when he heard anyone use that expression because *all* Amherst, Nova Scotia, was the edge of town. You came to the edge of most side streets and you fell into the marshes. Literally fell in when the heavy spring and summer rains pelted the area. They started to dry out a little come autumn and were covered with snow all winter. Sometimes the wind blew up from the Atlantic Ocean, or across from the Bay of Fundy or down from the Gulf of St. Lawrence, and it always brought with it the worst of the rain and snow.

Amherst had come into being as a slightly hilly yet solid stopping-off place for coaches coming up from Halifax on their way into the rest of Canada. The marshes lapped around the base of this elevated spot, and the coach overnight station soon had a hotel or two, then some rustic wooden cottages, then a couple of general stores and a couple of factories; then the usual number of elected civic officials, a newspaper, attorneys, and churches. In a little over a hundred years it had grown into an active but isolated village of about thirty-five hundred people. It had a main street, named after the Queen, "Victoria"; two streets that came from the north: Laplanche and Lawrence; and two from the south: Havelock and Church. When the railway came in 1872 and a passenger station was built, they called that street "Railway Station Street."

The house that Daniel and Olive Teed rented (and where Esther paced and looked out the window) was on Princess Street. Number 6 Princess Street. Princess was brief and narrow, running only between Havelock and Church streets just down from Victoria. It was very convenient because the Amherst Boot and Shoe Factory was just a couple of streets away, on Victoria, so Daniel didn't have to walk far to work each day. It was close enough that he could come home for lunch and then return for the afternoon shift. His wife, Olive, could go with Esther to the greengrocers and the butchers quite easily. Their sister Jennie, who worked for a tailor, only had a three-block walk. But when the rains came or the snow was melting, those short distances became quagmires that made sucking sounds as people pulled their boots up out of the ankle-deep mud. In 1878 paved streets and sidewalks had been heard of, but in other places. They could not yet be seen in Amherst.

And, of course, there were no automobiles, running water, refrigeration; no electric lights or electric anything else; and no toilets that flushed.

Esther heard the whistle blow at the shoe factory and hurried down the wooden staircase into the kitchen. This room, warm in winter and stifling in summer, was in the back of the house. The sun came in only from one window over the dry sink. On dark days an oil lamp burned from breakfast to way past supper.

Olive Teed had just put a large pot of water on the stove to boil, adding chunks of wood and shavings to the fire underneath. Supper that night would probably be a bowl of soup and some homemade bread and butter. Folks didn't like to eat too much when it was warm, as it was this August afternoon. And besides, the family had eaten their main meal at noon. They always ate heartily at mid-day and then lightly at night.

Esther took a small pan of boiling water and poured some of it into a teapot. She stirred the tea leaves inside with a long wooden spoon, then put the lid on the pot and waited for it to steep.

"Have you got everything ready?" her older sister asked her, even though she knew Esther had been fussing over that food basket all afternoon.

"Yes, except for the tea bottle. It'll be ready before he gets here."

"Did you remember to put in napkins? You must have something to wipe your fingers on after the chicken."

"I took three of them from the linen closet," Esther smiled. "An extra one just in case."

Olive was sitting at the small kitchen table, using the time waiting for the water to boil, to mend a tear in her son Willie's shirt. At five years old, that boy was into everything. George, the baby at seventeen months, was still controllable, but Willie was impossible. "Where did you say Bob was getting the horse and buggy?" she asked Esther.

"I didn't say. I don't know. He just told me he'd borrow one from somebody. Probably from the old man where he lives." She lifted the teapot lid and stirred the contents again. "Olive, do you believe in dreams?" she asked.

"In dreams? Why?"

"Well, I had one last night. It knocked me out of bed." Esther smiled. "Jennie didn't hear me awaken, she slept fast all night. But in this dream I saw the paint on the house here become green."

"But it's painted yellow," Olive said.

"I know it's yellow," Esther replied, "but it turned into an awful ugly green and instead of *us* being inside, the house was full of bears. Bears that growled at me and had red eyes." She shuddered.

Olive laughed. "There are more than enough bears out in the woods that you don't have to invent them here in the house."

"I know," Esther said, "but the bears tried to get me and I ran to the front door and when I opened it, all of Princess Street was filled with huge black bulls. There were dozens of them and they had bright blue eyes and blood was coming from their mouths and they saw me and started for the house. Well, I closed the door but they kept on coming and they charged right through the fence in the front yard and came crashing right into the house and knocked it over. Then just as I could feel the house falling over, I fell out of bed and onto the floor."

"Were you hurt?"

"No, I was just surprised. And glad, too, that the bears and bulls hadn't been for real." She picked up the heavy glass flask with the screw-top lid and began pouring the hot tea into it. "What do you think it means?" she asked. "I've never had anything like that before."

"I think it means you have Bob McNeal on the brain," her sister said with a laugh.

"Bob? Bob has nothing to do with the dream."

"Well, I read in that ladies' magazine a few weeks ago where animals in dreams are sometimes symbols. You know, one thing that really means something else entirely." Esther nodded her head. She usually listened to her sister. Olive was older and married and was more like a mother than a sister. Their own mother had died just three weeks after Esther was born. "That magazine said that men sometimes appear like animals in a dream. They can be a fox or a bull, anything. Even a snake."

"I don't like snakes." Esther shuddered.

"I think," Olive said, "that you turned Bob McNeal into a bull. And he broke down the house."

Esther made a face. "Well, how silly! Why would he break down the house? Why would I want him to do that?"

"If everything is a symbol," Olive laughed, "then the house could really mean your *heart*, and you want him to come crashing into your heart."

"And bump my backside on the floor in the bargain?" Esther blushed slightly. "No, thank you. I don't want any rowdy boyfriends. The Gypsies and the Indian girls can keep those kind for themselves." She turned the cap on the flask. "I want a good man like the one you've got. I want a man like Daniel."

"There are few men like him," Olive replied softly. "I got one of the best."

"But you didn't get them all. There must be one or two like him still out there."

"One or two?" Her sister laughed. "You mean one isn't going to be enough?"

Now Esther did blush. "Oh, you know what I mean," she said. "Just one. One good one. That's all I want."

They both stopped to listen to the front door being opened. "That's your good man now," Esther said. "And mine should be here shortly."

Daniel Teed came down the entrance hall toward the kitchen, stopping just long enough to let the baby, in a portable crib in the cooler dining room, grab his finger and gurgle at him.

"Did you see Bob?" Esther asked.

"I did. As we were leaving. He told me he was going to his house to change and get the buggy. He should be here soon. He told me to tell you not to forget about the ride this afternoon." Daniel drank from a dipper of cold water in a crock by the sink. He sighed and wiped his lips. "I reminded him that you had to be home at a decent hour." Daniel smiled at his wife. "I don't want some Cinderella coming back without her shoe after the stroke of midnight."

"Daniel!" Olive's voice raised. "You certainly didn't tell Bob anything like that!"

"No." He smiled. "I just said that to see Esther's face get all red."

Esther put her hands to her cheeks. "You did it. They're burning up." She tried to look angry with her brother-in-law but it was difficult. She owed him so much. He had taken her in, given her a place to stay and food to eat. She could never repay him with anger; even half-hearted anger in fun.

Esther was sure that the next half hour had a hundred minutes in it as she waited for the sound of Bob's knock on the door. When it finally did come, she was upstairs putting the brush to her hair one more time.

Bob stood on the small porch, his light summer cap in his hands. "Evening, Mr. Teed," he said.

"Evening, Bob." Daniel stepped aside and motioned the young man to enter. "Esther!" Daniel shouted up the stairs. "Bob's here."

The girl glanced in the mirror again, smoothed the high collar under her chin, straightened the folds of the long black skirt, took a deep breath, counted to ten, then slowly descended the staircase. Again the red color rushed into her face when she saw how handsome he looked standing there waiting for her.

"Esther," he said, extending his hand.

"Bob," she replied, taking the hand.

Olive came out of the kitchen carrying the supper basket. She had put a red cloth on top and it looked almost like Christmas. Esther turned to her sister, glad for a reason not to keep staring at Bob, and took the basket.

"It feels like rain," Daniel said. "I hope you two won't get wet."

"Oh, no, sir," Bob answered. "The buggy has isinglass curtains. I can roll them down, but I don't think we'll have to worry. The clouds look like they're moving toward the north." Bob opened the front door, and Esther passed silently in front of him.

"Where are you planning on driving?" Daniel inquired.

"Just around. Maybe take the stage road. Maybe to the end of Church Street. I haven't decided yet."

"Well, you be careful," Daniel said. "Don't get too far away if you see the rains coming."

"No, sir. I won't." Bob crossed the front yard to the picket fence where the horse and buggy was tied to the iron hitching post. He took the basket from Esther, then helped her into the seat. He untied the reins, walked around the front of the horse, and got into the driver's seat. Esther glanced up once, saw both Olive and Daniel standing in the doorway, smiled shyly, waved, and glanced away. Bob slapped the reins on the horse's rump and the animal pulled away and started clopping down the hard dirt street.

"That's real nice," Olive said as she and Daniel walked back into the kitchen.

"What's nice?"

"Esther and that young man. She needs a gentleman caller. She needs to get out more."

"Well," said her husband, "I'm not real certain that Bob McNeal is the right gentleman caller for her."

"I'm not talking about anything *permanent*"—Olive lifted the pot lid to see how much hot water was left—"just a gentleman friend who is interested in her. No other boy seems to be interested. Not right now, anyway."

"She's only eighteen," Daniel scowled. "She has time yet."

"That's what I said—there are no other beaus right now. Besides, you started courting me when I was eighteen. Or don't you remember?"

"Those were the old days," he replied. "Things move too fast in these modern times."

"Esther can take care of herself, I'm sure."

"Well, I don't like that McNeal boy." Daniel scowled.

"That's good," his wife laughed, "because he wanted *Esther* to go buggying with him, not you."

* * *

When they got to the corner of Church Street, Bob turned the horse to the right and soon they were on the main street, Victoria. The shoe factory was on one corner, and the courthouse with its white wooden columns and gabled roof was on the opposite side of the street. There was a small park beside the courthouse and there had been talk of putting a bandstand there for outdoor music.

Turning right again, up on Victoria itself, Esther could see that most of the shops were closed. Hatchford's. Chapman & Etter's for clothing for the entire family. The post office. Greenfields. The Bank of Nova Scotia. Only Lamy's Hotel seemed to have any activity around it. Esther waved at a girl who had been in school with her. The girl, with her mother and a basket of groceries, waved back. Then they stopped and whispered to each other. Esther knew what they were saying: "Esther Cox out buggying with Bob McNeal!"

Bob waved to a couple of men who were waiting to cross the street. He wanted them to see the fine buggy he was driving and to see that he had a girl with him. They shouted something but it was lost in the noise of the horses' hooves. Esther was just as glad she didn't hear it, yet she was proud to be out and to be seen with such a handsome boy as Bob.

As they continued out on Victoria Street the commercial section fell behind. There were only houses now, large houses with porches and turrets and scrollwork along the roofs. Houses with front lawns and shade trees and barns for the horses and buggies. Mrs. Moore, sweeping the afternoon dust from her front steps, waved at Esther. They passed Willow Street, then passed the four large homes (two on each side of the street) where the Blacks lived. They were doctors, merchants, and one was the publisher of the *Amherst Gazette*. Esther had never been inside those houses. They were a little too grand for her. They were "society." The Freemans owned the last two houses on Victoria. China oil lamps burned in the front windows of each house. They were like beacons, puddles of golden light in the darkness, warning the unsuspecting traveler that he was coming to the edge of town. To the edge of civilization. After the Freemans', after their manicured lawns and picket fences, the speck known as Amherst was no more.

Bob kept the horse on the narrowing dirt road. The dusk of sunset tinged the marshlands with scarlet while frogs and crickets stopped their singing long enough to watch the buggy go by.

Esther didn't ask the question but Bob replied to it. "I thought we'd go out a little farther before turning back," he said. "Old Nita here needs the exercise." The girl murmured agreement and stared ahead to a horizon that was getting darker and dimmer. Not only was the sun going down but rain clouds were welling up. They might have to roll down those curtains after all.

The horse continued down the road and at times Esther had to hold on when the wheels hit a rock or sank into a hole. Bob glanced at the storm clouds and slapped the reins harder. Old Nita stepped up her pace. Esther sucked in her breath and held it, becoming concerned that with the darkness and the oncoming rain they were getting too far away from town.

"Don't you think it's best we turn back?" she asked, her voice raised over the rattle of the carriage.

He didn't look at her. "Turn back? Why?"

"It's beginning to rain. There, look. You can see the sprinkles hit the road. We don't want to get wet."

"I don't mind," he said.

"Well, *I* do," Esther replied. She had wanted all along to tell him she was wearing her best dress. "I don't like the rain," she added. "Not when I have my good dress on."

"Perhaps we can do something about that," he said and smiled at her.

"Yes, we can pull the windows down."

"Not the rain." He grinned. "About getting your good

dress off." Again the slap of reins, and the horse trotted even faster.

A stabbing sensation plunged into Esther's stomach and spread up into her face. Did he say something about taking her dress off? She must have misunderstood. The carriage was making so much noise. "We don't want to eat in the rain," she said loudly. She must have misunderstood him. "We can't have a picnic in the rain!"

"I'm not hungry." He grinned at her again, and the last few colors of the sunset glowed red and purple against his skin. "Not hungry for food, anyway."

"Well, I packed that basket," Esther went on. "You said you especially liked chicken. I have a chicken in there. And potato salad, too."

"And what do you have in here?" Bob stretched out his arm and cupped his fingers over Esther's left breast. In the shock they felt like hot iron tongs.

Her right hand came up instinctively and tried to pull his clutching hand away. "Bob!" was all she could find the strength to say. "Bob!"

He relaxed his grip and dropped his hand heavily onto her lap. Busy fingers started kneading the flesh under the black cloth of her skirt. It took both her hands to fling his one hand aside.

"Bob!" she screamed. "What's the matter with you?"

He grinned and slapped the horse even harder. The buggy bounced through the raindrops and the dusk a little farther. Abruptly he yanked the reins. Old Nita slowed, pulled back, reared up slightly, and stopped.

"All right," he commanded. "Out."

He jumped down on the road and ran around to Esther's side of the buggy. "Out!" he said. "Over there."

"What?"

"Get out!" he ordered. "We're going over there." He pointed to a grove of trees that were just visible in the deepening darkness.

The girl's head felt as if it were going to burst. "What's the matter with you? Have you gone daft?"

"I said out! Get out of the buggy!"

The moment of shock swiftly changed to anger. "I'm *not* getting out of this buggy! And you stop acting silly!" She was amazed at how commanding her voice sounded.

"I told you I wanted you to get out!" he shouted and grabbed for her ankle as if he was going to pull her out.

She swung around (and later she would wonder where she got the courage) and kicked him with her other foot. He felt the thud in his chest and the hardness of the road as he hit it. "Now stop playing the fool," she said. "Get back in this buggy and drive me home."

The young man sprang up from the ground and ran back to the driver's side of the buggy. Rummaging around under the seat, he brought out a revolver, and waving it ahead of him, he came back onto Esther's side and pointed the weapon at her face.

"Get out of this god-damned buggy!" His voice was low and guttural. "Now!"

"I'm not!" she shouted.

"I'll blow your god-damned head off!" the rough voice bellowed.

"You won't!" Her voice had risen to the edge of hysteria. "That would be murder!"

"I've done murder before," he snarled. "You won't be the first one. Now get down off that damned seat!"

It was the click of the hammer being pulled back that made her crumble. With that one small sound, all the reserve and courage emptied from her body. She still wasn't crying. The events were too unreal to bring on tears.

He grabbed for her ankle again and she didn't resist. She could barely see the gun that he held at her head, yet she was all too aware that it was, in the darkness, a reality. It was all she could do to muster the strength to shift her body so that both legs were in a position to jump onto the ground. As she moved, she felt his hand slide upward from her ankle. Up her shoetop. Up her stockinged calf. Up to that place where the thickness of one leg touched against the other.

"No!" she screamed and kicked out at him again. Again he went flying onto the roadway. She heard the gun hit. It made a different sound as it hit than he did. She knew he had lost the gun. At least for a moment or two. "Help!" she screamed into the nothingness. "Oh, God, help me!"

Then there were two sounds. One almost atop the other. The first was a clap of thunder that made the horse rear up. The second the rattle and clopping of another buggy approaching them. "Help!" she screamed again.

A sheet of rain swept over her. The next sheet carried the sounds of the approaching buggy. "Help me! Please!"

A new sheet of rain brought a new sound: "Hello . . ."

"Here!" Esther shouted. "Over here!"

The buggy dipped to one side, suddenly, as Bob climbed back behind the reins. Esther pulled herself into a far corner as the young man slapped the horse and pulled it around. Old Nita understood. She was going home. Good. She trotted around effortlessly and began a rapid clip-clop back the way she had come.

That was when Esther started to cry. With the full understanding of what Bob had tried to do came the racking sobs. They passed the other buggy that had been approaching, but Esther didn't need its driver anymore. In fact, she didn't want the man even to see who she was. She wanted to ask Bob "why?" but the words wouldn't form around the tears. The images in her mind shone again and again: his grin; his gruff voice; that gun. And the worst—that hand. The one that worked itself up between her legs. She could still feel it there. Still burning.

They were racing now, heading straight into the layers of rain as fast as the horse could gallop. The buggy was open and the water washed over her again and again. She was soaked through to her skin, yet she didn't want him to stop and put down the windows. She didn't want him to stop for anything until she was safe at home. The rain served another purpose: It washed her. It sprayed her, tried to cleanse away the awfulness of what had just happened. To remove the memory. To soothe the places where his hand had been. To wash away the sin of it all. Her sin.

They clattered down Victoria Street, which was deserted in the darkness of the rainstorm. Esther was glad there was no one to notice her and wave to her now. All the way back Bob hadn't said a word. And she couldn't make any words come from her own throat.

They reached Princess Street, and the reins were pulled in front of the Teed home. Bob grabbed the unopened basket of food and tossed it into the yard, spilling the carefully prepared contents over the lawn. Esther turned her body outward to descend and felt his hand on her back. He shoved, and she fell. Before she had a chance to glance back at him, the carriage was out of sight.

Esther never saw Bob again. Neither did anyone else in Amherst.

PART TWO

Wednesday, September 4, 1878

The supper dishes had been washed, toweled dry, and stacked away in the wooden kitchen cabinets. Both boys, Willie and George, had been put to bed. Olive and Daniel were in the front parlor, relaxing, talking, winding down from another day.

Esther was already in bed. The heavy fog that had rolled in yesterday had come back again today, making it difficult to see even the house on the other side of the narrow street. It seemed to folks that the fogs were arriving earlier and staying later than usual. Everyone burned wooden logs to heat and cook with. The shoe factory emitted great belches of smoke all day long from its brick chimneys. The train puffed in and puffed out amid its own smoke. Then the cold air crept into town, bringing clouds that sat on the smoke and kept it at ground level. No wonder that by eight-thirty the town had gone to bed.

"She still hasn't told you anything?" Daniel asked his wife.

Olive shook her head. "She just doesn't want to talk about it."

"She didn't give you any explanation at all? The crying and the broken picnic basket?"

"She hasn't offered and I haven't asked. I figure she'll tell me when she feels the time is right. We have no claim to pry."

Daniel got up and limped across the room. He was only thirty-five but a touch of rheumatism made him favor his left leg, especially on cold, foggy nights. He rubbed the windowpane and tried to peer out. "Sure is funny," he said. "McNeal never showed up for work the next day. Hasn't been heard from since."

"It's only been a week," his wife reminded him. "A week ago tonight. Maybe the boy went to visit his folks."

"In the middle of the night? Old man Rumsfeld said he moved out his two suitcases in the middle of the night. The horse and buggy were found at the station the next morning. McNeal is gone. Run away."

Olive stopped her knitting needles. "There hasn't been any talk about him and Esther, has there? You know, down at the factory? The way you men talk."

Daniel shook his head. "If there has been, I haven't heard it. 'Course, they know I'm her brother-in-law and they'd shut up if I came around, but I don't think anyone's linked Esther with his disappearance."

"Maybe there isn't a link, as you call it. Maybe the boy just decided to go away and Esther is heartbroken because he's gone. Girls are like that," Olive said. "I know if I had a crush on a boy and he took me out one day and vanished the next, I'd feel badly."

"Then you'd think she'd want to explain it that way," Daniel replied, "instead of shaking her head and getting all teary-eyed whenever the subject is mentioned. She can't keep holding it in forever."

"She won't," his wife answered. "One of these days when she feels like it, she'll tell us."

Daniel turned back from the window and ran his hand over his light brown moustache. "You don't suppose that fellow tried to—"

"Tried what?"

"To . . . well, you know."

Olive put her knitting into a small canvas bag and dropped the needles in after it. "For heaven's sake, don't be silly. You *have* been listening to shop talk! I'm her sister. I should know. If anything like what you're thinking had occurred, I'd be the first one she'd tell." She picked up the oil lamp from the table. "Now let's go to bed. It's getting late and that imagination of yours is running on steam power! My sister is a good girl. Why, the very idea of it is ridiculous."

As they headed for the stairs, Olive lit a candle on a small table in the entrance hall. It was for Jennie, who was out visiting a friend. Olive liked her to have some light when she came home late like this. Then they went up to their bedroom, Olive going first because it always took Daniel's leg a little longer in this kind of weather.

The upstairs of this small cottage—that Daniel didn't own, but only rented from a Mr. Joseph Fillmore—contained four bedrooms. Someone standing in front and looking at the house could see Olive's shadow from the oil lamp in the upstairs window to the left. The other front window, dark now with the shade pulled, was the room where the two small boys slept. There were no windows on either side upstairs, so a person would have to go around back to see the windows of the other two bedrooms. One room was for Jennie and Esther, and the other room was rented out to "boarders." Right now relatives had it: William Cox (the only brother of Olive, Jennie, and Esther) and John Teed (a brother of Daniel's). Both young men slept in the same bed and worked in the same place: the Amherst Boot and Shoe Factory. They paid rent and took most of their meals at the house. The extra income was greatly appreciated by Daniel and Olive. Eight people lived and slept in the small cottage. There was a hall space around the staircase but no bathroom, of course. The "facility" was in the backyard, beyond the woodshed. Because of the mighty cold weather most of the year, no one ever spent longer than was necessary in the outhouse.

After Daniel was in bed, Olive turned down the lamp and lay there in the darkness listening for the front door to open. After a few minutes, the two boarders arrived and clumped rather heavily up the stairs. There must have been beer somewhere, she thought, smiling to herself. Shortly after that she heard her sister Jennie open the front door, pause long enough to take the candle, and come quietly up the stairs. When she heard the bedroom door close, Olive adjusted her pillow, pulled the light blanket up around her shoulders, and went to sleep.

Esther didn't hear Jennie come into the room or get into bed, but ten minutes later Esther's eyes opened wide. She lay there for a minute, waiting, then it came again. That feeling.

She jumped out of bed and started beating at the bedclothes. It was all she could do to stifle the scream that was welling in her throat.

"Jennie," she said anxiously. "Jennie, wake up."

The older girl, having just fallen asleep, was groggy. "What . . . ?"

"Jennie! There's a mouse in the bed! Get up!"

Jennie's eyes opened wide. "A mouse?" In a split second, she had bounded out from under the covers and was searching for a match to light the lamp.

"It's here!" Esther said. "Right here!"

Jennie shone the lamp in the direction her sister pointed. Sure enough, something was moving in the straw under the mattress ticking. Jennie held the light while Esther slapped at it with her hand.

The movements stopped.

"It can't hurt us in there," Jennie assured her sister. "Come on, let's get back to sleep."

The girls, tucking their long white nightgowns around their legs, got back into bed. They lay quietly for a few mintues, straining to catch any noise or movement of the uninvited mouse. Finally, they agreed that it must have gone. Jennie blew out the lamp. Soon they were both asleep.

Thursday, September 5, 1878

In the morning, Esther and Jennie agreed not to mention the mouse to Olive. Their sister hated mice and would have spent all day dragging the mattress into the backyard and beating it until she was sure the rodent had gone.

Breakfast was served in the dining room (there just wasn't room for an eating table in the kitchen) and the workers went off to their jobs—Daniel and William and John to the shoe factory, and Jennie to Dunlap's tailor shop.

The day was filled with the usual: Esther and Olive went shopping and cooked a hearty meal for the workers, who came home at mid-day. Then those dishes were washed and put away. The house was cleaned, some clothes were washed, others were ironed, others were mended, others taken in or let out. Then supper was prepared, which meant more dishes, pots and pans, and utensils that got dirty and had to be washed and put away. And, of course, amidst it all was the care and feeding and watching and loving of the two small boys.

The fog rolled in again that night, long before Esther and Jennie went to bed. The night air was chilly, so both girls put on their flannel nightgowns. Jennie had just turned out the lamp when they both heard the sound.

"Shhh!" said Jennie. "It's the mouse again."

Esther listened. "It is! But I don't think he's in the mattress."

"No, sounds more like underneath."

"In the box of patchwork scraps."

Jennie reached over to the oil lamp and quietly lit it. Each girl, placing a finger over her lips to tell the other not to make a sound, got out of bed slowly. They listened. No doubt about it, the sounds were coming from *under* the bed.

Jennie bravely reached in and grabbed the side of the green pasteboard box that held cloth scraps for mending and patches of material saved for quilts. She held the box out at arm's length and made a face as if she had the mouse by the tail. Carefully she set the box in the middle of the room.

Instantly, the box jumped into the air about a foot, then fell to the floor and tipped over, spilling some of the cloth pieces on the rug.

The girls looked at the box, at each other, and then back at the box.

"Did you see that?" Jennie whispered. Esther nodded her head. Jennie crept up on the box, careful to avoid any contact with the mouse inside, and turned it right side up.

The box immediately rose into the air, twisted onto its side, and fell back onto the floor.

Both girls screamed at once. That's the way Daniel found them, in the center of the room, holding on to each other and screaming. He could hear their screams all the time he struggled to get into his pants and a suit coat.

"What in blazes is going on?" he demanded.

"That box," Jennie said, trembling.

"It acted funny," Esther said in the same tone.

"It has a mouse in it," Jennie added.

"The mouse made it jump into the air," Esther continued.

"Now, wait a minute," Daniel said and walked over to inspect the box. He picked it up and rummaged his hand through the scraps. "There's no mouse in here," he said.

"There *was*," Jennie said. "It made the box jump."

"In the air," Esther added.

"No mouse can make this box jump in the air," Daniel replied. "That's impossible. And there's no mouse in here now. Where did he go?"

"He must have run away," said Jennie.

"And he *did* make the box jump," Esther insisted. "We saw it."

"Well," Daniel said, "you probably frightened him just the way you frightened me! Now you've either both been dreaming the same dream, or else you're both going crazy." He set the box back on the floor. "Go back to bed and let people get some sleep." He left the room, closing the door behind him.

"There *was* a mouse in there," said Jennie. "I saw the box move."

"I did, too," Esther replied. "It jumped twice."

They got back into bed and Jennie turned down the lamp. "Daniel says he thinks we're crazy," she giggled. "Too bad the mouse wasn't under the scraps when he stuck his hand in there."

"Wouldn't that have been something?" Esther snickered. "Can you imagine the expression on Daniel's face when the 'imaginary' mouse bit him?"

"Too bad it wasn't a snake," Jennie laughed.

"Or an elephant!" Esther giggled out loud.

"Shhh," Jennie cautioned, "or he'll be back in here with a net to take us to the looney bin."

"Maybe the elephant will get him first." Esther had to turn her face into the pillow to quiet her laughter.

The girls fell asleep. The box remained where Daniel had set it down in the middle of the room. Once during the night, the box moved, turned, and slid closer to the bed.

Friday, September 6, 1878

Esther refilled Daniel's coffee cup and pushed the sugar bowl closer to him. "There *was* a mouse in there, I tell you. We could hear it scratching and moving about. It was there the night before in the mattress, and it was in the box last night."

"We weren't dreaming, Daniel," Jennie said. "We both heard it."

"Well, what happened to it?" William Cox, their brother, asked. "Did you see it get away?"

"We didn't see it," Jennie said, "but it must have escaped while we were screaming, or else Daniel would have found it."

"Or the elephant," Esther giggled.

"What elephant?" Willie asked. Suddenly the five-year-old was interested in the conversation.

"Nothing," Esther said, laughing. "Just a joke."

"Was there an elephant in their room, Ma?" Willie asked Olive.

"Of course not," his mother replied. "That room's too small for an elephant. A mouse is just about the right size."

"Maybe the mouse escaped into your room, Olive. Maybe

he's hiding in a pair of your shoes just waiting for you to put them on." This from Daniel's younger brother, John.

Olive shuddered and involuntarily shuffled her feet. "He'd better not be, or you'll hear a yell that will make the shoe-factory whistle sound like a whisper. I hate mice!"

"There was no mouse there," Daniel said. "It was a lot of foolishness on the girls' part. Now let's be done with the subject before you have Olive passing the broom under all the furniture."

"With a baseball bat in the other hand," laughed William Cox.

"Bam!" shouted Willie. "Bam! Squish! Slam! Blood and guts all over the floor!"

"Willie," Jennie pretended to be shocked. "You are horrid. Stop talking like that when people are trying to eat their breakfast."

Olive reached over and grabbed Willie's hand. He was splashing his spoon into his oatmeal. "That'll be enough, young man. If you've finished with your breakfast, go on out and play."

"And take your mouse with you," Esther said.

"It's not my mouse," the boy replied. "You two invented him."

* * *

It was a normal day and it passed normally in Amherst. The family went to work, Esther and Olive went shopping. After the noon meal was served and the kitchen put back in order, Esther took a stroll along Victoria Street and stopped at the post office for a stamp and at Bird's Book Store for a bottle of ink. She would have walked longer, but the winds blowing in from the bay blew clouds of dust from the street into her face.

After supper, Esther complained that she didn't feel well. She had a headache and was feverish. She said good night to everyone and went to bed. That was at eight-thirty.

At ten o'clock, Jennie came to bed. Before she turned out the lamp, she placed her palm on Esther's forehead to see if she still had a fever, but the girl was cool. Esther, sleeping so peacefully and with her short brown hair spread out over the pillow, looked like an illustration from one of the Sunday school magazines. Jennie lay down, pulled the blanket up around her neck, and closed her eyes.

For fifteen minutes, the bedroom was calm.

Suddenly Esther screamed and sat up. She clutched at her face. In an instant she was out of the bed, taking sheet and blanket with her, standing in the middle of the room. "Oh, my *God*!" she cried. "Oh, my God!"

Jennie awoke instantly. "What's the matter?" she called. "Esther, what's the matter?"

"Oh, my God!" the girl screamed. "I'm dying! Please, dear God! I'm dying!"

Jennie fumbled for the matches, finally found them, and lit the lamp. There stood Esther, in her long nightgown, grasping the back of a chair. Jennie stared in disbelief, for her sister's short brown hair was standing straight out, as if a lightning bolt had gone through her. Esther's usually pale complexion was blood red. Her eyes bulged from their sockets.

"Help me! Oh, my God! What's happening?" She shouted but the words came out of her swollen throat thick and garbled.

Jennie jumped up and grabbed her sister, then pulled her hands away quickly. "You're burning up!" she said. "Your body's on fire!" She grabbed Esther's face, trying to hold the bobbing and twisting head between her hands. "Esther!" she screamed. "What's happening to you?"

The bedroom door burst open. It was Olive, wearing a shawl over her nightdress. Daniel, in his trousers and suit coat, was right behind her. They both stopped short, staring at the girl.

"Her *fingers*, Daniel!" whispered Olive. They had turned fiery red and had sunk into the wood on the back of the chair.

William Cox and John Teed then rushed into the room. Both had stopped to put on their trousers and suit coats. It would not have been proper to go into the girls' bedroom in just their nightshirts.

"She's mad!" William said aloud. "Look at her. She's lost her mind."

Esther's head rocked back and forth. Her protruding eyes stared blindly around the room. A dark brown fluid ran from the corners of her mouth.

Daniel ran behind the girl and encircled her waist with his arm. "Let's try to get her back into bed," he said.

William quickly grabbed Esther's feet and helped Daniel

lift her off the floor. The chair she was clutching rose as if it were weightless. John Teed tried to pry her fingers from it but she wouldn't release her grip. Then the chair fell, Esther crumpled, and they carried her easily to the bed. She didn't want to lie down and made motions for them to let her sit up. They stepped back and she raised her body, swung her legs over, and sat on the side of the bed. She didn't cry. She didn't make a sound. Her eyes looked normal now.

"Are you all right?" Olive asked her, placing the blanket around her shoulders.

Esther stared vacantly as if finding herself in an unknown place surrounded by strangers.

Jennie put her hand on Esther's forehead. "The burning's gone," she said. "She feels normal."

"Esther, what are you feeling?" Olive asked. "Can you tell us?"

"Can we get you something?" Jennie asked.

"Do you want us to call the doctor?" Daniel asked.

The loud voice boomed out of the teenage girl: "No doctor! I don't like doctors!" With that she jumped up from the bed and ran toward the door. William and John were right behind her, grabbing her and pulling her back before she could escape.

"Let me alone!" the loud voice came from her body. "Take your hands off me!"

The two men struggled to get her back across the room and almost threw her onto the bed. Olive quickly covered her with the sheet.

"No!" Esther shouted and ripped the sheet from her. "I'm burning up! I'm going to burst! My God, what's happening to me?" It was her own voice this time.

Then the swelling started. It began with her hands, ballooning them to three times their size. Then her feet, normally small feet, increased in size, the skin stretching white around her toes and ankles. Then it was her legs. Even under the nightgown they could see her legs swelling and enlarging until they stretched the flannel material almost to bursting. The torso was next, filling up the nightgown. Huge breasts pushed at the material, popping the buttons at the throatline. Then the arms swelled out of proportion, then the neck, then Esther's face became unrecognizable as her cheeks puffed up, her nose broadened, and her lips enlarged and stretched across her face.

From somewhere in that enormous, grotesque teenage body, a voice managed to cry out: "Help me! For God's sake, help me!"

No one moved. No one said anything. Olive gripped her husband's arm. Jennie backed up until she felt the wall pressing against her. The two men had managed to get closer to the door.

The monstrous creature that had been Esther Cox filled the bed, its skin stretched white and bloodless. The only way it remained human was the soft, pitiable cries that came from somewhere deep inside it.

Then the room shook. First there was the rattling explosion, then the shaking of everything and everyone standing around the bed.

Olive was the first to react. "A lightning bolt! It hit the house!" She pulled away from Daniel and ran out of the bedroom. "My boys! I know it hit my boys!"

"Olive!" Daniel shouted and ran after her. The two men did the same. But in their bedroom both Willie and little George were sound asleep. Olive started to cry and Daniel put his arm around her.

"They're all right," he said. "Thank God, they're all right."

"Where did that noise come from?" William asked. "I don't think it's raining. I didn't hear any rain."

Olive hurried back into Esther's bedroom. The girl was still monstrously swollen on the bed. Olive raised the window-shade. They could all see the stars. "It's not raining," she said. "That wasn't a lightning bolt."

"What was it, then?" John Teed asked. "Dynamite?"

"It sounded like it was hitting the house," William added. "It jarred everything."

As if on cue, there was another explosion. Again it rattled the people and the things.

"It's from under the bed!" William said. "It's coming from there!" He bent down to peer under the bed when a third loud report sent him crashing against the wall. Olive screamed and grabbed for Daniel. Then a fourth report, not as loud this time, but definitely coming from under the bed.

"Look!" Jennie pointed to Esther, who started to deflate.

There was no sound, no scent, just the incredible sight of the girl collapsing onto herself and returning to normal. In a few seconds, the monster was Esther once again. She smiled at them, turned her head on the pillow, and instantly fell asleep.

Jennie sat up all night watching her sister.

Saturday, September 7, 1878

Esther deliberately stayed in bed until she knew everyone had gone to work. Jennie had given her a good-bye kiss but she had pretended to be asleep. She just didn't want to talk to anyone about what had happened.

When she finally came downstairs, Olive had gone out shopping and had taken the boys with her. Esther usually ate a large breakfast, but this morning she had no appetite. She made herself a cup of strong black tea and spread butter on a small piece of bread. As she put away her dishes, she had the urge for something sour. There was a crock of dill pickles fermenting in the basement. She went down, chose one of the biggest from the batch, and wolfed it down.

She avoided Olive for most of the day, ashamed of the way she had carried on. Ashamed that everyone had seen her in her bedclothes. Ashamed that she had kept the household awake most of the night.

When everyone came home for lunch, she made sure she was out walking. The air was crisp. Fall was on its way. She caught her breath. Mr. Rumsfeld was riding by in his buggy, being pulled by Old Nita. The sight of it flooded her senses, and she felt Bob's hand up between her legs. She turned abruptly away, staring at nothing in Hutchford's window. If Mr. Rumsfeld noticed her, he didn't call out. She was thankful for that.

That evening, after supper, Daniel and Olive, along with Jennie and Esther, finally got around to discussing what had happened the night before. The two boarders were out with their girlfriends.

Nobody had an explanation, least of all Esther.

They had all seen it. Had all seen the same things happen in the same order. They had compared notes, and what they had witnessed was real. Yet, at the same time, it *wasn't* real. There was no explanation for it. Yet they all saw it.

"I think whatever it was," said Daniel, "was beyond our intelligence. Beyond what we normally can understand."

"Maybe we're not supposed to understand it," Olive said. "You know, like it says in the Bible. There are many things in Heaven and on Earth that are mysteries to us."

"Last night certainly was a mystery," Jennie said.

"More like a nightmare," Esther corrected her. "A terrible nightmare. I just hope it doesn't happen again tonight." Tears started in her eyes.

"It won't," her married sister assured her. "It was one of those once-in-a-lifetime things. You've already had it in your lifetime."

"I hope so," the girl replied. "I'm still exhausted from it. I don't know what I would do if it happened again."

"I think we should resolve," Daniel stated, "not to speak of it anymore in this household. What's past is past, and it can do no good unearthing it again."

They murmured their agreement.

"And don't tell anyone else, either," pleaded Esther. "It's really nobody's affair what happened. Nobody's but ours."

"I agree," said Olive. "We should keep this right here at home."

Esther gave her sister a thankful smile and patted her hand. "I'm most appreciative," she said.

The clock chimed nine times. Jennie looked at Esther. "Are you ready to try the bed again? To *sleep* this time?"

Esther laughed, but it was a nervous laugh. "I am ready to try. I've been praying all day that nothing happens tonight. I hope God answers my prayers."

"I'm sure He will," Olive said, standing up. "Now, can I get anyone something before we go to bed? Daniel, some tea? Jennie?"

"You know what I would like?" Esther said. "I'd like a glass of something sour. Do we have any lemons? Some lemons squeezed in a glass of water would be wonderful."

Olive walked toward the door. "I don't think there is a lemon in the house, but let me see what I can come up with. Daniel, do you want some tea or not?" He shook his head no.

In a few minutes, Olive was back in the parlor. There was a glass filled with liquid in her hand and a spark of devilment in her eye. "Esther, you want something sour, try this." Her smile got broader as she handed the glass to her sister.

Esther took a sip. "Oh, fine," she said and took a larger sip.

"Esther!" Olive almost screamed. "That's pure vinegar! Don't drink that! I was just joking."

But Esther tipped the glass upward and drained the glass dry.

Wednesday, September 11, 1878

Sunday was peaceful. So was Monday, Tuesday, and all day Wednesday. Everyone in the house hoped they had seen the last of Esther's "illness." As they had made an agreement not to talk about it, nothing had been said aloud for four days, but everyone had thought about it, tried to figure it out, and was terrified it would return.

That night it did.

It was almost 10:00 P.M. Esther and Jennie had washed their faces in the bowl on the dresser, put on their nightshirts, and brushed their hair. Jennie always took longer with her hair because, unlike Esther's, it was long and lustrous and golden brown. Jennie got into bed and smoothed the covers around her. "Did you see those shoes in Hutchford's window?" she asked her sister. "The red ones?"

"I did," Esther said, pulling down the cover on her side of the bed. "I walked past there yesterday and couldn't believe my eyes. Can you imagine wearing *red* shoes?"

"In Amherst!" Jennie laughed. "Only one type of woman would wear such a scandalous thing in broad daylight."

"Do you think they'll sell them?" Esther asked.

"Not to anybody decent. Not here. Only a painted lady or an American would wear those things." Jennie had admired them but was too embarrassed to go in and price them.

Esther put one leg up onto the bed when suddenly her body was shoved face down into the pillow. She gasped in surprise and tried to right herself, but a pressure in the middle of her back kept her from moving. "Jennie!" she protested, thinking it was her sister's doings, but one sideways glance showed both her sister's hands atop the covers. "Oh, my God!" she moaned. "Not again!"

Jennie jumped out of bed and ran around to the other side. She grabbed Esther by her shoulders, trying to pull her up. The girl wouldn't budge. Esther was moaning now as the pillow slowly worked its way up and over her face. Jennie grabbed the pillow and tried to pull it away, tried to get her some air to breathe.

Jennie kept muttering, "Be calm, Esther darling. Just be calm. It'll stop soon." No matter how hard she tugged, she was unable to free the suffocating pillow from her sister's face.

Esther was sobbing now, gasping for air, and choking on her own saliva. "Jennie, help me. I can't breathe. Oh, God, Jennie, help me!"

Then, like a thing alive, the pillow slid out from over Esther. She gulped in the needed air. Unseen hands grasped her shoulders and quickly turned her over. She went from lying on her stomach to lying on her back as if she had been a flipped playing card. The sudden movement knocked Jennie to the floor.

The swelling began. More rapid this time. More frightening to Jennie, who could only watch and do nothing. The feet grew four times their size. Then the hands. Legs. Enormous thighs. Horribly distended belly. Massive breasts. Ballooning arms. Trunklike neck. And a face with its features smeared like a mirror in a sideshow.

Jennie grabbed the sheet and blanket and covered her sister's grotesque and pain-filled body. "I'll get help," she could only whisper. "I'll get some help."

As if in answer, the sheet and blanket rose into the air, wadded into a ball, and tossed themselves across the room.

Jennie screamed. She stood alongside the bed and screamed and screamed and screamed. Then she fainted.

Olive and Daniel were the first to come through the bedroom doorway. John and William were right behind them.

Olive didn't know where to look, where to begin first. One sister swollen out of all human proportion on the bed. The other sister unconscious on the floor. "Pick up Jennie," she heard her voice commanding. "Put her back in bed." Two of the men placed her carefully at Esther's side.

Olive went into the far corner and got the balled-up bedclothes. She shook them out and covered the girls. As she smoothed the blanket around Esther, the sheet and blanket were ripped off the bed again. They rose into the air, twisted themselves into a jumble, and tossed themselves right back into the same corner.

Olive screamed and the men gasped. Then the pillow that was under Esther's head came sailing out as if pulled by powerful hands. It hovered over Esther's form for a second, then turned, sailed through the air, and hit John Teed square in the face. The young man yelled and tried to pull the pillow away as it forced him to fall over backward, his shoulder and elbow hitting the wood floor with a thud. He rolled away from it but the pillow just lay there, silent and harmless. "I'm sorry," he said loudly, "but I'm not going to stay in here and get hurt." He left the room quickly.

"William," Olive ordered, still in command of the situation, "go down and get some water. Esther's burning up. Hurry now." Then to her husband, "Daniel, get those bedclothes and let's keep these girls covered up."

Daniel took the sheet and blanket from the corner, and after untangling them, Olive spread them over her sisters. This time Olive sat on one side of the bed and Daniel on the other, the weight of their bodies keeping the cotton sheets in place. At the top, near the girls' faces, the materials rippled and flapped as if they were caught in a brisk wind.

Jennie remained unconscious. Esther was moaning and trying to call out from her bloated prison of a body.

"Daniel, we've got to do something," Olive said. "This can't go on."

He nodded. "I'll go and see Dr. Carritte tomorrow. He'll know what to do." Then he added, "I hope."

"I pray!" Olive said.

William came running back up the stairs and into the room with a bucket of water. Just as he was about to place it beside the bed, there was a loud explosion. As before, the room and everything in it shook. The noises came from under the bed. A second report was heard. Then a third, less loud, followed. The bucket of water rose into the air, floated directly over William Cox, tilted, and dumped its contents all over him.

Esther laughed, immediately lost her swelling, and fell asleep.

"Dr. Carritte tomorrow," Olive told Daniel. "Definitely."

Thursday, September 12, 1878

"Now, Daniel," Dr. Carritte said with a smile, "you really can't expect me to believe that story."

"It's true," Daniel insisted. "Everything I've told you is true. We've all seen it. Everyone in the house has seen it. And heard it."

The doctor got up from behind his desk and walked over to the window. "Look out there," he said, gesturing to the calm residential street on which his house and office stood. "*That* is reality. Those trees and those houses and that dog lifting his leg by that bush . . . that is reality. What you have been telling me is *not* real. Your story—or Esther's story, if you will—is not reality."

"But it's true," Daniel repeated.

The forty-eight-year-old medical man lowered his glasses and looked at Daniel. "I've treated your family as long as I can recall," he said. "Your mother was one of my first patients when I opened up here in Amherst. I brought both your Willie and your George into the world. When you cut your leg at the factory, I stitched it up for you." Daniel nodded. "And when Esther and Jennie moved into your house, I started seeing them, too. And now you come to me with this story—this cock-and-bull tale—of flying sheets and loud raps and swollen bodies. If I didn't know you—"

"But you *do* know me," Daniel broke in. "That's why you've got to believe me. Have I ever lied to you?" The doctor shook his head no. "Then why should this be a lie? Why should I try to get you to treat a hoax? What's happening at my house is very real!"

"What can I do?" the doctor asked. "Suppose what you're telling me is true. I'm a medical doctor. I'm not a witch doctor. I'm not a Spiritualist. Sounds like you need a priest or a devil-chaser. That's not what I am. I am a physician. I treat bodies that are ill."

"Esther's body is ill!" Daniel rose and walked over to the window where the doctor was standing. "Her body is ill. Maybe her mind is ill. Hell, I don't know. But you're the only person in town who can help her."

"Who else have you told? Who else knows about this?"

"Nobody!" Daniel replied quickly. "We don't want anyone to know about this."

"Not even your preacher, Reverend Temple?"

"Especially not him. It'd be all over town in a minute that Esther was possessed of devils. You know how he's always preaching against 'the demons amongst us.' Olive and I talked it over and we both agree he'd have Esther burning on a stake in front of the church just for special emphasis next Sunday."

"He does tend toward the dramatic," Dr. Carritte smiled. "I find his sermons an excellent time to review my schedule for the rest of the week." He reached out and put his hand on

Daniel's shoulder. "How can I help you?" he asked. "I must tell you I don't believe your story. I must tell you I don't believe in ghosts or demons. My training has taught me to believe only what I can see with my eyes and hear with my stethoscope. I can treat only what's real. I can't treat something I can't understand."

"I know that and I appreciate your honesty. You've always been fair with me and with everyone around here." Daniel put his hand up to touch the doctor's hand, to feel the assurance that this man could give him. "All I'm asking of you is to come and see Esther. Come and examine her. Come and examine her as if she had a bad cold. That's all I'm asking. Just come and see her."

The doctor sighed and moved away from the window over to his desk. "My appointment book says that I have an operation this afternoon and Mrs. Grady at seven. I have to be back here for supper by eight or my wife will be most upset. I suppose," he said, turning the page and then turning it back again, "I suppose I could be at your home by ten this evening. Is that all right?"

"That'll be fine." Daniel sighed deeply. "I truly appreciate it."

"I haven't done anything yet for you to appreciate," the doctor replied.

"Just being there will help," Daniel smiled. "I know it will."

After Daniel had gone, Dr. Carritte stayed looking out the window. "What are you going to take in your bag?" he asked himself aloud. "A cross and a bell and a candle? A sharp-pointed stake? Maybe a gun with a silver bullet. Maybe," he said slowly, "maybe you shouldn't be going at all."

* * *

Everyone stiffened just a little bit when they heard the doctor's horse and buggy clatter up to the front gate. They had been waiting for him in the parlor, the entire household, waiting to see what he had to say about Esther's condition.

Daniel opened the door, and Olive rose to greet him when he came into the room. "Thank you for coming, Doctor," she said. "It means so much to us."

Dr. Carritte glanced about him. He said good evening to Jennie and to her brother, William, and Daniel's brother John. The young men mumbled their greetings, then stared at the floor. They hoped he wouldn't ask them any questions because they could only give him crazy answers.

"Esther is already in bed," Olive said. "I thought it best if you saw her upstairs, and alone." She took the doctor's arm and guided him toward the staircase. "If you need anything, please call," she added. "We'll be right here . . . waiting."

There was a candle burning in the wall sconce halfway up the stairs, and the doctor cast a long shadow as he passed it, clutching the handle of his medical bag tightly in his right hand. At the top landing, there was light coming from just one room. He poked his head in the doorway. "Esther?" he called softly.

"In here, Dr. Carritte," she responded. She had put on her best nightdress and had combed her hair and put a ribbon in it just for him. She had even rubbed a few drops of rosewater over her body to mask any natural odors that might displease the medical man during his examination. Even though he had examined her several times since she had moved to Amherst, he had never seen her naked. Doctors never saw their female patients naked. Even an expectant mother kept her petticoat on when being examined and when she gave birth the doctor was expected to reach in blindly, under a tent made from a sheet. But then, the majority of decent married women made sure their husbands never saw them naked, either. They undressed in a closet or in the dark and always blew out the candle before their men started pulling up their nightgowns.

"Esther," he said, sitting on the edge of the bed, "how are you feeling? Your brother-in-law tells me you had quite a fright."

She reddened. Even though the doctor was an old friend, he was the first "outsider" to know about her attacks. "Yes," she said softly. "Last night and then before that on Friday night."

"What was it?" he asked.

"I don't know. It was most unusual. I was feeling fine and then I started to get bigger. Just blow up like a balloon. My arms and legs, they got so big. And my face stretched and . . ." she paused. A tear shone in the corner of her right eye. "It was horrible," she said. "It hurt so much."

"What hurt?"

"My body. When the swelling came, my skin stretched so far! My skin burned so! I was terrified it would split and my insides would come rushing out through the rip. You know when you put a sausage on the fire? And it starts to boil inside and puff up?" The doctor nodded yes. "Well, that's how I felt. Like I was boiling inside and any minute I would burst open and things—particles of my body—would come running out onto the bed. It was terrible." Now the tears came more rapidly. "And with the whole family watching," she sobbed. "Daniel and Olive and Daniel's brother. Watching me here in bed. With my nightclothes on, stretching and crying." He reached up and wiped away her tears. "And Jennie fainted. I didn't know about it till afterward. Jennie fainted." She was sobbing now. "Doctor, I don't want to do this to my family! I don't want to make them suffer. Please! Please do something. Give me something to make this go away!"

He dug into his bag and brought out an unmarked brown bottle. "Here," he said, taking off the cap and placing it near her lips, "take a drink of this. It'll calm you a bit." Esther did as she was told and felt the slightly bitter liquid warm her throat and stomach as it slid down. "Now let's see what I can discover," he said. "You just lie there and let the medicine take its effect and I'll see what ails you." He brought out his stethoscope and listened to her heart. Then he checked her pulse. He pulled the sheet down near her waist and started making thumping noises all over her upper body, then asked her to turn over. He listened to her breathing, thumped on her lower back, and ran his hands up and down her spine. Esther was calmer. The crying had stopped. "You can turn over now," he said finally. She did and he pulled the sheet and blanket up over her shoulders. He walked to the door and called downstairs. "Daniel. Olive. You can come up now."

They came quickly up the stairs and into the room, Jennie and the two young men right behind them. The doctor was sitting on the side of the bed.

"It is," he said, "as I expected. She is suffering from nervous excitement. I don't know from what exactly, but it appears that her system has had a shock and is trying to adjust to it." He scanned their faces. "Do you know of anything that could have caused this? A sudden fright? A disappointment? The death of a loved one? A change in plans?" They shook their heads no. "Nothing like that?" he asked. Again, the negative head shakes. "Well," he said, "it's nothing serious and it will go away in time. Meanwhile, I'll leave a prescription for a calmative. She'll need to take it for a few days until she is restored to health."

The pillow under Esther's head raised itself and floated out past her face. It hovered in the air with only one corner still behind her head. It hung, alone and unaided, in the air, with the faint flutter of a small bird.

The group standing around the bed stood stock still in amazement. Dr. Carritte's glasses slid down his nose as his mouth dropped open.

Then the pillow gave another flutter and silently slid back into place as Esther's head lowered and sank back onto it.

"Did you see that?" the doctor gasped.

"Did *you* see it?" Daniel demanded. "That's what I've been telling you about."

"I don't believe it," the doctor said.

"Yet you saw it," Olive put in.

"Yes," he replied. "Of course I saw it. You all did." He looked rapidly at their faces. "You did, didn't you?"

"Yes." "Yes." "I saw it," came the replies.

Then the pillow started out again. Alone and unaided, it floated from under Esther's head. This time it went as far as the wall before it reversed itself and started back toward the bed.

John Teed took three large steps and grabbed the edge of the pillow. For a second it shook, then pulled away from him and started back toward the girl's head. John tugged on it, trying to get it away from Esther. His face grew red with the effort and everyone could see his knuckles whiten as he used all his strength to control the thing. He planted the heels of his boots onto the floor but the pillow gave one fierce tug of its own, yanked itself out of his grasp, and slid back under Esther's head.

The doctor was the first to speak. "How wonderful!"

The doctor was the first to jump. A loud report, like a gunshot, shook the bed he was sitting on. Instantly he was on his knees, peering under the bed. "It came from under there," he said aloud. Then it came again, but this time directly under his feet. The vibration of it jiggled his glasses and made the watch chain across his vest sway. The sounds moved out into the center of the room. The family members moved against the wall, but the doctor followed the sounds, trying to step in exactly the spot where each noise came from.

"Amazing," he said to no one in particular, "simply amazing."

That was when the bed covers repeated their act. The

sheet and blanket covering the frightened girl rose swiftly into the air, twisted themselves into a ball, and threw themselves straight at the doctor. He ducked and they sailed over his head and fell lifeless into a far corner.

Dr. Carritte stood looking at the jumbled pile when Olive's voice called out sharply: "Look out!"

He turned to see a large piece of plaster, torn from a side wall, come hurtling through the air at him. He put up his hands to shield his face, but the object stopped just inches from him and fell straight to the floor, never touching him. In wonder, he picked up the hunk of plaster, examined it, and put it on a chair.

"My word," was all he could say.

"Now do you believe me?" Daniel asked him. "Now do you believe that we need help?"

"I believe you," the doctor replied, "but I don't know *what* I'm believing. This is all so strange. I've never seen anything like it. I don't know if anyone else ever has either. Of course, I'll see what I can do, but—"

They all heard it at the same time. All eyes turned toward the wall beside the bed. Esther heard it, too, and her eyes opened wide.

Into the plaster of the wall, an unseen hand started to carve large letters. They were about a foot high, uneven but deep. The plaster fell away in hundreds of fragments as the letters appeared one after another. No one spoke. No one tried to stop the invisible writer as he gouged the wall with his terrible message:

ESTHER COX, YOU ARE MINE TO KILL!

Friday, September 13, 1878

As he had promised the night before, Dr. Carritte came calling on Esther right after breakfast. Instead of finding her in bed—as he had expected—she was up and dressed and helping Olive with the housework.

"How did you sleep?" he asked Esther.

"Right after you left, I fell sound asleep," she said. "It must have been that medicine you made me drink."

"And how do you feel?"

"I feel wonderful," she replied with a smile. "I have all

sorts of energy and am truly refreshed by the sleep. I want to thank you."

"I haven't done anything yet to be thanked," he said. Olive pulled out a chair from the dining-room table, and he took a seat. "I should like to write you a prescription for more of that calming medicine," he said. "Have it filled today and take some before you go to bed tonight." He started to write on his prescription pad. Then he looked up at both of them.

"We did see what we thought we saw last night, didn't we?" he asked.

They nodded.

"I mean the bedclothes and the loud noises and all."

They nodded.

"And that message on the wall?" He couldn't look at Esther as he asked: "Was it still there this morning?"

"It's still there," Olive said.

"Then we didn't imagine it." He sighed. He had been hoping it had been some kind of mass hypnosis. Mesmerism was all the rage in some sophisticated circles, and he had read how entire groups of people could be convinced of the reality of things that really were not there. Audiences of people had sworn they saw things—cats; flames; palm trees in the snow—when it had all been a mesmerist's trick. That thought had come to him in the middle of the night as he lay in bed unable to sleep, thinking about the happenings in the Teed house. "It's still there," he repeated. "Too bad." He sighed deeply. Then he smiled. It was his bedside-manner smile. "Well, maybe it will go away. Perhaps it will never happen again. I mean, we don't understand why it *came*, so we won't know why it leaves. Nothing is permanent." He smiled at Esther. "Nothing. Everything goes away with time."

"I hope so," she said.

"Esther," Olive spoke up, "why don't you run down to the cellar and get the doctor a glass of cold milk? Would you like one, Doctor?"

"Very much. Thank you."

Esther took a clear-glass tumbler from the cupboard, opened the cellar door that was in the dining-room wall, and went down the steps.

Olive used her absence to speak to the doctor. "Do you really think she'll be all right?" she asked.

"Olive, I don't know. I'm a medical man. What I saw last

night was not medical. It was something else." Olive started to speak, but he held up his hand. "Don't ask me. I don't know what that 'something else' is. I've tried to categorize it, but I can't. It could be hypnosis. It could be mental aberrations. It could be just imagination."

"Or it could be demons," Olive said.

"Yes," he replied slowly. "It could be demons."

First they heard Esther scream, then heard her clumsily running back up the stairs. The glass in her hand had a little milk in it, the rest of the milk had been spilled down the front of her skirt. "There's somebody down there," she panted. "He tried to hit me with a board." She looked down at her clothes. "Oh," she groaned, "look what I've done to my clean dress!"

Dr. Carritte quickly pushed past her and ran down the stairs. There was enough light coming in from the side windows that he could see there was no one down there. Everything looked in place except for a length of two by four that was in the middle of the floor.

"Esther!" he called. "Esther there is no one down here."

"Yes there is," she answered.

"No there is not. Now you come down here. I want to show you there is no one here." He waited. "Esther! You have to start facing these things. There is no one down here." Another pause. "Come down and see for yourself."

Olive gave her a smile and then a gentle nudge toward the cellar steps. Esther took a deep breath and slowly descended the stairs. The doctor came over to her, took her hand, and led her into the center of the room.

"You see, it's empty. There's nobody down here but the two of us. Your imagination is playing tricks on you. After last night," he said with a smile, "I'm not surprised."

"But that board," she said, pointing to the two-by-four, "it came right at me."

The doctor bent over and picked it up. He handed it to her. "You see, it's quite harmless now." She took it in her hands. "It can't hurt you."

It was her turn to smile. "I guess you're right," she said. "I've just been distraught over everything. I'm seeing things where nothing really—"

A large potato hit her on the side of the head. She cried out and dropped the piece of wood. Then another potato came flying up and out of the vegetable bin, striking her on the shoulder.

Two potatoes sailed at the doctor, one hitting him in the back, the other on his elbow.

They turned to look at the source of the bombardment and gasped as several large potatoes rose straight up from the bin and pointed in their direction.

Dr. Carritte grabbed Esther by the arm. "Let's get upstairs, quick!" he shouted.

They ran for the stairs, the heavy vegetables striking them, missing them, thudding against the wall and floor. They continued to bounce against the cellar door after the two were in the dining room and the doctor had slammed the door.

Esther ran into Olive's arms and burst into tears. The doctor brushed the dirt off his clothes, threw his prescription pad into his bag, snapped it shut, and picked it up.

"I'll be back at ten tonight," was all he said as he quickly left the house.

* * *

Esther was in bed when the doctor returned at ten that night.

"I tried to sleep," she said to him, "but it was impossible. I feel funny. Funny inside."

"What do you mean?"

"Like pins and needles are moving through my veins. Like long thin worms are inside me, crawling and running. Sometimes it feels as if things with hairy legs are walking across my face, and when I try to yank them off, there's nothing there." Her eyes were red. Olive had told him Esther had been crying most of the afternoon. "Isn't there *anything* you can give me to stop this?" She touched his hand with hers. "This . . . whatever it is . . . has got to stop. It's upsetting everyone."

"I know," he said soothingly. "I've got something here I want you to take." He placed his medical bag on the dresser and opened it. He took the tumbler that was beside the water pitcher and shook it upside down. Then he carefully measured an ounce of potassium bromide and watched the white crystals as they settled to the bottom of the glass. Then he added an ounce of crystal morphine. He had given morphine for years as a sedative for his patients. Then a carefully measured table-spoon of opium mixed with alcohol. The crystals began to dissolve. From another bottle, he filled the glass with a brown pungent liquid. It was brandy, another calmative he had found that worked. He stirred it all with the spoon.

"Here," he said, handing the concoction to the girl. "Drink this. It'll help you relax." He stood there while Esther, rather slowly because of the smell of the alcohol, drained the glass. "There," he said, "that should put you to sleep."

He sat on the edge of the bed and listened to her heart with his stethoscope. Then he took her pulse, checking it with the watch that he kept in his vest pocket. "Your pulse is high," he said, "but the medicine you just took should bring it down."

"Did you find the reason?" she asked.

"The reason?"

"This afternoon . . . in the books in your office. Did you find the reason why those potatoes flew at us?" Her gaze was steady on his face.

"No, I didn't," he confessed. "There is nothing in my medical books to explain that. I wish there were."

"But you saw it, too. You saw that it wasn't my imagination."

"I saw it," he replied. "And," he smiled, rubbing his elbow, "I *felt* it, too. No, at first I thought it was imagination. Or hypnosis. In fact, that's what I told Daniel when he first asked me to come to see you. I thought you, or someone, were playing mental tricks. Parlor games, if you will."

"But these aren't games," she said.

"No. They're not, but I don't know what to call them, how to classify them. If they are brought about by human magnetism, then I can treat that. If these things originate because of something physical your body is going through, then I can help. But Esther," he said softly, "if these are mental things . . . then there is nothing I can do."

"Mental?" the girl repeated the word. "Do you think I'm crazy?"

"No."

"Do you think I'm *going* crazy?"

He sighed. "I don't know. We'll have to wait and find out. I don't believe so, but then, yesterday I didn't believe any of this was really happening." He rose and pulled the sheet up around her chin. "I'll let you get some rest now. I'm going down and sit with Daniel and Olive for a spell and I'll check to see that you're asleep before I go."

He was halfway to the door when the first loud banging noise shook the room. Then another. Then another. Then a rapid staccato of them, constant and ceaseless and loud.

He ran down the stairs, almost bumping into Daniel and John as they were rushing up.

"It's coming from the roof," the doctor said. "Someone's on the roof."

The three men ran out the front doorway, across the small lawn, and through the gateway to the street. The pounding noises were as loud outside as they were in the house. There was a full moon, illuminating the clear night sky and the rooftops.

"It sounds like someone hitting it with a sledgehammer!" Daniel shouted above the noise. "Like they were trying to break through the shingles."

No one was on the roof.

"What's going on?" a male voice asked. They turned to see Mr. Simmons, the neighbor from across the narrow street, standing there in his nightshirt. "What's all that pounding?"

"I . . ." Dr. Carritte started to say, ". . . we don't know."

"It's just there," John Teed added. "Up there." He pointed at the roof.

"I don't see anything." Mr. Simmons squinted into the night.

"Good," said Daniel, "because we don't either."

"It woke me up," Mr. Simmons said. "It woke me and the missus up."

"I'm sorry," Daniel said.

"Can't you make it stop?" Simmons asked him.

"If we could see who was doing it," the doctor said, "we could ask him to stop. I can't see him. Neither can you."

"Well," Simmons said, turning back toward his front door, "it's damned annoying."

"Yes," Daniel said, "it certainly is. I'm sorry for it."

The pounding kept up.

Olive and Jennie were in the bedroom with Esther, sitting on each side of the bed and holding her hands. Tears streamed down the girl's face as the steady noise on the roof cut jagged edges into her nerves.

The pounding kept up.

On Princess Street, everyone was awake. Even folks on King Street, the next block up, were awakened by the incessant pounding. A crowd began to gather in front of the Teed home. Some carried oil lamps, others lit candles to see better. They stood in their nightclothes, pointing at the roof, hearing the loud reports, and seeing nothing.

At the exact moment a church bell struck midnight, the noises stopped. Esther instantly fell asleep.

Thursday, September 19, 1878

"I knew they would eventually get to it." Daniel sighed and handed the newspaper to Olive. "It's basically what the *Amherst Gazette* printed earlier this week."

Olive took the paper, hesitating to read Esther's name in print. The *Gazette* had been very good about it, keeping her sister's name and Daniel's name out of the story, even though most of Amherst knew what was happening and who the people were who were involved.

"No names, yet," said Daniel. The *Chignecto Post*, a weekly newspaper from Sackville, was widely read in the area. Sackville, about ten miles to the northeast, in New Brunswick, was an important town with more industry and commercial houses. There were more churches than in Amherst, more schools, and more people. The weekly four-page paper was always crammed with local gossip scattered between display and classified ads, national and international news. "It's right there on the front page," he said. "They call it 'An Amherst Sensation.'"

Olive's eyes scanned the first few paragraphs, which seemed to be reprinted from the story the *Gazette* had run. She relaxed. She didn't see the names Cox or Teed. Then she came to the new part, the editorial comment the *Post* had amended to the facts:

> The affair has created great excitement, crowds having gathered about the house nightly, so that a policeman was required to disperse them.
>
> We have taken pains to obtain our information from trustworthy sources, and believe the description given to be as it *appeared* to those present.

"'Appeared'?" Olive's voice rose. "After their reporter spent two hours here asking us questions, they use the word 'appeared'?"

Daniel shrugged his shoulders.

Olive continued to read:

> The most probable explanation of the phenomenon is that the girl chiefly affected with magnetism, is unconsciously a mesmerist, her nervous condition, caused by ill health, rendering her imagination very susceptible . . .

"'Her imagination'?" Olive was indignant.

"Read on," Daniel replied.

> . . . rendering her imagination very susceptible, and others coming within her influence partaking of the delusions which forced themselves upon her mind. We would be glad to hear from anyone who has met with similar experiences.

"So that reporter has it all figured out," Olive said, tossing the paper onto the floor. "Dr. Carritte couldn't figure it out, but the reporter did with just one visit. In other words, Esther imagined it all and that made us imagine it, too. Correct?"

"I guess that's what he's saying," Daniel replied, "and it's our imagination that keeps the Simmonses across the street from sleeping until midnight every night." The rooftop thumping had gone on each night—except Sunday—since it started.

"I showed their reporter the bedroom wall," Olive said. "Does he think Esther's imagination gouged out the plaster to make those awful words?"

"The human mind is a pretty powerful thing," Daniel said with a smile.

"Yes, but this human *newspaper* is a pretty poor thing. And I know just where I'm going to put it. In the fire."

"You aren't going to show it to Esther?" Daniel asked.

"No," she said. "The story in the *Gazette* upset her sufficiently. I don't want her to know people over in Sackville are talking about her. Anyway, this makes it appear that she's some king of mentalist freak."

"Or something worse," Daniel said.

Olive stopped on her way to the kitchen, newspaper in hand. "Yes," she said softly, "or something worse."

Saturday, September 28, 1878

The good people of Amherst continued to discuss Esther and her strangeness. Even though the loud poundings on the roof had ceased, there were still other odd goings-on inside the Teed home.

A bucket of clear drinking water on the kitchen table suddenly turned murky yellow and bubbled up and over the top and onto the floor as if it were boiling. Reverend Temple saw that. He and his wife were visiting the Teeds that morning. He explained to anyone who would listen that it was his "spiritual duty" that took him there. After all, Esther and Jennie were his parishioners, and during these terrible times he would have been remiss not to have been there to give them guidance. His wife rarely went with him on house calls, but she was right there on that day, determined not to miss a thing and to gather as much information as possible to pass along to her friends.

"It's perfectly understandable," she said to Olive after the shock of seeing the water pail bubble over, "that you don't want every nosey person in town in here."

Esther was on the floor, wiping up the water with a rag. "This happens all the time, Mrs. Temple," she said. "Just suddenly. For no reason."

"There must be a reason, child," the woman replied. There is a reason for everything in the Lord's world."

"Well," Olive spoke up, "I wish the Lord would give us a sign as to why this is happening here. To us. Daniel and I have tried to examine it, to figure out what's wrong, but it's beyond our ken."

Esther got up and twisted the wet rag over the sink. "I'm sorry again for the way I acted," she said. "It was very rude of me."

"We'll just put the blame on 'it'," said the minister, "whatever 'it' is."

When Olive had opened the door to the reverend and his wife (Esther never went near the door now), the girl had heard their voices and had shouted: "Don't let that fool in!" Esther had felt the words coming from her throat, but they weren't her voice. It was a low, masculine voice, and once everyone had recovered from the shock, Esther couldn't apologize enough or do enough to make the visitors feel welcome. "It really wasn't *me*," she said softly. "I don't know where the voice came from."

Mrs. Temple made a mental note to tell her friends about the ventriloquism the girl was using. "Of course it wasn't, dear," she said. She smiled. Esther and Olive returned the smile.

"Incapable," repeated her husband. He sighed. "But we must find the source of your troubles. We must turn over every stone until the truth is known and the font of all this unhappiness is banished."

Bam! Something hit the outside wall of the kitchen and hit it hard.

They froze for a moment, then the minister dashed to the window and looked out into the backyard.

Bam! Bam!

"It's out there!" his wife screamed.

"I don't see anything!" he shouted at her.

"Well, it's there!" her voice rose higher. "What is it? Go get it!"

He turned to her. "Go *get* it?" he said incredulously. "Go out there and *get* it?"

"Well, do something!" the woman insisted.

"There's not much he can do," Olive said as the pounding stopped. "There's not much any of us can do."

"I could pray," he suggested. He bowed his head and put his palms together when they all heard the scratching. It was coming from the pantry. In a few steps, all four of them were at the pantry door, peering in.

Large even letters, written firmly by an unseen pencil on the pantry wall: "What a fool! What piss! Esther don't want your prayers. Me neither. Get out!"

In their race to the front door, the reverend outdistanced his wife by at least four paces.

* * *

In the past week, Daniel had dismantled the large double bed in the girls' room and replaced it with two cots. It had been Esther's idea. She knew that Jennie wasn't getting any sleep, and Jennie had to go to work every morning. Jennie had protested at first but now liked the idea of not having pillows snatched from under her head, and covers lifted off and tossed across the room. It also calmed her somewhat to know that whatever "it" was, it wouldn't make a mistake, in the middle of the night, and attack *her*, thinking she was Esther.

The experience that afternoon with the bubbling water and the writing on the wall had upset Esther more than usual, but what really concerned her was the strange voice—the harsh, masculine voice—that had come out of her throat when the minister and his wife had arrived. To have called the Reverend Temple "a fool!" To have felt the rough sounds vibrating from her own throat, without having thought them first, without knowingly having moved her lips to say them. It was bad enough that she rarely left the house anymore, afraid of what would happen around her in the streets or in the shops. True, the manifestations took place only inside the small frame house, but who knew what to expect? Mr. Cole, who owned a store that sold china and glassware, had jokingly asked her not to visit his shop because he "didn't want everything crashing around." He had said it with a laugh, but he had been serious. If Mr. Cole was concerned, then other merchants were concerned as well. They obviously talked of her illness and what was causing it. William Cox and John Teed claimed, at the shoe factory, that nobody ever mentioned Esther to them, but she knew they were not telling the truth. She knew men there asked the two boarders about the goings-on at the Teed house. After all, it was in the papers. Perfect strangers were reading about it and coming to their own conclusions. At least, thank God, those terrible loud banging noises on the roof had ceased. The Lord had answered *one* of her prayers.

"Are you all right?" Jennie asked her as she came into the bedroom.

Esther was already in bed, the covers pulled up to her chin, waiting for her sister to turn down the lamp. "Yes," she said. "Just awfully tired, but nothing else."

"Are you going to church with us tomorrow?"

She shook her head. "I don't think so. I just couldn't face Reverend Temple after what happened today."

"That'll make three Sundays in a row you haven't gone," Jennie reminded her.

"I just don't feel like it."

"You can't be a stick-in-the-mud forever," her sister said.

"I know, but I'm afraid. Suppose I get inside the church and the rappings start? Or the hymnbooks fly? Or the flowers land in somebody's lap? Then what?"

"Nothing ever happens on *Sunday*," Jennie said. "You know we've all talked about it. Monday through Saturday, yes, but there is never anything on Sunday." She brushed her long brown hair, staring in the mirror that hung over the dresser. "Not a rap, not a movement, not a thing. It's almost as if 'it' takes Sunday off."

"After working all week 'he' needs a day off," Esther said.

"So I think you can go with us tomorrow," the older girl answered. She finished running the brush across her hair. "You have to get out *sometime*. You can't go on being a lady hermit."

"I won't," Esther said.

"You don't go shopping anymore, you don't take Olive's little boys for walks, you don't do anything but stay cooped up in this house!"

"I *know*," Esther said. She almost added that she was getting tired of hearing about it, but she didn't.

"Then it's settled," Jennie said, getting into her bed and turning the wick down on the oil lamp. "You'll go with us tomorrow."

"I'll think about it."

"No thinking. You'll go." There was a long pause as Jennie listened to her sister breathing in the darkness. Her voice softened. "You really have to get out, Esther. You really do." She waited for an answer, and when none came she adjusted the pillow and closed her eyes. Sleep came quickly.

* * *

By 11:30 P.M., all the oil lamps in tiny Amherst had been dimmed. No horses' hooves clomped on the hard dirt streets nor buggies rattled their wheels. Everyone was asleep, most of them under light blankets. Even though it was only the end of September, the chilly nights had come back. The cold evening breezes from off the bay had returned.

That wasn't all that returned.

Esther awoke with a start. There was someone in bed with her, someone lying beside her on the narrow cot. She tried to sit up, but she couldn't make her muscles work. She couldn't co-ordinate them, couldn't get an arm up, couldn't make a leg bend.

Something was holding her down.

She screamed—opened her mouth and screamed, but

nothing came out. No sound. No voice. Just the straining of her throat. Just the stretching of her lips. No sound.

It was a hand. It was a hand on her leg. A large hand. She could feel all five fingers sliding along her skin. Five fingers caressing, stopping to knead her flesh, moving higher.

She tried to get strength into her arm, strength to grab that searching hand and yank it off, but her arm wouldn't move. She tried to scream again. Still no sound.

Her eyes grew wide and she jerked her face away as someone's warm breath exhaled against her cheek. Then it breathed into her ear. The hand was still moving, still searching her naked skin. She could feel the folds of her nightgown where it had been pushed up to her waist. She could feel the warm cloth, then feel the chill on her nakedness below.

She groaned and tried to lift her body, to shove whoever it was onto the floor. Her body wouldn't move, wouldn't rise. The breath was back again on her face, warm and foul-smelling and insistent. She twisted her head, tried to avoid the warm lips that came down roughly on her mouth. She could feel her stomach writhe as the insisting tongue forced itself between her teeth and licked at the roof of her mouth.

Her face became wet. Tears. At least she could still cry. The tears welled up and over her lids and ran down her cheeks. Silent tears, for no sound came from her throat, no matter how desperately she tried to scream.

Then another hand touched her leg. Two hands now, kneading and caressing and exploring. They gradually slid higher. Then higher. With an incredible shock, she realized they were touching her *there*. Down *there*! Between her legs. Her privates. Rubbing and fondling and scratching at the entrance to her private parts! No one had ever done that before. No one had ever even *seen* her private parts! Oh, my God! Who was this? Where was Jennie? Why didn't Jennie stop him?

Suddenly, with a painful push, her legs were spread apart, like someone had taken a roast chicken and yanked apart the drumsticks. The figure, the body, the unknown presence rolled from beside her to be on top of her. She could feel his weight, feel the disgusting movement of his chest and stomach as he breathed. The rancid breath was full in her face again. The reeking mouth was back against hers, pressing and working with its tongue. She still couldn't move, the heavy masculine body atop hers making it even more impossible.

She felt the two hands come up under her nightgown and touch her breasts. They were rough as they cupped them, then pinched her nipples. Her stomach churned again with the terror of what was happening to her.

Then the pressure on her ceased for a moment. The hands were still on her breasts but the body—his body—had raised. It was no longer pushing against hers. Esther dared hope for a second that her attacker was getting off her, getting out of bed.

Then the plunge. The unimaginable, unbearable pain as he plunged with one brutal thrust deep inside her. The fire raced from between her legs up into her throat. It seared everything inside her as he pulled out some and then plunged back into her. Again and again the violent thrustings tore into her body. She tried to scream, but the mouth was tight against hers. She could hear the cot moving, creaking under each of his thrusts into her. She could hear her own gasps as she forced herself to breathe through her nose. She exhaled loudly each time he pushed down on her . . . in her.

"Esther?" Jennie sat up in bed. "Esther?"

There was no answer, just the sound of heavy breathing and the creaking of the wood and canvas cot.

"Esther!" Jennie screamed and searched for the matches. Shaking as badly as she was, it was a wonder she was able to light the lamp, but when she did and turned it in the direction of her sister's bed, she almost fainted.

There was her teenage sister, lying flat on the cot, her nightgown up over her abdomen, her arms stretched out, and her legs up and open. She was crying as the cot continued to sink and rise and sink and rise by itself.

"Esther!" she called again and scrambled out of bed. "Esther, what's happening?"

The girl didn't answer. She just moaned and twisted her face.

"Esther!" Jennie reached down and grabbed her sister by the shoulders and shook her. The girl opened her eyes and stared in terror into her face. Jennie grabbed the twisted nightgown, trying to yank it over her sister's legs. It wouldn't budge. Then she ran to the foot of the cot and picked up the sheet that had fallen to the floor. Quickly she brought the sheet up over Esther's body, covering her nakedness.

Then Jennie staggered against the wall. The sheet was moving. It rose and fell, and under it she could see the outline of a man's body. His back, his shoulders, his thrusting buttocks. She almost fell against the lamp in her terror and confusion. Thoughts raced through her mind a mile a minute but she couldn't function. She couldn't move toward the bed. To that sheet. To that form. She felt nailed to the wall, unable to do anything but watch in fascinated horror.

Then it stopped. The masculine figure under the sheet dissolved. Jennie watched the sheet float lazily down around the contours of Esther's body. The cot stopped rocking. The room became unbearably still.

Then Esther cried out. It was a long, low wail that came from someplace deep, someplace that had never been touched by such misery before.

Jennie ran to her and cradled her in her arms. There was no attempt to call any of the others, to awaken them and tell them what had happened. The sisters could read the thoughts in each other's eyes. This was their own private secret. Their own shared horror. No one else must ever know.

Tuesday, October 1, 1878

Sunday passed, as always, without incident. Esther did not go to church, nor did Jennie insist. They did not talk of what had taken place. Jennie instinctively knew it was not a subject to discuss with Esther. Esther was so ashamed of what had happened that, at first, she would look away from Jennie when she spoke to her rather than look her sister in the face. In 1878, decent girls never talked about such things, and certainly no decent girl ever *did* such things. Esther felt dirty. Felt used. Felt that she was sinful, had been abandoned, could never marry. At least a decent man. What decent man would want her if he knew that she had been . . . that she was no longer . . . that she was no better than a wanton woman? She prayed that Jennie would never slip and tell anyone of this. Everyone in Amherst waited for gossip and more gossip of "the Amherst mystery girl." They took each incident and blew it into a major event, and once the item had become public gossip it became public news in either the *Gazette* or the *Post*. What would they call her now—"The Amherst Whore"?

* * *

On Monday, the rappings began. Not loud pounding noises, but knockings on the walls, on the furniture, on the doors and staircase. They followed Esther like flies around spoiled fruit, always with her, only rapping where she was, interrupting, insisting, upsetting.

By Tuesday, the others in the house had gotten used to them. Esther swore she never would. Daniel said it was like the ticking of a clock, the noise was always there, so after a while you didn't notice it. That night, Esther chose to sit in the dining room after supper rather than in the parlor with the others. That way, she said, they wouldn't be bothered by the rappings. They could relax after a busy workday and discuss things without being interrupted. Everyone protested, but the girl was insistent. As long as these noises continued, she would make them as unobtrusive as possible on the others.

"I went to see Dr. Carritte today," Olive told her husband as they sat in the parlor. "I needed some more of that sedative for Esther. Jennie says she hasn't been sleeping well these nights."

Daniel looked at Jennie, and she nodded her head in agreement. "She tries to stay awake long after I turn down the lamp," she said. "I can hear her talking to herself or humming just to keep awake. She told me this morning that she was going to take a hatpin to bed with her and stick herself with it so as not to fall asleep."

"Did you tell her it was a crazy idea?" John Teed asked.

Daniel gave his younger brother a scowling look. "You know," he said through his teeth, "that's one word we never say to Esther!"

John flushed, "I didn't mean it like that, Daniel. I meant that the *idea* was crazy." He sighed. "That's all."

"No," Jennie replied, "I didn't say anything. She's at her wits' end with this thing. I just wonder where it will end."

"*If* it will end," John said. "It's been a month now since it started."

"A month Friday," Olive corrected him.

"That's a long time," John said. "That's a lot of pressure all at once."

"She's strong," Daniel added. "She'll make it."

"I'm not so sure." His wife shook her head. "Have you noticed the way her hands shake when she has to do something like pour coffee or write a grocery list? There is a tremor there that wasn't there before. I've watched her when she didn't know I was watching, and sometimes her arms will jerk suddenly or her legs will twitch. You can see the sudden movement under her skirt."

John Teed refilled his pipe and after taking a long draft on it said, "Ralph Torgelson asked me at work today if I thought Esther was possessed by demons."

They all stared at him. "What did you say?" Olive asked.

"I told him I didn't believe in demons," he said. "Then he asked me if I ever read the Bible. I told him I did, read it every day."

Jennie snickered. "What did he say to that?"

"He asked me why then I didn't believe in demons if I read my Bible. Didn't I believe the words in the Bible were the words of God?" He inhaled another puff of the rich smoke. "I said I didn't know about God and that no man did, but I did know about Esther because she is my sister-in-law, and I know she isn't evil. I said demons are only around evil people, and Esther is an innocent child."

"What'd he say to that?"

"He told me I'd better be careful and wear a cross." He laughed. "Oh, yes, and to keep my bedroom door locked at night."

"Your door?" Olive exclaimed. "What has your door to do with this?"

"If my door is locked, the demons can't come in and get me." He laughed again. "I told him that if they can get up and pound on the roof without a ladder they can sure as hell get into my room and pound on me, locked door or no."

"Nobody has dared to ask me about it at the tailor shop," Jennie said.

"They see the way you handle those scissors," Daniel laughed, "and they don't dare mention the subject."

"I've had a couple of women inquire about Esther's health when I go to market," Olive said, "but none of them ever come right out and ask me for details."

"Which they're dying to do, I'm sure," Jennie added.

"But I can feel a difference out there," Olive continued. "I get treated differently in the shops. The clerks wait on me quicker than they used to, and then hurry to another customer. Maybe it's my imagination, but I feel people giving me more space on the street. You know, like walking farther around me and pulling back when I pass."

"Did Dr. Carritte give you the medicine?" Daniel asked.

Olive nodded. "Has he any new thoughts on what's causing all this? Has he written to anyone outside Amherst to try to solve this thing?"

"He says he's been going through his books and medical journals but so far her case seems unique."

"He doesn't think it's demons, does he?" John asked.

"He hasn't said what he thinks it is. But he's a scientific man. I rather doubt he would think it was demons. He wants to do some more reading on it before he examines her again. He told me he'd be over Thursday night and asked me to give the sedative to her that night. He wants her with a clear head."

"That's not going to be easy," Jennie put in. "She's getting more confused the longer these things keep tormenting her." She wished she could tell Olive about the attack Saturday night, but it would mean breaking her silent promise to Esther. If the girl wanted Olive to know, she would tell her herself.

"I . . . I'm going up to bed now." Esther stuck her head in the doorway to the parlor.

Olive rose. "I have some medicine that Dr. Carritte wants you to take. He gave it to me this afternoon and wants you to swallow two tablespoons before you go to bed."

"It's not to make me sleep, is it? I really don't want to *sleep*, I just want to go to bed. To rest a little."

"No, it's not to make you sleep," Olive lied. "It's to relax you."

"Are you sure?"

"I'm positive. Have I ever not told you the truth?" Esther shook her head. "Then why should I start now?" She put her arm around the girl's shoulder and led her into the kitchen, where the medicine and a tablespoon were already waiting.

On her way upstairs, Esther called out good night to everyone still in the parlor. The rappings began again, on the steps, on the bannister, on the walls: light, rapid, almost playful as if they delightedly anticipated having the teenage girl back in bed.

Thursday, October 3, 1878

The supper dishes were put away quickly and the parlor was given a light dusting. The antimacassars on the sofa and chair were straightened. The lamp wicks were trimmed. The two young boys were bathed and already in bed when the doctor called.

Esther was waiting for him in the parlor. The doctor had sent around a note that afternoon that he didn't want to examine her in bed but to be up and dressed. She breathed a deep sigh when she read the note, for she was certain he would discover, on his first examination since Saturday night, that she was no longer a virgin. She didn't know *how* doctors knew those things, but he would find it out. She heard a story when she was in high school of a young lady who was about to be married and had been examined for one thing by her doctor only to have been found out that *another* thing was wrong with her. The doctor, of course, had told her husband-to-be and, of course, the marriage had been canceled. Nobody blamed the groom for his action. Nobody even blamed the doctor for telling him. All the blame was heaped on the young woman, who protested she had *done* no wrong. It didn't matter. A few days afterward, they found her body floating in the bay. There was almost no one at her funeral.

Dr. Carritte extended his hand, and Esther took it. "Good evening, my dear," he said. "How do you feel?"

"Better, thank you, sir," she replied softly.

The doctor shook hands with Daniel and his brother John as well as William Cox, Esther's brother. Olive and Jennie came out of the kitchen carrying a tray of coffee and small gingerbread cakes. The doctor greeted each one by name.

"I appreciate your being here," Olive said.

"It's been all of three weeks since the last visit," he replied, seating himself on the sofa. He smiled at Esther. "It's awfully serene in here tonight," he said and laughed. "The last time I was here I was pummeled with potatoes in the afternoon and almost hit with plaster at night." No one laughed at this, just smiled politely. If the doctor had expected laughter he was mistaken; no one in the house saw anything funny about what had been going on. "You have been taking the medicine I've sent?"

"Yes, sir. Every night."

"Good. Has it helped?"

"To do what?" Esther asked.

"To put you to sleep," he replied. "Have you been sleeping better with the medicine?"

Esther shot a glance at Olive, who lowered her head. "Yes, sir. Much better, thank you."

"There hasn't been any more of that pounding on the

roof," Daniel spoke up. "The night you were here was the worst. It tapered off after that. It's been at least a week since we've had any of that going on."

"I know," the doctor replied. "I mean, people have told me the poundings have stopped."

"People?" Esther's voice raised just a bit.

"You know, the folks around town. They tell me things." He paused, then added, "And they ask me things."

"Ask you things?" Esther said. "You mean about me?" The man nodded. "What . . . ?" She felt her throat tightening. "What do you tell them . . . about me?"

"Just that I don't know what is causing your ailment. That's about all. And I don't, you know. I don't have any clues. Just a few ideas." He opened his medicine bag and looked for something in an inside pocket.

"What ideas do you have?" This from Daniel.

"That it may be electro-magnetic influences, for one," the man replied.

"You mean lightning?" William Cox asked.

"Not exactly lightning. More like some electric current moving through Esther's body and causing things around her to happen."

"Like a lightning rod," William continued. The doctor shrugged his shoulders. "Like on a barn roof. The lightning hits the rod and bounces off onto something else."

"Yes," the doctor replied.

"Except that's not how a lightning rod works," William continued. "The idea of a rod on the roof in the first place is to capture the lightning so it *won't* bounce around."

"Oh," the doctor said. "I guess you're right."

"Do you think it's hypnosis?" Olive asked. "The *Post* seems to think so. In fact, they've come to that conclusion."

"I know," the man replied, "I read that story myself. I don't know too much about hypnosis, but I've been reading up on it and it doesn't seem to be the same thing."

"I once saw a hypnotist onstage in St. John," Daniel's brother spoke up, "and he didn't do any of the things that Esther can do." He looked at her proudly.

"I don't *do* anything," the girl insisted. "It just happens."

John Teed blushed at the reprimand. "That's what I meant," he said.

"What about demons?" Olive said the word aloud,

another word the family had agreed never to say in front of Esther. "Do you think she is possessed by demons?" No one looked at Esther. She held her breath.

The doctor shook his head. "I don't know anything about demons. I'm a man of science. Demons are Reverend Temple's territory."

"I thought Christianity was his territory," Daniel interrupted.

"Same thing, really," the doctor replied. "He deals with all aspects of the soul. My training has been with the body."

"And with all your training," Daniel continued, "you don't know what's ailing Esther."

"No." He shook his head. "I must confess, I don't."

Esther got up suddenly from her chair and walked toward the door. "I was expecting some good news, Doctor. I can't stand much more of this around me."

"I'm sorry, child," he said. "I was hoping I could get rid of it by now, too." He went over to her, put his arm around her, and led her back to her chair. "But I do have one idea," he said. "It's a new one and, frankly, it may not be the right one, but we can try it." He smoothed her hair. "Do you want to hear it?"

There was a murmur from everyone in the room as he went back to the sofa and pulled a thin book from his bag. "I came across this yesterday. Actually, I've had it for quite a while but never really gave it any serious consideration. It's about three girls, three American girls down in New York State, who had similar rappings and flying things."

"Similar?" Olive was interested.

"Yes. Their names are Fox. Three sisters named Fox. About twenty years ago they heard rappings in their bedroom and, of course, it frightened them. Then somehow they came to the conclusion that the noises were being caused by spirits—"

"Demons?" Daniel interjected.

"No, no, no. Spirits. Not demons. It appears there's a difference. Anyway, once they got over their fright they tried to communicate with them . . . these spirits . . . and managed to do so. With great accuracy, apparently."

"And these weren't demons?" Esther asked again.

"No, they were spirits. Ghosts, if you will. Ghosts of people who had died and were trying to get messages back to people who were still alive."

"I think I heard something about that," John Teed spoke up. "They lived in this farmhouse and the rappings said there was a skeleton in the cellar and by following the information the rappings gave, they dug up the floor and found the skeleton."

"Of the spirit that was sending the messages, yes." The doctor smiled. "That's the very case."

Olive asked: "Why would this spirit or ghost or whatever want his body dug up? Why not just leave his remains alone?"

"As I recall it," John said, "the body was that of a peddler who had called on the previous tenants of the farmhouse and they robbed and killed him. They buried his body in the cellar so the police wouldn't find it. The ghost wanted his family to know what had happened to him."

"Dead people care what's happened to them?" William Cox laughed.

"Live people care, don't they?" Jennie told her brother. "If you died away from home, wouldn't you want us to know about it? And not worry and wonder forever?"

William shrugged. "I don't know. If I was dead, it wouldn't matter, would it?"

"It would matter to *us*," Jennie insisted. "We would want to know what had happened to you."

"Well," her brother conceded, "perhaps you're right."

Esther's face had grown ashen during this conversation, and she sat stiffly in the chair, her hands clasped tightly together. "Dead people?" she said. "Do you mean there are *dead* people around me?"

"It's possible," the doctor replied.

"Dead?" She rose and walked nervously to the other side of the room. "If there is one thing I can't *abide*, it's a dead person! I hate it when someone dies and I have to go and look at their body. Jennie, you recall how it was when Aunt Bessie was laid out in the parlor of her house?" Jennie nodded. "And how everyone insisted I kiss her farewell before they closed the casket?"

"What you feel is perfectly understandable," the doctor said soothingly, "but I am not referring to dead *bodies*, I'm referring to spirits. Spirits that have already left their bodies. Their bodies have long gone . . . been buried . . . but the spirit, for some reason, remains."

"Why?" Esther asked.

"Why?" the doctor was surprised by the question. "I . . . don't really know *why*. It's just that that's the way it seems to happen. For 'why,' perhaps you'd better talk to Reverend Temple."

"He won't know 'why,'" Olive said flatly. "He and his wife were so frightened in here last week that they had a footrace to the front door."

The doctor suppressed a smile that had started to form. "He deals with spirits every day," he said. "That's his business."

"Not the way he dashed out of here, he doesn't deal with them," said Olive. "I really don't think we can count on him for any help if what you say is true."

"Then who *can* we count on?" asked Daniel. "You say medicine doesn't have the answers and the preacher doesn't have them. Then who does? What happens to Esther? Where do we proceed? Doesn't anybody care?"

"Are they going to lock me up in the crazy house?" Esther spun around and glared at the doctor. "I'm not crazy, you know. I was fine until all this started. I'm not crazy." She started to cry and slumped against the wall. "Oh, God, why is this happening to *me*? What have I done?"

Bam! Bam! Bam! The knocking came on the wall just above her head.

"There! That's it! That's what I was telling you about!" Dr. Carritte jumped up in excitement. "That's what the Fox girls were experiencing!"

"I don't want anything to do with dead people," Esther cried. She put her hands over her face and slid slowly down the wall until she sat crumpled on the floor. Both Olive and Jennie started for her, but the doctor motioned them away.

"If we are going to find anything out, we have to do it now," he said sternly.

"But let me help her—" Olive said.

"No! Let her stay where she is!" he barked. "I'm sorry, but I'm going to take charge here."

"Then *do* something," Daniel said loudly. "Get this misery over with."

The doctor stood in the center of the room, facing Esther. "Let me handle this," he said. "You all be quiet and let me handle this." He took a deep breath and then in a commanding voice said: "Whoever or whatever you are, can you hear me?"

Bam! Bam! Bam!

"Does that mean 'yes'?"

Bam! Bam! Bam!

"Do three raps mean 'yes'?"

Again, the hard knocking came three times.

The doctor turned and smiled at the stunned family members. "You see, it's working. If three raps are for 'yes,'" he said loudly, "what is the rap for 'no'?"

Bam!

"Just a single knock?"

Bam! Bam! Bam!

"So an affirmative answer brings three knocks and a negative one brings only one knock?"

Again, three loud raps.

Daniel spoke up. "May I ask a question?" This was followed by three of the raps. "Are my two boys in this room right now?" One rap.

"That's correct," Olive said. "The boys are in bed."

The doctor continued. "Are you a spirit?" Three raps. "Are you dead?" Three raps. "Are you a relative who has passed on? One rap. "You're not a relative. Are you a friend who passed on?" One rap.

"You're not a relative or a friend," said Daniel. "Then we don't know you." No answer.

"Make it in the form of a question," the doctor said.

"Are you the ghost of someone who is dead and none of us ever knew in life? Is that correct?"

Three raps.

"What are you doing here?" Olive spoke up. No answer. "Why are you bothering us?" No answer.

"To get a response, you must ask a question that can be answered with either 'yes' or 'no,'" the doctor told her. "Reword that."

"Are you here to help us?"

Bam!

"Are you going to leave Esther alone?"

Bam!

"Are you a good spirit?" Jennie called out.

Bam!

"Are you evil?" she asked loudly.

Bam! Bam! Bam!

Esther was unconscious. They had to carry her to bed.

Friday, October 4, 1878

"Well, Reverend Temple," Olive said as she opened the front door, "I didn't expect to see you here again."

The Wesleyan minister stood with his hat in his hand. "Reverend Clay and I thought we should come by to see if there is anything we can do to help the poor afflicted girl."

The Baptist minister finished tying the horse to the post by the gate and came onto the porch. "Good afternoon, Mrs. Teed."

"Good afternoon, Reverend Clay." Olive smiled to herself. This was the first time the Baptist preacher had been inside her house. She wasn't a member of his church and he never even nodded to her when they passed on the street, but now that she had the town curiosity inside . . . "Won't you come in, gentlemen." She held the door wider for them and wiped her hands on her apron. "You'll have to excuse my appearance, I'm in the process of fixing noon dinner. My husband and the others will be here shortly." She motioned them toward the parlor.

"Where is Esther?" Reverend Temple asked.

"In the kitchen. I'll get her."

"No, that's fine. We can go to her." He touched Olive lightly on the arm. "I want to show Reverend Clay the bucket of water that boiled over."

"Yes," said the Baptist preacher. "Mrs. Temple has talked of nothing else since she witnessed it."

Olive smiled. "I'm sure she has."

"Mrs. Clay wanted to come today but I thought she'd better stay away for a while. Until Esther gets stronger, anyway."

"Stronger?"

"Dr. Carritte told us she fainted last night, so we figured she'd not be too strong today."

"You've talked with Dr. Carritte?"

"We had breakfast at the cafe this morning. A group of us. We always do on Friday mornings. Helps to understand what's happening in the community."

"Of course," Olive said. "To let the . . . news . . . get around."

"Exactly. This is a growing community, and we must keep our fingers on its pulse."

"Indeed."

They entered the kitchen. Esther, at the sideboard paring potatoes, looked up quickly. She had not been expecting intruders. She recognized Reverend Clay and blushed when she saw Reverend Temple. After all, she had called him a fool the other day. She turned her attention back to the potatoes.

Reverend Temple spoke first. "Esther, we heard from Dr. Carritte this morning that he has discovered what's been ailing you." The girl didn't answer. "He says that you are either a conduit for electricity or else you have benign spirits around you."

"Benign spirits?" Olive's voice rose just slightly.

"Well," Reverend Temple said, "at least not *demons*."

"No," said his companion, "not demons. We were all very happy to learn they are *not* demons."

"So were we," Olive said flatly.

"There had been so much talk in town about demons and devilish spirits that we are certainly glad those rumors can be laid to rest." Reverend Temple pulled out a chair and sat down at the table. "I had always thought they were benign spirits, myself. Poor lost souls trapped between earth and heaven, unsure which way to go. Now my Baptist colleague here believes the electrical theory over the spirit theory."

"I don't believe spirits can manifest themselves to humans," the other man stated. "The souls of the dead are not permitted to remain on this planet."

"Who doesn't permit them?" Olive asked.

"Why, God, of course. He is all-powerful and He is always in command. The Bible tells us that."

Esther raised her head. "The Bible talks about spirits roaming the earth."

"Oh, yes," the Baptist minister replied, "but that was back in the olden days, in the days of Jesus. These are modern times. God will not permit spirits to roam the earth until the Second Coming."

"Now, see," put in Reverend Temple, "I don't believe that. I believe there are spirits all around us. Good and bad."

"Like good and bad people?" Esther asked.

"Exactly."

"How can you die and still be bad?" the girl asked.

"If you don't go to heaven," Reverend Temple said.

"Do good spirits go to heaven?"

"Oh, yes."

"So just bad spirits stay here."

"No, I didn't say that. You can have both good *and* bad spirits here on earth."

"But I thought the good ones went to heaven," Esther insisted.

"Not *all* of them," the preacher tried to explain.

"That doesn't seem very fair," she said. "Some good ones get to go and some good ones have to stay. Does that seem fair to you?"

Reverend Temple got slightly red in the face. "It's not whether I consider it fair or not, it's just the way of the Lord."

"Then *He's* not very fair," she said and took a slash at a potato.

"Esther!" Olive said loudly. "I'm surprised at you."

Reverend Temple smoothed things over. "That's perfectly understandable. We are discussing theology and God's reasons for doing things. None of us can understand why the Creator does some of the things He does."

"And we dare not question," said the Baptist. "We must only accept."

Esther poured water onto the potatoes in the pot. "I find it very difficult to accept what's been happening to me. I never went to Church a lot and never went to ministers' college, so I don't have any of the answers. I just wish if God has put this thing on me He'd take it off."

Reverend Temple decided to change the subject. "That's the bucket there," he pointed out to his companion. "The one I told you about. The one that boiled over."

Olive brought the bucket from the sideboard and put it in the center of the table. Reverend Clay carefully put his hand in it. "It's cold water now," he said.

"Of course it is," Olive said. "I just drew it from the well."

"And it just foamed up and over?" he asked. "Without being near a fire?"

"Just as you see it now," Reverend Temple said proudly, as if he had had something to do with the manifestation.

"It certainly would have been marvelous to have witnessed it," the other man said. "To have been able to see something that unusual."

Bam! The single knock shook the table. Reverend Temple

jumped up from his chair, his ruddy complexion suddenly ashen. Bam!

"Look!" the Baptist minister shouted. "Look at the water!" They all stared as the clear water started to turn yellow. Then it began to bubble. Then it acted as if it were boiling. It rose to the top of the pail when Olive grabbed it.

"No, you don't," she said. "Not over my clean floor again!" She set the pail in the sink, where all movement abruptly stopped.

"Well, you saw it," Esther said flatly.

"Yes, yes, I did." The Reverend Clay's eyes were still quite wide.

"I suppose you might as well see the wall upstairs, too," Olive said. "As long as you're here." She led the way out of the kitchen and up the stairs. Both men paused at the entrance to the bedroom, unsure if they wanted to go in or not. "Over there," Olive pointed.

They could see the gouges in the plaster from where they stood. The large, crudely printed letters were still there, exactly as they had first appeared: "Esther Cox, you are mine to kill!"

Reverend Clay ventured into the room first, then the other man entered. They ran their hands over the letters, letting their fingers feel the deeply cut lines. The Baptist minister took off his hat and pulled out the handkerchief he always kept in it. He placed his hat on Esther's cot. "It looks as if someone did this with a large nail or a railroad spike or something," he said, wiping the white dust from his hands.

"We didn't see what did it," Olive said. "They just appeared, scattering plaster over the rug."

"The entire family saw it?" The minister touched the wall again. "Even Dr. Carritte saw it?"

"Yes," Olive replied, "even the doctor. We all saw it."

That's when the minister's hat rose off Esther's cot and floated slowly up to the ceiling. Olive saw it first, shouted, and pointed. The men stared upward and, for a second, the preacher was sure he had lost his hat forever. Then it came down, quickly, and fell on the floor.

"Can I try it again?" Reverend Clay picked up his hat, dusted it off, and put it back on the cot. Again it floated up and touched the ceiling. He had just uttered "remarkable!" when the hat spun several times in the air and came rushing at him on a forty-five-degree angle. He ducked as it sailed past his face, then stopped, spun again, and aimed. With a plop, the hat landed squarely on the man's head. With a rip, the brim tore loose as the hat was yanked down over his eyes.

The Reverend Temple won this race to the door as well.

Sunday, October 6, 1878

The Baptist church was full to overflowing after word circulated (posters had quickly been printed and tacked to trees) that the Reverend Clay would lecture on Esther and the phenomenon he *personally* witnessed. The curious, including a number who never went to church, filled the pews. After the singing and a brief Bible message, the learned man of God delivered a one-hour lecture based on what he had seen in about ten minutes at the Teed residence.

"It was not demons." (A sigh of relief from the congregation.)

"Esther did not in any way produce these manifestations herself." (Another sigh.)

"The Teed family was not responsible." (Nodding of heads.)

"It is Dr. Carritte's theory that the girl's nerves have received a shock of some kind." (Murmuring of inquiring interest.)

"It is my contention that it's caused by lightning." (Lightning?)

"It is my contention that invisible flashes of lightning leave her body in some mysterious manner and that the sounds that everyone has been able to hear so distinctly are nothing more than peals of thunder." (Sideways glances one to another.)

"Therefore, we here in Amherst have nothing to fear. This is not the work of the Devil." (Scattered applause.)

"We will now pass the collection plate."

Monday, October 7, 1878

"Olive, my *dear*!" Olive felt the perfumed cheek touching hers before she even knew who was at the door. "Dear Olive, it must all be such a trial for you!"

Olive stepped back to get a better look at her visitors. "Why, Mrs. Talbot," she said. "What a surprise."

"I know, dear, and I've been meaning to visit you before but I've just been so busy and all." The middle-aged woman in the long black dress with all the ruffles pushed past Olive and came into the hall. "You know Mrs. Lewis, of course? And Mrs. Braithwaite? And Olive, this is my sister-in-law Mrs. Timmons. She's visiting us from Halifax."

Olive extended her hand to each of the ladies as they filed into her hallway and headed toward the parlor. She knew Mrs. Talbot from church, but it was only a nodding acquaintance. The Talbots and the Teeds were not on the same social level. The other two women were wives of businessmen. She knew their faces, but they had never had her to their homes. Now they were in *her* home. Again she suppressed a smile.

"And how is dear, dear Esther?" Mrs. Talbot arranged herself on the sofa, making sure her full black taffeta skirt was displayed to its best advantage.

"She's fine, thank you," Olive said.

"Is she here?" asked Mrs. Lewis. "I mean, *here* in the house?" When Olive said "yes," the ladies giggled nervously.

"I think the others would like to meet her," Mrs. Talbot said. "Of course, *I* know Esther *personally.*" She beamed indulgence at the others. "She was in my daughter's Sunday school class. Such a sweet child."

"Thank you," Olive replied. "I also think my sister is a sweet child."

"It must be terrible for you," Mrs. Timmons spoke up. "It's been in the Halifax papers ever since it started. Everyone is so curious about it. All my friends were terribly excited when I told them I was coming to Amherst and that my sister-in-law actually *knew* Esther! And then yesterday in church when Dr. Clay explained what was really happening—"

"Dr. Clay?" Olive hadn't heard about that. "Dr. Clay is a Baptist, Mrs. Talbot. Why didn't you and your sister-in-law go to the Wesleyan church as usual?"

"Well," said the lady from Halifax, "when I heard that there was going to be a lecture about the Amherst demons, I insisted we go to the Baptist church instead. It was my idea."

"Anyway," Mrs. Talbot chimed in, "I have no prejudices. I can go to the Baptist church once in a while if I choose. I don't have to believe everything I hear, of course."

"And yesterday," Olive questioned, "the sermon was about Esther and her demons?"

"No demons! No, no," Mrs. Braithwaite said quickly. "The Reverend Clay made a special point about that. There are no demons involved, and you and the others in your family aren't responsible, either."

"That's good news," Olive answered.

"It's all lightning," Mrs. Lewis put in. "Lightning. Isn't that interesting? Even on a sunny day. Fascinating!"

"Lightning." Olive rolled the word around her tongue. "Yes, that is a fascinating theory. From the sky?"

"Oh, no," Mrs. Talbot exclaimed. "From Esther!"

"It comes from her."

"Invisible."

"In all directions."

"No control over it."

"Fascinating."

"Obviously, Olive," Mrs. Talbot said confidentially, "we would not be here if there were *demons*. Wild horses wouldn't drag us in here if that were the case. But lightning, well, that's . . . that's normal. I mean, everybody has seen lightning. We *all* have seen lightning. It does take it out of the supernatural, now, doesn't it?"

"No," said Olive, "it doesn't."

"Doesn't?"

"I cannot agree with the minister that what's been happening here is natural, like lightning. I've seen too much of it and witnessed things that mere lightning is incapable of doing."

"But after all, dear Olive," Mrs. Talbot said, "in all respects to you and your opinion, Reverend Clay is a learned man. He has *studied* theology and scientific matters. If he says it is lightning, then you must give him some credence."

Olive decided it was now or never. She could smile and be pleasant and let these women—and the dozens who would come around later—interrupt her chores, disturb her home, and upset her family life. It was already more than Esther could handle, and it was becoming more than Olive wanted to handle.

"What we have in this house is a spirit," she said. "A spirit who is mean and troublesome and evil."

"Evil?" Mrs. Braithwaite pulled her collar closer to her chin.

"Evil. He torments my poor sister, he throws things

across the room, he makes fires go out and cold water boil. He also writes obscenities on the walls. Lightning doesn't do that."

"But the Reverend Clay—"

"I don't care about the Reverend Clay," Olive stated. "He came over here, *uninvited*"—she emphasized the word—"with Reverend Temple. He heard knocks, saw the water boil, and had his hat ruined. All that took less than ten minutes. We, who have been shut in here for over a month with these manifestations, do not know what they are. And we have had to live with them. *Live* with them. Not pay a quick *uninvited* visit and run."

Mrs. Talbot's feathers began to bristle. "You're saying that Reverend Clay is incorrect?"

"I'm saying that Reverend Clay doens't know what he's talking about. And neither does Reverend Temple. I'm not sure that even Dr. Carritte knows what he's talking about. But that's all they've been doing. Talking. It's been all talk and nothing has been accomplished and my little sister has been made to suffer because of it." Olive was standing near the doorway. "Now if you ladies will excuse me, I have food to prepare and little boys who need my attention."

"We would like to see Esther," Mrs. Talbot said.

"Yes," Mrs. Timmons added. "I'm leaving for Halifax tomorrow."

"No," Olive heard her voice say. "I'm sorry, but you can't."

"But I came all the way from Halifax—"

"That is not my concern," Olive interrupted, "nor is it Esther's concern."

"Is she in the kitchen?" Mrs. Talbot rose from the sofa. "I think I should be allowed to speak to—"

Olive was firm. "She is not in the kitchen at the moment and you can't speak to her."

"But back in Halifax—"

"I really don't care about Halifax," Olive said, "I care about my sister."

"But so do *we*," Mrs. Talbot replied. "That's why we are here."

"You are here to see the freak in the side-show," Olive replied firmly, "and there will be no performance today. Nor tomorrow," she added. "My sister is suffering. She is ill. She is not on public display."

"But Esther was with my daughter in Sunday school—"

Olive opened the front door. "Mrs. Talbot. Ladies. I must ask you to leave."

"Well, I have never been so insulted. . . ." Mrs. Braithwaite marched past Olive.

Mrs. Talbot didn't budge.

"This is my house . . . my home . . . Mrs. Talbot, and I can have whomever I want in it. And I don't want you or your friends. I'm presiding over a family here, not a circus."

"Well, I will inform Reverend Temple and Reverend Clay just how you have acted, Mrs. Teed," Mrs. Talbot flustered. "And they will see to this."

"If necessary, Mrs. Talbot," said Olive, "I will tell Sheriff MacLean how you have acted. He has told us to call him whenever we have a problem with gawkers."

"Gawkers!" Mrs. Talbot pressed her hand against her ample bosom. "Gawkers! I have never been called a 'gawker.'"

"Well then, that's just one more name to add to your list, isn't it?" Olive said as she slammed the door behind them.

Thursday, October 17, 1878

> The *Chignecto Post:*
> The mysterious knocks and other manifestations of the spirits or of animal magnetism or of humbuggery, have recommenced at Amherst, a young lady being the supposed "Medium." A number of gentlemen, including some physicians have been investigating the case and have so far detected no natural or apparent cause for the manifestations.

Esther was virtually a prisoner by now. If she went into a shop people stared, tried to touch her, or pulled their children out of harm's way. Groups of people stood in front of the house, pointing, gossiping, waiting to hear or see something they could tell others about. Once a church group nailed a letter to the front door demanding that "Esther's satanic friends" leave town. The milkman stopped delivering because his wife didn't want him to "bring the demon home" with him. Someone tossed a hammer through the parlor window, smashing one of the panes. Daniel boarded up the window and hoped that no one would do anything to the upstairs windows.

Stories circulated about the horrible things that went on inside the small frame house. Children had been sacrificed there, one story said. A horrible face could be seen exactly at midnight in an upper window, went another. Neighbors complained to Daniel that their friends and relatives were afraid to visit them on "the Devil's street" and for him to do something about it. Daniel insisted he was trying to do exactly that. More than once John Teed or William Cox had to slip out the back way to call the police and get the front yard cleared of troublesome, and sometimes drunken, gangs. And local wags referred to the rappings in the house as "Esther's farts."

Sunday, October 27, 1878

That morning, Daniel hitched the horse to the buggy and drove Esther to a friend's house a few miles away. She had covered her face with a shawl so no one would see her and torment her. Olive insisted it was the only way the girl—and the family—would get any rest.

After a few days, of course, the *Chignecto Post* found out about it:

> Miss Cox, the heroine of the mysterious manifestations that have created such a sensation in Amherst, the past two months, is now in Upper Sackville, stopping at Mr. Gideon Snowden's. The manifestations on Princess Street have ceased.

Indeed, the manifestations did cease. Esther was gone from the house, and some semblance of normality returned to the Teed residence. The curious no longer gathered in groups in front of the house. No more nailed letters or broken windows or insinuated rumors for Daniel and his family. Olive noticed a "warming up" from the neighbors and citizens she met on everyday chores. Neither she nor Jennie socialized as before. They missed going to church and to the community functions but they had seen the true face of their society and it frightened them. The Teed family became a small gathering unto themselves, preferring their own company and their own "truth" to that of the troublesome and even vicious world around them.

Friday, November 1, 1878

"But you promised," Esther was almost in tears. "You promised. No visitors. No callers. You *promised*!"

"But it's Mr. Milner," Mrs. Snowden whispered. "He owns the *Post*. He's very important."

"I don't want to see him. Or anyone. Olive and Daniel asked you especially."

"I know," the older woman replied. "Here, brush your hair and pinch your cheeks a little. You looked peaked."

"He's going to ask me a lot of questions."

"Maybe not. Maybe he just wants to say hello."

Esther put the brush down on the dresser top. "Please make him go away." The woman shook her head. "I don't want to see anyone."

"This man is very important around here," the woman replied. "I wonder if you should change that dress. He *owns* the newspaper. He could do you a great deal of good. Don't you have a different hair ribbon than that one?" She handed the brush back to Esther. "A couple more strokes and then come down. He's in the parlor. I guess that dress will do. He's very important. I've never had such an important man in my parlor before. Pinch those cheeks." And she was gone.

Esther descended the staircase slowly. She could smell his cigar and hear Mrs. Snowden's rattling voice before she entered the room. Mrs. Snowden was dusting a side table with the edge of her apron while the tall, silver-haired man examined a Staffordshire figurine on the mantlepiece.

"Here she is!" Mrs. Snowden took several small steps and grabbed Esther by the hand. "This is our Esther," she beamed. "Esther, this is Mr. William Milner. He owns the *Chignecto Post*." Esther took his large outstretched hand, touched it lightly, and then sat stiffly on a chair beside the fireplace. While Mrs. Snowden fluttered, Mr. Milner sat on the sofa.

"I hope you're feeling better, Miss Cox," he said. His voice was deep.

"Yes, thank you." Her voice was soft and unsteady. He was the first stranger she had been forced to meet since fleeing Amherst, and she wasn't ready for him.

"I trust I'm not intruding," he said.

"Oh, my, no," Mrs. Snowden chirped, "goodness gracious. It's an honor to have you. An honor."

"Thank you, ma'am." He looked around for an ashtray, and Mrs. Snowden almost flew across the room and back retrieving one for him. He smiled at her and crossed his long legs, showing the tops of his expensive leather boots. "I'm pleased you agreed to see me, Miss Cox."

Esther started to say something, but the woman cut her off. "Why, indeed! It is us who are pleased by your visit, sir!"

"Thank you," he said. "Most kind." His eyes never left Esther's face. "We've heard a great deal about you. From Amherst. You've become quite a little celebrity over there." Esther didn't say a word. "Everyone hereabouts has heard of you and are anxious to meet you. You've not been out much since coming to town." Esther shook her head. "Just here to rest up?" She nodded. "Well, I'll try not to take too much of your time."

"Oh, for heaven's sake, take as long as you want," Mrs. Snowden almost sang out. "I was telling Esther just the other day that she ought to get out more, to mingle more. She needs fresh air. Fresh air always does a body so much good. I recall one time when I had been a sickroom shut-in for a month, how good it felt to get out of the house and into the fresh—"

"Yes, I'm sure," he interrupted her smoothly. "I'm sure. Now, Esther, if you don't mind, I'd like to know exactly what has been happening to you." He kept staring at her.

"Why?"

"Why? Well, because as a newspaperman, I'd like to have the truth. My readers depend on my newspaper for the truth."

"I've already told the truth," she said with a sigh.

"We have heard *stories* over here . . ." he said.

"That's been the problem," the girl replied. "I've told the truth and people have told stories."

"Well, maybe I can rectify those stories. What hasn't been true?"

It was her turn to stare at him. "What *hasn't* been? I can't answer for what *hasn't* been. I can only answer for what I know. For what's really happened."

"Can you tell me?"

"I've already told it a hundred times." She caught a quiver in her voice and fiercely told herself to stay in control of the situation. "Your reporter came and talked to me in Amherst. He spent a couple of hours talking with me and my sister

Olive. He took all sorts of notes. He should still have them. You can read his notes. What he wrote down was the truth."

"I'd prefer to hear it for myself. With my own ears." The man took another puff on the cigar. "To make my own judgment."

"I'm really awfully tired of it," she said. "Tired of talking about it and tired of hearing about it."

"Well, I'm not," he said.

"You don't have to live with it. I do." She thought of Olive and hoped she had some of her sister's strength.

"I understand that and appreciate that," he said, "but my readers have a right to know."

"To know what?"

"The truth."

"I've *told* the truth. To your reporter and to the doctors and to the ministers and to the neighbors, to everybody. All I have ever told is the truth." She looked him square in the face. "Why do you think I *haven't* been telling the truth?"

"I didn't say that."

"No, Esther," Mrs. Snowden butted in, "he didn't say that."

Esther sighed. "Once the truth is told it always remains the truth. My sister told me that."

He puffed again on the cigar. "So I'm not going to be told anything new?"

"There is nothing new."

Another puff, a long silence, and then he ground the cigar out in the ashtray. "You are rather flippant for such a young girl," he said. "It appears you have little respect for authority."

"I have respect for the truth, and that's all I have been telling."

"This truth of yours," he said, "this collection of stories about boiling buckets of water, hats flying across the room, rappings and writings on the wall, all this is the truth? Your idea of what *truth* is?"

"Olive says you can't change the truth. It just is."

"Are you a Christian person?" he asked abruptly.

"What?" the question stunned her.

"A Christian person," he repeated, "a believer in Jesus Christ and that He was the true son of God."

"I . . . I . . . yes, of course I am," she stammered.

His eyes were on hers. "Why do you hesitate? Why don't you answer me directly?"

"Well," Esther felt her face burning red hot, "no one has ever asked me that question before. I always assumed that everyone knew that I—"

"That you were what?" he asked quickly.

"That I was a Christian. Everybody is a Christian." She looked at Mrs. Snowden. "Aren't they?"

"There are those who profess it with their right hand while doing the Devil's work with their left," he said. "Which side are you on? The right or the left?"

"The right or left of what?" She could feel her inner composure melting away.

"The right or the left hand of God?" he said loudly.

Tears formed in her eyes as she tried to understand what he was saying, trying to find an answer he would believe. "I've done no wrong—"

"It's not wrong to call demons?"

Esther felt as if she had been slapped. "Demons?" The tears were larger now.

"To invoke demons in your work? To call upon the forces of Satan to frighten innocent people? That's not wrong?"

The tears started down her cheeks. "Of course it is," she said.

"Then why do you do it?" he demanded. "If you know it's wrong?"

"I *don't* do it." Her voice broke. "I don't call anything. It just happens."

"It just happens!" His voice rose. "And it happens to you? And only you?"

"Yes," she sobbed.

"Just by happenstance these demons choose you? These devils choose a simpleminded teenage girl from Amherst. *Our* Amherst. Just by accident." He got up and stood over her. "Do you expect me to believe that?" She was crying so badly she couldn't answer. "Do you? Do you expect the good people of this country to believe all this just happens? You are involved in witchcraft! In some kind of Devil-worship! You call down these satanic forces! Admit it!" He grabbed her shoulders and shook her. "Admit it!" he shouted.

Esther felt a surge of strength running through her arms. Quickly her hands went up to the hands that were on her shoulders, and she dug her nails into their flesh. The man pulled back in pain. Then she placed her hands—those hands with the new power—around his waist and squeezed. He yelled again, and the yell continued as she tossed his body up over the sofa and heard it thump onto the hardwood floor.

She jumped up and ran past the hysterical Mrs. Snowden, toward the door. She was headed for the staircase and the safety of her bedroom when she stopped, wheeled around, and glared at the fallen man. They all heard the words boom out of her throat in a harsh masculine voice:

"Old man! Keep your damned hands off my girl!"

Thursday, November 7, 1878

For a full week before the article appeared in the *Chignecto Post*, Dr. Carritte and Reverend Temple had been talking to its news reporter about Esther. Instead of a stranger writing the story, they demanded and got permission to write their own version of what happened and to correct any errors before it went to print. Rumor had it that the *Post* was going to do a story—the definitive story—on Esther Cox and what had been labeled "The Amherst Mystery." The moment the paper hit the front porches, all other activity ceased.

THE ESTHER COX MYSTERY

> Below will be found the testimony of the physician and minister of the Gospel who attended the house of Mr. Teed at Amherst during the period when mysterious knocks and rappings attending Esther Cox took place. Both of these gentlemen have themselves revised this account made by our reporter, ensuring absolute accuracy.
>
> Our reporter questioned several other citizens of Amherst. Dr. Nathan Tupper visited Miss Cox on one occasion for the purpose of witnessing the manifestations, but none whatever occurred. He was incredulous as to their being any serious character. Several others were of the same opinion. At the same time, a great majority of the persons who visited the house, gave an experience nearly identical to that of Dr. Carritte and Rev. Mr. Temple.
>
> DR. CARRITTE'S STATEMENT:
>
> The first manifestations I witnessed was when I was called to see Miss Cox professionally. She was

suffering from nervous excitement. My attention was first called to taps apparently on the wooden slats of the bed. Then the taps left the slats and commenced on the walls, like beating a tattoo. Then from the walls it ran to the roof, sounding like a heavy hammering. I heard these sounds repeatedly after my first visit. Sometimes other persons were present and heard the same. At first the family were much alarmed, but in time became quite used to it. I saw the pillows force themselves out on the floor, when by no possibility could Miss Cox have moved them. I tried a great many experiments with pillows. Two persons took hold of a pillow; it would appear to be impelled towards the bed. Placed pillows at the foot of the bed. They would move towards the head. They would stiffen up and swell out. They, in fact, appeared to be animated with life. I placed on the bed a hat. It danced up on its edge. Sometimes there were a number of ladies and other spectators in the room.

On one occasion, when sitting near the door, the bedclothes commenced to move down towards the foot of the bed in folds. The two Misses Cox were lying on the bed at the time. I turned my head to call the attention of Mrs. Teed to the movement, when suddenly bang against the door a lot of plaster fell in connection with the pillows and bedclothes. An examination of it showed what would seem quite incredible. The plaster could not have reached the door, no matter in what direction it was impelled from the wall from which it was forced, because the door was around a jog or corner of the room. After starting from the wall it must have received a new impulse. Possibly it may in some way have come in contact with the bedclothes, and thus have had its position changed. About a foot square of plaster fell. I am quite satisfied that neither of the Misses Cox moved the plaster.

I sent her down cellar on one occasion, and the pounding on the floor was loud. She became alarmed and ran back, and the pounding continued until she got above the steps. I stood in the recess in the cellar watching her, and the pounding went on, satisfying me that she could not have done it, and no other person did. I have been sitting in the room day and evening, when the rappings went on. I have repeatedly put her in a room alone, and the rappings would be loud. By opening the door suddenly, I was quite assured that she was not in that part of the room where the poundings occurred, and could not have been done with her hands or feet. One night I heard the rappings on the roof. I ran out of the house but saw nothing on the roof. It was a bright moonlight night, and I could have seen any visible object that might have caused it. I heard it that night as far as Blair's Stables, about 75 yards distant, several houses filling up the space. I have sent her in the woodshed and the sounds came from there. The rappings and knockings appeared to proceed contiguous to her, and to change from place to place as she moved round.

These manifestations were always preceded by nervous excitement, twitching of the muscles and unnatural sleep. During this sleep no rappings took place. When she awoke the rappings would recommence. Then when she became wearied and exhausted, and recovered her natural sleep, the rappings would recommence and continue during the sleep at intervals.

The writing on the wall and the matches setting fire to the house I know nothing about. I have seen the writing going on at different times. I have often heard scratching on the wall, like a person writing, at a time when she was in full view and some distance from it. The most remarkable feature in the affair that I personally witnessed was the manner in which a pillow held in my hand swelled up and writhed and contorted itself as if animated by life. This took place before a number of persons present, and it operated in other persons hands in the same way, proving conclusively to all who witnessed it, that some unseen power or agency was operating. What that agency is, I have no theory whatever to offer. I only give the facts as I witnessed them. I heard of these manifestations before I went to the house, and believed they were idle talk till I witnessed them for myself. I do not believe I could have been deceived in my own sensations of hearing and seeing, or that many others could have been deceived.

REV. R.A. TEMPLE'S STATEMENT:

Mrs. Teed and Mr. Teed, are members of my church. I was in the habit of visiting the house in discharge of my duty as pastor, nd saw Miss Cox about the time of the commencement of the phenomena. I was naturally enough quite assured of the honesty and sincerity of Mr. and Mrs. Teed and Miss Cox, and of the fact that they would not willingly lend themselves to any imposture, but any confidence I reposed in them did not prevent my examining for myself and testing, as far as I was able, the manifestations in order to satisfy myself they were not the result of fraud or collusion. When I first visited Miss Cox, I found her suffering from intense nervous excitement. The restless movements and nervous twitchings of her body, showed she was laboring under exciting influences. She received me with evident repugnance, which as I talked calmly gradaully wore off, and I thereafter visited her a number of times both day and evening. The phenomena I witnessed took place indifferently, both in daylight and after dark, so that I was able to scrutinize the house and surroundings in broad daylight, and when I could have scarcely been deluded by the testimony of my own senses. The manifestations of whatever kind appeared to wait upon or attend the movements of Miss Cox. They took place under no circumstances during her absence. During the days I visited the house, I saw very many strange occurances, that were not only without any visible cause, but were totally inexplicable to my mind, as far as my acquaintance extends to the laws that govern force and matter. I have seen pillows and bedclothes move round on the bed without visible or human cause whatever impelling them. I have heard tappings on the walls, bedstead, floors, and with noises on the roof and sides of the house, sometimes almost as loud as thunder. I could not very well have been mistaken in these noises. On one occasion in particular—it was in the forenoon—I was conversing with Miss Cox in the kitchen of the house. I was standing between her and the window and I heard a loud rapping, apparently on the wall outside. Miss Cox could not have done it herself, as I was between her and the place where it occurred. I quickly glanced out the window and saw no one in the vicinity of the outside and no possible means whereby it could have been done. Even while I looked, the noise continued. The occurance of the noise at such a time when the senses are most on the alert quite satisfied me that it was no ordinary occurance. I have seen writing on the wall in the pantry, done by Miss Cox when she was said to be under exciting influences, and at the dictation of some outside agency or power. I did not see her do it. It has been done, I understand, in the evenings in the dark. I do not know whether she can write, but understand she can write but slightly. I do not know whether the handwriting differs materially from hers or not. The writing is made in right lines, as perfectly as if made in daylight. The spelling is execrable. It is the most abominable trash, blasphemous and villainous in a degree that could only emanate from some depraved creature. I do not think that Miss Cox herself could inspire such curses and foul thoughts. I do not know how she held the pencil, whether she herself guided it or whether she merely touched it. My testimony ought to deal only with what I have myself witnessed. On one occasion I was sitting in the front parlor and Miss Cox in the dining room. I heard the sound of an open-handed slap and an exclamation of "Oh!" I hurried into the room and found Miss Cox holding her hand to her face. She said, "He has slapped me." I looked at her cheek closely. There was a bright red spot on it, as if the blood had gathered there after a smart blow. She of course might have done that herself, if inclined to deceive, or in a state of hallucination she may have imagined some other power did it. But on another occasion, in daylight, I was sitting with her, when suddenly I heard the same noise, and the same exclamation of pain from her, and the same red spot appeared. I was quite satisfied she did not strike herself. Her hands were before her, and she could not have raised them without my seeing her. I had heard that when she went into the kitchen the water in the pail often bubbled up almost in a state of effervescence. I was much inclined to doubt it, but one morning I satisfied myself the statement was true. I went out into the kitchen. She was there. There were knockings and rappings on the roof and walls. Directly the water in one of the pails became violently agitated. The pail was about half full of water, and it assumed a yellowish hue, as if drawn from a muddy brook or well. It retained that color. The water in the other bucket was quite clear, not a speck in it. I was told they were both drawn at the same time from the same well. The buckets differed in no appreciable way, except the one that appeared agitated was not painted on the inside, the other was.

I cannot give any solution of this mystery. Miss Cox herself imagines she is under the influence of a young man, who appears to have picked up some books on Mesmerism and becoming versed in it, has been experimenting on her. She is fully imbued with that idea that he controlled and influenced these movements.

By this secret power, she says she has conversed with him, has been informed of his locality, knew by intuition when he was passing on the street. One day when he was thus (as she says) talking to her, she turned to her sister, and asked her if she did not hear him speak, and appeared to be surprised when her sister replied "No." This may be an hallucination on her part, but the impressions on her mind ought not to be cast aside in seeking the bottom of this mystery. I have no theory or explanation to offer. I believe these phenomena to be worthy of scientific attention and investigation as I have no doubt they are reconcilable with known laws. I have not come to regard them as supernatural, or as manifestations from the land of spirits. The meaningless character of

> the performances forbids any such conclusion. The age with all its discoveriees has only reached their outskirts—the borderland of the great world of electricity, of which these may only be phases.

Daniel stopped reading aloud and lowered the newspaper to his lap. There was silence in the parlor after he finished. It had been Olive's idea that he read it to the entire family after dinner. Jennie had heard about it but hadn't seen it. William Cox and John Teed could "draw" their names, but neither could read or write. Daniel had taught himself to read when he was a teenager. It was this same ability that eventually made him foreman at the Amherst Boot and Shoe Factory. "What do you think?" he asked.

"Well," said Olive, "it took courage for both those men to say in print what they did. One being a doctor and the other being a minister and all."

"Doctor Carritte didn't tell about being hit by potatoes," said Jennie, laughing.

"No," Olive remarked, "I think the incident was a little beneath his dignity."

"Nor did he mention the code," William put in. "The three raps for 'yes' and the one rap for 'no.'"

"He didn't, did he?" Daniel frowned. "I wonder why he left that out. We all witnessed it."

"Probably," added Jennie, "he didn't think anyone would believe him. I know when I mentioned it at work, everyone laughed. Nobody thought it was true."

"But it was!" Olive said sharply.

"*We* know it was," Jennie replied, "but nobody else does."

"Maybe nobody wants to," Daniel said. "People don't like the idea of ghosts."

"Not in Amherst," John said with a laugh.

"Not *anywhere*," Daniel said.

"You know," Olive said slowly, "Dr. Carritte never really came to any conclusion. Never really said what he thought it is."

"Neither did the preacher," William spoke up.

"They don't know what it is," Jennie said. "They have reputations to maintain. I thought they said more than was necessary as it is."

"Well, at least they didn't make Esther sound like a

looney," Olive said. "Or a witch or a satanist or whatever they're called." She sighed, "We're lucky there."

"I don't think Reverend Temple said anything at all," Jennie spoke up. "He used a lot of words but what did he say?"

"That he had seen things he couldn't explain," Daniel said.

"He didn't say Mrs. Temple also saw the bucket boiling and the writing on the wall." Olive laughed. "She must be furious with him for not mentioning her name in the newspaper."

"It's all over town anyway," Jennie said. "Everyone who is anyone in Amherst has heard of her close call with the ghost." She laughed. "I wish I could have been here to see her face."

"It was the color of yesterday's ashes," Olive snickered. "And her hat became tilted to one side." Now, she laughed aloud. "Esther and I fell into each other's arms with the giggles after they had gone."

"Then no wonder he didn't mention it," Daniel said. "What's this nonsense about Esther and some young man who read about Mesmerism? Where did Reverend Temple get that story?"

"From Esther," Jennie said. "She'd told me about it, but I paid it no mind. She must have told him and he remembered it."

"Who is the young man?" Daniel asked. "Do I know him?"

Jennie stared down at the carpet. "Bob McNeal."

"Who?" Daniel's voice rose. "Bob McNeal? Why, he hasn't been around Amherst for months. Where in the world did she get that idea? Bob McNeal, indeed!"

"She claimed once or twice," Jennie tried to explain, "that she just *knew* when he was near her. Knew even when he was *thinking* about her."

"I'm surprised she never mentioned him to me," Olive said. "After all, we spend entire days together."

"It is one of her secrets," Jennie said. "She asked me not to tell anyone."

"And now the whole world knows," Olive said flatly.

"Well, you know how Esther is with her secrets," Jennie kept on explaining, "she gets these ideas and you can't reason them out of her."

"Bob McNeal hasn't been in town for months," William remarked. "He just left. That's all."

"Right," John said. "He used to work at a table near mine. One day he didn't come to work. Nobody ever saw him again."

"Where did she get this idea about Mesmerism?" Daniel asked Jennie. "Did Bob tell her he was studying it?"

"I don't know," Jennie answered truthfully. "She didn't elaborate on it, and I didn't ask. Bob is a subject she doesn't like to discuss."

"After that picnic," John said.

"And she came home wet," William added.

"The way he threw the food basket into the yard and practically threw her out of the buggy as well," Olive said sharply, "there certainly was no call for those kinds of manners. I, for one, was glad he never called on her again. He's not the kind of man I want for my sister."

"Where'd he go?" William asked. "Anybody see him again?"

"I heard," Daniel said, "that he was working on the docks at St. John, but I don't know for sure. He was a strange one, he was. But for Esther to put all the blame for this on him, when she really doesn't know—"

"It's better than blaming it on ghosts," Jennie said. "The minister wouldn't have believed her if she said it was ghosts, but he did believe her when she said it was Mesmerism. Esther *wants* to be believed. You know, *we*"—and she waved her right hand at the small group in the parlor—"we are the only ones who believe her. Nobody else does. Not her friends, the girls she went to school with, the neighbors. Not Reverend Temple and probably not even Dr. Carritte believe her. I can understand her inventing imaginary stories when people refuse to believe the true ones."

Daniel took a deep breath. "Which brings me," he said slowly, "to another item in today's *Post.*"

"Another?" said Olive. "About Esther?"

"About Esther. I didn't want to read it to you first. In fact," Daniel wasn't smiling, "I didn't want to read it to you at all, but I knew you'd eventually hear about it."

Olive put her hand to her mouth. "Oh, God," she whispered. "Don't let it be bad, please."

"It is," her husband replied. "It's bad."

"Who wrote it?" Jennie asked.

"The owner of the paper himself," Daniel replied. "Mr. William Milner, publisher and owner of the *Post.* It's an—" he paused—"an editorial."

"About Esther," Olive said, almost not breathing.

"About Esther," Daniel replied. "Do you want me to read it, or not?" After they murmured their consent, Daniel folded the paper back to the front page. He settled farther into his chair, getting a better glow from the oil lamp on the table beside him. "The Cox Phenomena," he read aloud, and then continued for several minutes to read what was basically a scholarly paper on ghosts, spirits, demons, and Devil-worshipers. The publisher cited cases in mythology, in antiquity, and the modern Spiritualist movement. They tried to follow this pedagogical, yet negative, dissertation. "This is the part coming up that I was talking about," he said, looking up from his reading.

"He hasn't mentioned Esther by name," Olive said. "Only in the title."

"He doesn't," Daniel said. "Let me finish." He folded the newspaper again and started reading the last two paragraphs.

> There are some citizens in this area who firmly believe in these spirits, in these helpers from the underworld. They believe these demons are able to set back those laws of the Universe made by the Almighty Himself and which the Christian world sacredly believes, stand fixed and immutable from everlasting to everlasting.
>
> If a "demonic" influence exists in Amherst, as has been suggested by a contemporary, the laws of James the First had better be re-enacted, making it a capital crime, "For anyone that shall use, practice or exercise any invocation of any evil or wicked spirit or consult or covenant, or employ any wicked spirit to or for any purpose."

Daniel looked at the faces around him. They were unmoving. He resumed reading: "Under that law three thousand persons were hanged during the long Parliament and thousands both before and after."

The room was silent. Then Olive started to cry. "My God," she said, "that man wants Esther *killed*!"

Sunday, November 24, 1878

"Now, let's not get overly excited," Olive said to the family at breakfast. "When she gets back home, let's just pretend that everything is all right. And nobody mention those stories in the *Post*." She looked at William and John. "Perhaps she hasn't seen them. After all, she's been too sick to read anything."

The family had learned that the very day the articles—and the death-penalty editorial—appeared, Esther became very ill. Mrs. Snowden had called a doctor, and the diagnosis was diphtheria. For two weeks the girl lay in bed, sweating, having chills, not being able to eat anything and vomiting up whatever she did get down. Mrs. Snowden had cared for her, given her the medicines and was, frankly, relieved when Esther recovered and could go back to Amherst. During that time—over two weeks—there had been no manifestations of any kind. It was as if the energies respected her illness and left her alone. Daniel called for her that morning and drove her back to the house on Princess Street.

Of course, they fussed over her when she came home. Olive and Jennie both remarked on how pale she looked and how much weight she had lost. The two young Teed children had made crayon drawings of what they thought Esther had looked like when she was in bed. John and William had scoured the marshes and picked a bouquet of the last remaining wild flowers and handed them to her as she opened the door. She cried and hugged everyone and was genuinely glad to be home. While Mrs. Snowden had done everything possible for her, the woman's constant and unthinking chatter had begun to fray at her nerves. She longed for the peace and quiet of the Amherst house, even if there *was* a ghost in it.

Olive helped her upstairs with her suitcase and unpacked for her. Esther just sat on the bed and watched. "We truly missed you, dear," Olive said. "The boys were so alone all day with no one to play with. They asked about you all the time."

"I missed you, too," she replied. "I missed everybody!" She looked around her room, and her smile faded when she saw the wall with the letters gouged on it. "You haven't plastered that over yet," she said. "I thought maybe you'd do it while I was gone."

"No, I wanted to, to cover up those hideous words, but

Dr. Carritte said it was 'evidence' and it was too soon to destroy such 'evidence.'"

"Evidence of what?" the girl asked.

"Of what's been happening, I guess," her sister replied. "In case another doctor or another expert comes in to study the case. He has been trying to find someone, but without much success."

"Has there been any"— she paused and looked at Olive— "anything happening since I went away? In the house, I mean."

"No." Olive hung one of Esther's dresses in the wardrobe. "Not a sound."

"No knocking or writings or things flying?"

Olive shook her head, "It's been mighty peaceful here"— she closed the wardrobe door—"and let's pray it stays that way. Was there anything at the Snowdens'?"

"You didn't hear about Mr. Milner?" she asked hesitatingly. "Mrs. Snowden didn't tell you about that?"

"You mean what he wrote in the paper?"

Esther shook her head. "I didn't read the paper, because Mrs. Snowden said it had been unkind. So I didn't ask her to show it to me. I was too sick to get more upset." She paused. "You didn't hear that I picked the man up and threw him across the parlor?"

Olive steadied herself against the dresser. "No, I didn't. Let me sit down first." She came over and sat on the cot beside Esther. "Now," she said, "tell me about it." Esther related as much as she could remember. She recalled him shouting at her and saying she was evil, but she swore to her sister that she didn't recall picking him up and throwing him. Nor did she recall saying anything to him. She had gone straight to her room; passed out on the bed, and awoke feeling miserable. The diphtheria had started to come on shortly after that.

"Mr. Milner is a tall man, Olive. He's big-boned. Look at me—I'm small and pudgy. How could I have picked him up and tossed him? I have difficulty helping you turn a mattress! But Mrs. Snowden said I did it. I don't remember."

"Did you see the man after that?"

She shook her head. "No. Never again. I got sick and didn't see anybody but the doctor and Mrs. Snowden. I didn't want to see anybody. Did he put *that* in the paper? That I had tossed him over the sofa?"

Olive had to smile. "No," she said, "that was one item he didn't mention. Probably you bruised his ego more than his backside." She laughed. "You know, perhaps those ghosts around you are good for something after all."

Esther smiled. It was good to be home and to hear her sister laugh. "I hope they are, but so far I can't see any use for them. They frighten me. I'm getting accustomed to them, but they still frighten me."

Olive almost asked her about this Mesmerism business and Bob McNeal but decided against it. Mentioning Bob always uspet Esther, Olive didn't know why, but she was not about to upset her sister the first day back home. "I do have some good news for you," she said. "Mr. White is coming over later this afternoon and wants to talk to you."

"Mr. White?" Esther asked. "Of the Oyster Saloon?" Olive nodded yes. "What does he want with me?"

"He wants to give you a job."

"A job?" Esther's mouth dropped open. "With pay?"

"Of course with pay. He and Daniel have discussed it, and I agree with them that it would be perfect for you." She smiled. "And you could use the money."

"I've never had a job," Esther said, stammering. "Why me? What would I do?"

"Why don't we wait and ask Mr. White when he stops over? A job would take your mind off things."

Esther got up and walked out of the room with her sister. "Everything's happening so fast. I don't feel in control anymore."

"You'll be all right"—she patted Esther's shoulder—"and getting into commerce will do you a world of good." Olive didn't see the frown Esther wore all the way down the stairs.

* * *

Both Mr. and Mrs. White had come calling. They were in their mid-forties and rather wealthy, for Amherst. John White was a big man with a hearty laugh who had opened a coffee and sandwich shop, then increased it to seafood and fresh oysters when in season. He fried them, sautéed them, broiled them, and served them raw with side dishes of potatoes and vegetables; fresh homemade bread and butter; and tangy, cold beer. It was a popular eating spot, especially for the men. Some of the ladies in town didn't think it was proper to be seen in a place that served beer, but other ladies dined there and gossiped to their friends about who else they saw eating there. Most times it was just loud and crowded, but sometimes it got rowdy and the air grew blue with English and French cuss words. That's when John White would come out from behind the serving bar and knock heads together.

"Why me?" Esther repeated the question to John White as they sat in the parlor. "I've never worked in a saloon before."

"I need somebody, and you're a strong and healthy girl. Daniel and I have known each other for years, so you have all the references you need."

"And it will be good for you to get out of this house now," Daniel added. "Olive can take care of the boys without you. She saw that when you were over with the Snowdens."

"And you'll be bringing in money," Mrs. White said. "You'll see what a blessing it'll be when you have your own income. I wanted to work when I was a girl, but my folks wouldn't permit it. I work some in the restaurant now but we have a new house, so I'd prefer to stay home and mind it."

Esther had heard that they were building a new home, a large place outside town, and people had wondered how Mrs. White would manage the home and still work at the saloon. So she would be taking Mrs. White's place. "That's a great deal of responsibility," Esther said. "Are you sure I can handle it? Waiting on tables and carrying those trays?"

"Oh, I won't have you do any of the heavy work," John White said. "I've got a fellow for that. I want you behind the bar and to help clear the tables and maybe do a little of the cooking, but mostly to be out front and see that everything goes right. You can do that," he said. "What you don't already know, I'll show you. It's really very easy."

"When do you wish me to start?" she asked. "I just returned home, and I have been ill. I'd like a little more time before starting the job."

"This is Sunday," John White replied. "Let's say you begin Friday. That's the day before Saturday. We get really busy then."

"In the morning?"

"Eight would be perfect."

The Whites stayed for a little longer, having a cup of tea and talking of local happenings. No one mentioned Esther's "troubles." She was glad of that. When they left, Esther went up to her room to lie down. She felt good about things. She had recovered from the diphtheria. She was back in her home with people who loved her. She was about to start a job and have her own money. Her life *was* getting better. Perhaps now she would be able to lead a *normal* life. She smiled. How good it was to be back where people—like the Whites—needed her.

In the buggy, John and Mary White grinned at each other. The horse was heading down La Planche Street past the Oyster Saloon, across the tracks, and out where their new home stood. "I really didn't think she'd do it," he said. "Damn! I really didn't think she'd do it!"

"Wait till the word gets out," his wife said. "There won't be an empty seat in the place."

"When they know that the famous Esther Cox is going to be there and they can see her and talk to her for the price of a drink, we'll have to turn 'em away with a billy club. Damn!" He grinned again.

"How much did you have to pay Daniel?" his wife asked.

"Not a thing. Daniel didn't ask, and I didn't offer. He just kept telling me how good it would be for Esther, and I just kept agreeing with him."

"People will come from all around to see her," Mrs. White said. "Are you still going to put those ads in the Halifax and St. John papers?"

"Course I am." He slapped the horse with the reins. "Hot damn! Yesterday I had me a restaurant, and today I got me a restaurant and freak show combined! Move, Patsy. We've got lots to do before Friday!"

Friday, November 29, 1878

Olive walked Esther to White's that first morning, and both were surprised at the crowd of people already inside. There wasn't an empty chair at any of the tables and the bar was, at that hour of the day, lined two-deep. There was a silence as she first walked in the door, followed by a murmuring and nudging as she stood there bewildered, wondering where Mr. White could be.

It was Mrs. White who came out of the kitchen and took her arm. "Good morning, my dear," she said. "Olive. Good morning."

Olive nodded. "I didn't expect to see so many people here this time of day," she said.

"It's not our normal crowd," Mrs. White beamed, "but of

course we don't want to do anything to chase them away." She laughed, and Esther reached out and took Olive's hand. Mrs. White steered Esther toward the back of the saloon. "Come with me, child. Mr. White's in the kitchen. I'm sure he'll be glad to show you what to do."

"You do understand, of course," Olive said to the woman, "that Esther is a little nervous right now. This is the first time she's ever had an outside employment. I would appreciate"—and she smiled at Mrs. White—"if you and your husband would go a little easy on her at first. You know, kind of let her observe things rather than expect her to do them right away. Of course," she added quickly, "I don't presume to tell you folks how to run your business."

Mrs. White was still smiling. The large crowd with money in its pocket would have made a dead man smile. She patted Olive on the arm. "Of course. I understand," and she said, laughing, "big sisters are always there to protect little sisters, aren't they? Don't concern yourself, Olive, your little sister will be treated as if she were one of the family."

Back out on the street and walking home, Olive stopped suddenly and remembered: Rumor had it that Mrs. White's father used to beat his children unmercifully and her mother died at home under very mysterious circumstances. "Like one of the family?" Olive said aloud.

* * *

Mr. White held out his large hand and took Esther's small one in his. "Glad you could make it, child," he said. "All those people out there, I really didn't know how I was going to get along without you." He took a long white bib apron off a hook on the wall and handed it to her. "Put this on—you don't want to soil your dress." As Esther tied the belt behind her, he led her out of the kitchen and over behind the bar. The loud talking hushed almost instantly as the crowd saw her. "All I want you to do for a while," he said, "is to take the empty glasses you see on the bar and wash them. You put them in this sink with the soapsuds, then in this sink with the clear water, then you wipe them off with one of these towels. You can see where they go after that." He gestured to the glasses that were stacked and organized by type and size on the bar shelf. "Mr. Crowe here will do all the serving, and he has to have clean glasses. Mr. Crowe?" White signaled to the white-haired man who was drawing a pint of beer. "Mr. Crowe, this is Esther. Esther Cox. She's going to be working with us from now on."

The man wiped his hand on his apron and shook Esther's hand. "Pleased," he said, but there was no pleasure in his eyes or in the tone of his voice. "You ever did this before?" Esther shook her head no. He shrugged his shoulders and glanced at the owner. "Just keep the dirty glasses clean and the clean glasses where I can get 'em." He walked to the far end of the bar and drew another beer.

There were several empty foam-spattered glasses already on the bar, and Esther gathered them and put them into the tepid, soapy water. She wiped their edges with a sponge and squished the water in and out of them several times. She held each one up to the light to see that it was perfectly clean before she dipped it into the rinse water. Then she dried each glass with a large cotton dish towel. That finished, she straightened up to admire the clean countertop only to see that there were another dozen dirty glasses there. As she reached for them, the one waiter in the place came and deposited another full tray of empties before her.

"'Lo," he said and flashed a toothy grin. "My name's Chip."

"Chip?" She had never heard of anyone with that name.

"It's really Ronald, but my mom hated that name so they call me Chip. For 'Chip off the old block.'" He was in his mid-twenties and handsome in a gangly sort of way. "Don't pay these people no mind," he said softly. "They don't know whether to drink or gawk."

It was the first time that Esther really looked at the patrons along the bar. They were all staring at her. Some had their glasses in their hands; others held them halfway to their mouths as if they were about to drink but their real reason for being there was to stare at her. She felt her face turn bright crimson, and she grabbed some dirty glasses and plunged them into the soapy water. She kept her hands under the water; that way no one could see how they were shaking.

"Let's see you do something!" A man's voice called loudly from somewhere along the bar.

"Yeah," two others chimed in. "Show us, Esther!"

Her face burned hotter and she didn't dare look up. She took a deep breath and told herself it would be all right. This was her first day, and it was natural she would be nervous.

"Let's hear some knockings."

"Make my glass of beer boil!"

Esther felt the tears come to her eyes, and she had been trying so hard to control them. She gave her complete concentration to the soapy water.

"Got any ghosts with you?" a man shouted.

She smiled, timidly. Maybe a smile was all they wanted.

"Come on, Esther"—this time it was a woman's voice—"let's see what you can do!"

Esther kept smiling, kept her head lowered, kept her tear-blinded gaze at the dirty glasses in the sink. After a while it'll be all right, she said to herself. They'll get used to it. After a while.

"Come on, Esther!" shouted another voice. "White put beer up two cents a glass. We should get something extra for it!"

She started to raise her head in reply but lowered it again. She didn't want the whole saloon to see she was crying.

"She's a phony!" the same woman said loudly. "I never did believe all those stories!"

Then it happened. The man at the farthest end of the bar had just set his half-empty beer glass on the counter when it started to slide down toward the glass of the customer on his right. The two glasses met and slid toward the next one down. Then the three beer glasses headed for the fourth, the fifth was snatched up by its owner just in time, and the sixth was nudged into the seventh. By this time those at the bar had taken a giant step backward, while those at the tables came crowding behind them. The beer glasses—some full, others empty—continued their movement down the bar. One by one, glasses were added to the parade. They reached the end of the bar. There was silence in the room. They stopped and spun around on their bases, slopping beer everywhere. The crowd gasped and stepped back. Then like a flight of self-destructive crystal birds, the glasses rose into the air, sailed toward the wall, and smashed, one by one, their shards falling on the sawdust floor.

"Oh, my God!" the woman said with a gasp, and hers was the only voice to break the silence.

Esther, sobbing openly now, yanked the apron over her face to hide the tears and shame and stumbled toward the kitchen door. She had to get out of there. Two large hands grabbed her by the shoulders. She stared into John White's face. "I'm so sorry!" The words came out in breathless stops and starts. "I'm so sorry! I'll pay for the glasses. I really will. I'll pay for them," and she started crying even harder.

John White pulled her to him and held her close. "Don't you fret," he said, and she could smell the cigar smoke on his breath, "don't pay it no mind. It wasn't your fault."

"But," she stammered, "it has followed me here! It's breaking things in here!"

He patted her back and said soothingly, "Never you mind. If it happens, it happens. I won't have you paying for any broken glasses around here. If it happens again, just let it. Don't try to stop it. That wouldn't be natural." Esther couldn't see the big grin he had on his face. "You just let it happen. That's the best way." He moved and opened the kitchen door, admitting the girl to the safety of the back room. He closed the door and went behind the bar.

"Ladies and gentlemen," he said in a loud, happy voice, "drinks are on the house!"

Thursday, December 5, 1878

A news item from the *Chignecto Post:*

> The Cox—electro-magnetic—dynamic—mesmeric—diabolic—hair lifting—thunder pealing—chair dancing performance is again in operation: this time at White's Oyster Saloon, Amherst.

Saturday, December 7, 1878

It had been a long week for Esther. A Monday through Saturday of hell. She hated to go to sleep at night knowing she would awaken only to go to the saloon the next day. No matter what she told Daniel and Olive, they were positive it was the best thing for her. They reminded her she was making money and getting her meals. They also told her how much she was helping the Whites. Business had never been so good at the Oyster Saloon. Extra customers meant extra tips for both Mr. Crowe and Chip. Extra money for them just when Christmas was coming up. Her being there would assure everyone who worked at White's of a better and more prosperous holiday season. Even Esther would be able to buy presents for the family this year instead of giving them handmade things.

Olive didn't mention it, but it was a blessing for her as well that Esther was away most of the day. She did the shopping and the housework by herself with just a little added effort, but not to have "those ghosts" around the house was wonderful. There had been no raps, no boiling waters, no writings on the wall. Potatoes didn't fly around the cellar anymore. Chairs in the dining room didn't tip over. No more poundings on the floor meant the naps of her two small sons would not be disturbed.

Daniel hoped that "whatever it was" would tire itself out in the restaurant and not be active when Esther came home. Indeed, it seems as though "it" was much calmer in the evenings than it had been. Daniel hadn't taken long to see the *real* reason the Whites were anxious to have the girl in their restaurant: She was a drawing card. She had become, in fact, the town's new source of amusement. It became fashionable to go to White's and wait for things to happen. Those who hung around for a while were almost always rewarded.

One afternoon, just as lunch was about over, the few empty chairs around the tables began to move. They slid—some rose through the air—to the front of the saloon. The patrons watched in amazement as the chairs, like acrobats, rose up and sat one atop the other. Then the bottom chair in the center was abruptly yanked away and the pyramid of legs and seats came crashing to the floor. Esther observed it all in horror from the back of the room.

On Wednesday, the saloon served what it called a "blue-plate special." It was a cut-rate meal served, literally, on special blue plates. Regular customers looked forward to Wednesday's at White's. Chip wove his way among the crowded tables placing the blue plates—piled high with fried oysters, coleslaw, mashed potatoes, a roll, and butter—when his tray was lifted from his upstretched arm. He stood and stared at it, mouth open, as it hovered just above his reach. He jumped for it; it rose higher. Then those sitting nearby scattered as the thought came to all of them at once that maybe the tray would tip and dump that food on them. The tray turned one way, then the other, and then sailed toward the table that had ordered the food. Unseen hands lowered the tray, picked up the plates, and set them carefully in front of the astonished diners. John White stood in the kitchen doorway observing it all. Esther crouched behind him.

The plates at all the other tables began to move. Only the blue ones. They rose, passed through the air, and came down in front of a different patron. At least two dozen of them sailed through the air, coming close to one another but never touching, never breaking, to be deposited carefully on other tables. Once the movement ceased, several of the fainthearted ran from the restaurant.

That Saturday, the last workday of the week, had started off with few problems. True, a sugar bowl had dumped itself onto someone's plate of spaghetti. Salt-shaker lids had been loosened so that Chip had to return several salt-dumped meals to the kitchen. The door to the outhouse stuck several times, not letting the sitter free until John White tugged lightly on the handle.

Esther was tired and more nervous than usual. White had her working in several areas at once. No longer was she just an ornament behind the bar. She now helped the cook pare and chop vegetables, helped the dishwasher scrape the plates, carried food scraps to the garbage cans, brought in wood for the cookstove, and did whatever else White decided she would do. He had discovered it didn't matter if she was in the dining area for the manifestations to occur. He could have it both ways: the happenings in the front of the house and the worker in the back. Esther didn't mind being in the kitchen; it kept those staring eyes from her face. Each time she had to go behind the bar or out to the tables, all conversation—all noise—ceased. Then her cheeks would flame up and her eyes would blur with tears. The kitchen was a place to hide.

She was passing a damp mop near the cookstove when she heard the noise. It was a clashing, slamming sound of metal against metal. She jumped back as the heavy oven door on the stove opened by itself and clanged itself shut. It opened and clanged, repeating the movement over and over. John White ran in from the dining area, looking for the source of noise. As if the stove could hear, he shouted "Stop that racket!" and ran to get an axe handle from the pantry. When the door began to swing shut, he shoved the wooden handle between the stove rim and the door. "Now, that's enough of that," he said, and dusting off his hands, returned to the bar.

Esther backed away from the stove and watched in terrified fascination as the long metal screws that held the door to the frame of the stove worked their way upward and out. Then the door lifted from its hinges and pulled away. Esther was able to scream just as the axe handle was yanked out of position and the heavy metal door went flying across the room. The crash, as it hit the far wall, could be heard even out in the street.

White ran back into the kitchen, followed by a friend of his, Bill Rogers, who had been having a drink at the bar. All activity had stopped in the kitchen. The cook was standing like a statue, and Chip had pressed himself up against the wall. The oven door had missed him by inches. Esther had fallen to the floor and was sobbing in fright.

"Look at that god-damned thing!" White shouted to nobody in particular. He tried to pick up the door, but it was too heavy for him, so he and Rogers together put it back in place. White replaced the screws in the hinges, tightening them with all his force. Then he put the axe handle in place. "Let's see you do that again, you bastard," he said, and then, as if on cue, the screws came up and out, the door came loose, the axe handle rose into the air, and the door crashed with a thunderous noise against the far wall.

Chip, after regaining his breath, dashed out the back doorway and ran to the next block, where Jennie worked at Dunlap Tailors. The girl didn't think twice about leaving and ran back with him to the restaurant. She found her sister on the floor, rigid with fear. In all the noise and panic, no one had thought to console the girl.

Jennie helped her sister sit up, then helped her onto a stool in the center of the kitchen. Esther was so terrified of what had happened that her sobs were dry, coming with each breath. Jennie called for a damp rag, and as she bathed the girl's face she held her close and kept telling her over and over again it was all right. She hadn't been hurt. She had only been frightened. "I think you'd better get Dr. Carritte," she said to John White. "He knows how to calm her down." White nodded to Chip, and the waiter ran out the back doorway again.

"Okay, okay," White said loudly as he opened the kitchen door, "form a line and come on in!" Almost everyone in the dining room scurried to see. They filed into the kitchen, marveling at the heavy stove door and the broken plaster around it. They stared at Esther before they went back to their tables, oohing and aahing over the door but not saying a word to her. Just staring. She put her face into Jennie's warm shoulder and kept shuddering.

When Dr. Carritte arrived, he brought the Reverend Clay with him. The minister had been in the doctor's office when Chip came running. The doctor asked for a glass and some water and from his bag he mixed several powders and liquids together and stood watching while Esther drank it. While John White explained about the door, the dry, racking sobs inside Esther subsided.

"She's feeling better now," Jennie said. "I think I'd better take her home."

Bam! Bam! Two loud knocks came from under the floor. Esther clutched at Jennie and buried her face again.

"What was that?" Chip asked.

"Rappings," said the preacher. "They came from over there. Under the floor." He turned to White. "Quick," he said, "how do we get down into the cellar?"

"There isn't any cellar under here," the man replied.

"No cellar?" said the minister. "Then how could anyone get under there to—"

Bam!

"Oh, God," said Chip. "Now what?"

Bam!

"Just keep calm," the doctor commanded. "All of you. Keep calm. I think I know how to handle this."

"How?" asked the minister.

"This happened once before. Not the stove-door thing, but these raps. It was when I was at the Teed home. We came up with a way to—" he looked around at the expressions on faces—"to communicate with them." Nobody said a word. The cook and the dishwasher hardly breathed. Chip gripped a towel between his hands. "If we ask it questions," said the doctor, "it will answer with knockings. Three raps are 'yes.' One rap is 'no.'"

"What do you mean 'it'?" John White said worriedly. "Who is 'it'?"

The doctor shook his head. "I don't know who or even *what* 'it' is. All I know is that we are able to communicate."

Bill Rogers, as well as being a friend of John White's, was an important man in town: Inspector of Fisheries for Nova Scotia. He took charge. "Give us one loud rap!" he called.

Bam!

"It worked!" he shouted in amazement. "Now two raps." Bam! Bam! "Now three." Bam! Bam! Bam! "Amazing!" he laughed. "And I'm standing right here. I can see Esther on that stool, see right through the legs of that stool, and she didn't make those noises!"

"No," said the dishwasher, "something else did."

"Or *somebody* else did," added the cook.

"I'm going to try this again," Rogers said. He looked past where Esther was sitting. "Who are you, anyway? The Devil?"

Bam! Bam! Bam!

Both the cook and the dishwasher eased themselves toward the open back door.

"Are you here for me?" Rogers asked.

Bam!

"Are you here for John White?"

Bam!

"For Dr. Carritte?"

Bam!

"Do you want Miss Cox?"

Bam! Bam! Bam!

Tuesday, December 10, 1878

"Doesn't all this bother you?" The young man spoke as Esther came behind the bar with a tray of dirty glasses.

She stopped. "Bother me? What?"

"All this uproar about your ghosts and all. Having everyone knowing about you."

She stopped again.

"It does," she said, "but it'll go away soon and then . . ." She stopped again. What a nice-looking young man! Her face turned red as if she had said her thoughts aloud. The tray trembled and she held it tighter, with both hands.

"And then?" he asked.

"Then it'll go away and things will be back to normal." She laughed. "Whatever 'normal' means. I've almost forgotten." Did everyone have blue eyes *that* blue? "It's just a phase."

"Well," he said, "I sure hope you get rid of it soon. It can't be the most pleasant thing in the world."

"It isn't!" She smiled at him. That blond hair looked so good above those blue eyes! "But what can I do? Just bear with it till it's over with."

"I wish you luck." He smiled.

Then she smiled. "Thank you."

Chip came over to the bar and put his arm around the young man's shoulder. "I see you've already met her," he said.

"I was going to wait for you to introduce us"—the young man kept smiling at Esther—"but when she just passed by me like that, I decided to introduce myself." He paused, looking at her, still smiling. "But I didn't, did I. I didn't introduce myself."

The red started back in her cheeks. "No, you didn't."

"Let me do it," Chip said. "That's what he came in here for. Esther Cox, I'd like to present my friend Adam Porter. Adam Porter, Esther Cox."

"Hello."

"Hello."

"Now that that's done, I've got two tables to set up." Chip patted Adam on the back and went into the kitchen.

"He's a nice boy," Esther said. Adam nodded agreement. "He's been such a help to me around here. So any friend of his is a friend of mine."

"Delighted to hear it," he said.

She put the tray down and wondered if her hair was less than perfect. She didn't dare glance into the bar mirror to find out. "I haven't seen you in here before," she said. "You don't live in Amherst."

"No. Up in Port Philip. With my mother and my two boys."

"Two boys? You have two boys?" She felt herself deflate a little. "How nice." Would her luck ever change? "How nice," she repeated.

"It is, I guess. A little difficult, though, in these times to raise children. My mother isn't in the best of health, and she finds them a chore. She loves them, but they take a lot of work."

"Your mother?"

"My wife passed away last year. Diphtheria. She never was very strong."

"I'm sorry," she said.

"One of those things that happen," he said. "You never know."

"No, I guess not."

"Hey!" Mr. Crowe called from the end of the bar. "Could I have some clean glasses down here? If you don't mind."

Esther turned quickly from the young man and grabbed several beer steins by their handles. She took them down to the bartender. When she glanced up, she saw Adam Porter near the door talking to Chip. Then Adam left.

"Hmmm," Esther said to herself, "I suppose I should be sad that his wife is dead. Funny, but I'm not." The memory of that smile and those blue eyes—especially those blue eyes—kept her going for the rest of the day.

Thursday, December 12, 1878

The *Chignecto Post*, between an article on what local merchants had for sale this Christmas and a report on General Roberts's victory over the Afghans:

> The Cox Mystery
>
> As our readers are aware, the manifestations returned last week with redoubled power, and White's Saloon, Amherst, where Miss Cox was stopping, became the center of public interest. Taps and raps on the floor and ceiling became almost continuous, and chairs and other moveable objects walked about in the most independent manner. As there was no difficulty in obtaining access to Miss Cox, many visited her who had not done so during her previous stay in Amherst, and if any one in Amherst doubted the fact of the manifestations taking place as described, there was no difficulty in getting them set at rest pretty effectually.
>
> From the circumstances Dr. Carritte found he could subdue the manifestations, by the administration of sedatives to Miss Cox, seemed to point conclusively to the fact that the force exerted came from her and not from any external source, thus dissipating into the air high flown speculations as to their spiritualistic or mesmeric or demonaic origin. Could the unseen devil be vanquished by an opiate? This theory was quite confirmed by an experiment of Dr. Carritte's last week. In the midst of these manifestations, when the spirits appeared to be more lively and mischievous than ever, he stood Miss Cox on glass, securing electrical insulation as far as

possible. *The manifestations suddenly ceased.* When the glass was removed *they again recommenced.* This was repeated sufficiently to show the force exerted belonging to the class of electricity, and thus ends the much discussed Cox mystery. It is a matter of extreme congratulation that the phenomena has been reduced to operations under natural laws, and that no supernatural agency, no spirit of the damned in this world or of the world to come is chargeable with upsetting the laws of dynamics and infusing new elements into the laws of force and matter. How Esther Cox was controlled by mesmerism, how a "colossal fist" pounded the walls about her, how she was persued by spirits of evil who sent messages to this sphere through her handwriting, are stories that told around the evening firelight, will no longer send a thrill of horror to the youthful heart or hang like a nightmare over the minds of the faithful.

Daniel lowered the paper and looked at the family members assembled around the dining-room table. "And that is how the *Post* has dismissed the entire thing." He looked at Esther, who had listened to the reading with her hand up to her mouth. "Does it make you feel better," he asked her, "to know Mr. Milner has solved the mystery and that everything is all right once again?"

Esther shrugged. "I suppose he is entitled to his opinion. It's his newspaper. I know what's been happening to me. He doesn't."

"People believe anything they read in print," put in Jennie. "It's almost gospel if it's in the paper."

"Then maybe they'll leave me alone," Esther sighed.

"The people or the spirits?" Olive asked.

"Both," the girl replied. "I'm tired of them all. I just want to go away somewhere and dig a hole and cover myself with leaves and not see anyone or talk to anyone until all this has been forgotten."

"Do you think it ever will be?" Olive asked.

"I think so," Daniel replied. He pushed back his chair and rose from the table, laying the newspaper next to his plate. "Something new and more interesting will come along, and folks will forget. And so," he said, bending over and touching Esther lightly on her hair, "so will your 'spirits.'"

At that the copy of the *Post* jumped into the air, rose to the ceiling, crumpled, and tossed itself against the wall.

Friday, December 20, 1878

It was the beginning of the fourth week for Esther at the restaurant, and how she hated it. White, of course, loved it. Never had there been so many customers in his saloon, and never had he taken such amounts of money to the bank. Everyone in the area talked of Esther and the "spooky" things that happened around her at the restaurant. Spiritualists accepted it as "proof of survival." Skeptics claimed it was "merely Mesmerism." Christians were adamant it was "the work of the Devil." White and his wife didn't care what it was called as long as it brought in the customers and didn't cause too much damage. A few broken glasses, some dents in the kitchen wall, and the breaking of a few chair legs were all expenses they were more than glad to pay for the privilege of having Esther and her spirits working for them.

Esther had grown more nervous with each workday, not from being stared at or called to or backed away from, but from the tension that at any moment—and always without warning—something horrendous would happen. Something that she would be blamed for. Yet, she had told herself, time after time with amazement, the Whites didn't seem to mind. They never made her responsible for the breakage or the confusion. They never deducted a penny from her salary. She had offered to pay each time something was ruined—even kept a list of the things she felt were her fault—but they refused to hear of it. She marveled at their patience with her, and even though she hated working there, she was grateful that they were so considerate. Any other employer, she reasoned, would have fired her long ago.

The manifestations on Princess Street ceased. When she started at White's, the energies had quitted the small frame house and turned their full malevolence on the Oyster Saloon. Olive was delighted that things had returned to normal. So was everyone else in the house. Esther was happy that by being away her sister and her children could live in peace. It was a strange mixture of feelings inside her: She hated to go to work, and yet she was glad the work was there to go to.

It was easier getting there now that the winter snows had arrived. Before the bad weather, she met many people on the streets who would stare at her and back away from her or else stop whatever they were doing and point at her. Now the harsh winds and the stinging snow allowed her to bundle up in heavy coats, pull a cap down over her head, and wrap most of her face in a scarf. There were fewer pedestrians out now, and she came to enjoy the peace and quiet of the ten-minute walk to and from the restaurant every day. She was eighteen years old.

On Monday of that week two men unloaded a box of oysters from their wagon. The mollusks were packed in ice to keep them alive and fresh. Esther watched the men struggle with the wooden crate as they carried it inside and put it on the kitchen floor. As lunches were being prepared, the cook opened the crate and took out only the oysters he needed. Esther was behind the bar filling the overhead racks with clean glasses. That noon those early-bird drinkers standing at the bar got more than their money's worth. The door to the kitchen was banged open, and everyone stared in disbelief as the heavy oyster-filled crate slid effortlessly out of the kitchen, past the bar, and stopped in the center of the dining room. When some of the drinkers tried to push it (they were sure it was on wheels), it wouldn't budge.

On Tuesday, the chairs did their balancing act again. Not just the empty ones this time but even several that were occupied. Diners who had been comfortably seated found themselves sliding to the floor as their seats were pulled out from under them. The outcries and embarrassed groans were silenced by the spectacle of the chairs moving toward the front of the room and placing themselves in line. Then some of the chairs in the back sailed up onto those in front and straddled the seats with their legs. Line by line the remaining chairs were invisibly lifted into position until a pyramid of legs and seats blocked the entire front wall. Esther sank against the bar, afraid to look at what she knew would happen next as a few adventurous customers approached the balancing act and tried to pull the chairs out of position. They wouldn't be moved.

Then everyone in the restaurant—except Esther and a few intelligent others—ran delightedly to the chairs, trying to force them apart. With much laughter, they found there was no way the chairs could be separated. What a wonderful trick this was! You sure got your money's worth at White's! Wait till the boys at work hear of this! They pointed, they posed, and they laughed. The laughter ceased suddenly when the entire construction collapsed on top of them, banging them with backs, slamming them with seats, and jabbing them with legs. No one was seriously injured, but John White had to hear complaints about bruised shoulders and painful bumps. Esther, shocked by the noise and the screams of the customers, ran out the back doorway. As she stood bareheaded in the snow, the entire episode suddenly struck her as terribly funny, and she folded her arms across her chest and laughed.

On Wednesday, the laughter continued as the blue-plate specials lifted off, hovered, and came down carefully in front of the diners. Chip had hated Wednesdays before, but now he looked forward to having all those unseen hands helping him.

On Thursday, it wasn't so funny. A customer came in with four large railroad spikes. He had Esther sit down on a chair in the center of the dining room, and he placed the iron spikes in her lap.

Esther spread her legs enough so the heavy metal things could be cradled in the material of her floor-length dress. The object of the test, said the customer, was to see how far the ghosts would throw the spikes and at what.

Everyone watched from a safe distance. If there was to be any funny stuff with those spikes like there had been on Tuesday with the chairs, folks wanted to get out of the way in a hurry.

But the spikes didn't move. They just lay there on the dark blue homespun skirt. People waited. Nothing happened.

"I guess that's all we're going to see," said the man, and he reached to remove the spikes but pulled his hand back with a yell. "Damn! Those are hot!"

Then everyone could see the spikes begin to glow. They started off light pink at the tops and gradually turned to a darker red as the heat moved to the points. Esther jumped up, feeling the warmth in her lap and sniffing the odor of singed cloth. The spikes scattered on the floor. Booted feet moved away. Then one at a time the glowing metal spikes were raised from the floor and thrown into a corner at least twenty feet away.

"She seems more upset about her old skirt than she is about the hand that threw those spikes," a female customer was heard to say.

On Friday, it wasn't funny at all.

The Whites had a small son named Fred. The boy was in the restaurant that day, by himself at a corner table, waiting for his mother to come back from her shopping. To keep him quiet, he had been given a block of wood and a small pocket-knife. He was hard at work trying to carve a bird when Esther came out of the kitchen. She carried a tray of fried oysters and bite-size pieces of fish. In the center was a glass bowl of White's special tartar sauce. It was part of the "free lunch" that sat on the bar every Friday.

There was some question about how many in the room saw it coming. Even if they had shouted or called out, it's doubtful that anything could have been done to stop it. Those sitting near the little boy said they saw the expression on his face as the knife was yanked from his hand, as it turned in the air, and as it pointed itself before sailing over everyone's head toward the bar.

Esther screamed and dropped the tray, sending oysters and sauce and fish and broken glass over the floor behind the bar. She groped toward the pain in her back, then her body twisted and she fell atop the mess that had been the "free lunch."

Mr. Crowe, the bartender, was the first one to reach her. He was the first one to see the knife sticking into her back. John White had been sitting with a friend at a table, and he ran behind the bar when he saw Esther go down. The two men stared, unsure of what to do.

Little Fred squeezed between his father's legs and demanding his knife, yanked it from Esther's back. The blood spurted up and out onto her white blouse and her long gray skirt.

Fred wiped the blood from the blade, closed it, and put the knife into his pocket.

Immediately the knife squirmed up and out of his pocket, hovered in the air in front of the startled group, opened its blade, and plunged back into the bleeding wound.

Fred grabbed the knife and pulled it out. White grabbed his son's hand, took the still bloody weapon, opened the cash register, and threw it into the drawer.

Esther was helped to her feet and aching from the wound as well as the fall was guided to a quiet spot in the kitchen. White, himself, drove her in his buggy to Dr. Carritte's. Her sobs were all he heard.

"I'm not going back there, Doctor," she said as the man dressed the wound. "I'm not. I'm sorry, but I can't bear any more of this! Those people and their stares and the things they say to me! I can't live with it any longer!"

"It'll be all right," he soothed.

"When?" she demanded. "*When* will it be all right? It's been going on for months now! Nobody knows what it *is*. Nobody has any answers! And you know something?" She turned her head to look at him. "Nobody even *cares*! Nobody cares what this awful thing is. They think it's some kind of vaudeville act, some sideshow they are getting to see for free!"

"Your sisters care." He was still soothing. "Daniel cares."

"But nobody *does* anything." She was angry now and unable to cry. "They just push me away and hope that whatever *it* is will go away with me! I don't deserve this kind of thing. I've never done anything to anybody to be treated like this."

"But this is the first time *it* has ever hurt you, really drawn blood."

"And what will happen the *second* time?" she demanded. "Olive always says, 'there's a first time for everything.' Well, this knife is my first time. When will the next time be? And the time after that?" She was on her feet now, not caring that he hadn't quite finished with the bandage. "You saw the wall. You saw those words that I was *his* to kill! Well, he's starting, isn't he? Like everything else *he's* done, it's been little by little. First a pocketknife in the back. What will his last thing be? A butcher knife in the heart?"

Christmas Eve 1878

"A new skirt!" Esther quickly pulled the gift out of the fancily wrapped box. "Oh, Jennie, thank you!"

"Well, you needed one after what happened at White's. Anyway," she said with a smile, "this one is not homespun. It's factory-made. The saleswoman at Chapman's said it came all the way from Boston."

"It must have cost a fortune!" Esther stood up and fitted the waist of the skirt around her midriff. She was thinner now, she noted with satisfaction. The events of the past few months had caused her to lose weight. She wasn't the pudgy little girl any longer and, as she approached nineteen, she was metamorphosing into an attractive young woman. She whirled around so everyone could see. "It is lovely. Thank you." She kissed her sister on the forehead.

The Christmas branch sat in the center of the dining-room table. It had been cut from a live fir tree, and Olive and her two children had decorated it with ribbons, loops of colored paper, and strings of popcorn. Leaning against the branch was a chromo-lithograph of the baby Jesus and three small black-and-white camels that Olive had discovered in a magazine illustration. She had pasted them onto the lid of a shoebox (courtesy of the Amherst Boot and Shoe Factory) and cut them out. A bottle of real French wine stood near the branch. It had been a gift from John and Mary White. It had been given to the Teed family but ostensibly it was for Esther and all she had been through in the month she had been at their restaurant.

She had not gone back to work after the knife attack. Dr. Carritte had told the Whites he didn't think Esther was in the right physical or mental condition to return there "just yet." White, unhappily, understood. He would miss the extra revenue she unsuspectingly brought in, but it *was* the holiday season, and the restaurant business always slowed down around this time, anyway. When he had pressed her for a definite date on which she would return, she shrugged and said, "When the doctor thinks I'm ready." She had enough confidence in the doctor to hope he would *never* think she was ready to return to that terrible place.

Yet the place had had its rewards. White had paid her very well for what little she did, and with this newfound wealth she was able to buy Christmas presents for everyone in the house. In other years, she had *made* them gifts. This year she had *bought* them gifts. It was an entirely different feeling.

After all the packages had been opened, the paper and boxes gathered up, and the exhausted children put to bed, Daniel opened the Whites' bottle of wine. The six adults held their glasses high and clinked them delightedly after Daniel's toast: "May all our happiness be ahead of us and all our sorrows behind us. Merry Christmas!"

* * *

"Jennie!" The voice was a hoarse whisper in the blackness of the night. "Jennie! Jennie, wake up!"

Jennie stirred at the sound, then rolled over and sat up when she felt the hand on her shoulder. In the darkness, she could see Esther standing beside her, ghostlike in her long woolen nightdress. The older girl groped for the lamp and turned up the wick. The flame, burning softly every night, rose and illuminated the glass chimney, then sent rays of light across the bed and onto the two girls. "What's the matter?" Jennie asked sleepily.

"Jennie, I'm afraid." Esther pulled back the patchwork quilt that covered her sister and slid under it. It was good to feel her sister's warm body close to her own.

"Of what?" Jennie looked around the room. Nothing seemed to be out of place.

"Of *that*!" Esther whispered. "Listen."

Jennie listened and heard nothing. "I don't hear anyth—"

"Shhh! Listen! There it is again."

Jennie cocked her head to one side. Maybe that would help. "I'm sorry, Esther, I don't hear anything. I don't know what you're talking about."

"The voice!" Esther insisted. "*That* voice. Listen to what it's saying, Jennie." A pause of silence. "Oh, my God, Jennie, just listen to what it's saying!" She started to cry. "What are we going to do? What am *I* going to do?"

Jennie pushed her sister's head back onto the pillow. She held her face in her hands. "Just a minute now, Esther. I don't hear any voice. I don't know what you're talking about." Esther sobbed, and Jennie felt the warm tears on her hands. "If you keep crying, I can't understand what you're saying, and I can't help you. I want to help you, but I can't if you don't get control of yourself."

Esther blinked away the tears, and Jennie wiped her face with a corner of the sheet. "You don't hear it?" she asked softly. "You really don't?"

"I don't. I don't hear it, and I don't know why you're so frightened." Jennie glanced about the room again, trying to find something out of place as in times before. Things like flying blankets, animated pillows, and writings on the walls. This wasn't the same room where those other things had happened, but the front room that the children had been sleeping in. After Esther returned from Mrs. Snowden's, Olive had changed bedrooms. The boys got the back bedroom (with the writing on the wall), and Jennie and Esther took the front bedroom. It was smaller but it was on the street (in case they had to shout for help) and it was right beside the stairway (in case they had to run). Olive also hoped that by moving the room, the ghosts wouldn't find Esther in the usual place and would go away. As Jennie's gaze went around the room, she saw nothing to indicate that Esther's tormentors had returned.

"It . . . it's a voice," Esther said slowly, exhaling and trying to breathe normally and speak naturally. "It's a voice . . . of a man . . . or that used to be a man . . . and he tells me over and over again that he is dead . . . and"—she paused and swallowed—"and he wants me to tell everyone that he is angry . . . and that"—and here the tears came silently—"that he is going to burn down this house and kill everyone in it!"

"He *what*?" Jennie almost shouted.

Esther sat up and hugged her sister tightly. "He says he's going to burn down the house. *This* house. Oh, God! What are we going to do?"

Jennie had seen too much in the past few months to doubt anything her younger sister told her. She got out of bed and grabbed for her winter robe. "The first thing we're going to do is get Daniel and Olive in here and tell them what you just told me."

Olive was already awake when Jennie rapped on their bedroom door. Olive had always been a light sleeper, and since this business with Esther started, she joked that she slept with one eye open and the other one awake. She shook Daniel, and while he fumbled into his trousers and suit jacket (over his long johns), she hurried into the girls' bedroom. By the time he got there, Esther was halfway through the explanation and had started crying again.

". . . and he said he was a ghost and he was going to set fire to this house and kill us all!"

"Who said?" Daniel demanded.

"A voice," Olive explained. "a loud voice that only Esther can hear."

"The voice of a ghost," Jennie added.

"Oh, now." Daniel was exasperated and sleepy. "Let's not commence that again."

"I'm sorry." Esther was still crying. "That's what he told me. Burn us all out."

Both the boarders were now in the room. They had become light sleepers, too. "But it's *not* a ghost," William Teed said. "I thought everyone—the newspapers—agreed that there *were* no ghosts."

"It's Mesmerism or electricity," John Teed added. "Or whatever. I agree with Daniel, so let's not commence that again. We've had enough ghost talk."

"Nothing's different in the room," Jennie said. "It's normal."

"But I *hear* him," Esther insisted. "I hear his voice, and he's telling me the same thing over and over!"

"Darling," Olive sat on the bed beside her sister, "you're just worked up. The things at the restaurant and all the excitement of Christmas have worked you up. You just got over the diphtheria. You're overwrought. It's understandable. What you need is rest. I'll go warm up a glass of milk and bring some of that medicine Dr. Carritte left for you." She kissed Esther on the forehead as she rose. "You just lie here calmly and I'll be right back."

Esther reached out and quickly pulled her sister back down on the bed. "Don't go!" Her voice was sharper now. "He says for none of you to go! He says for all of you to look up at the ceiling."

They did. They stared at the ceiling above the bed and saw nothing.

"Really, Esther." Olive started to rise again when she heard the others gasp.

There, against the ceiling, directly over the bed, a lighted match appeared. Its red and yellow flame had a halo of white around it, and its brightness grew in intensity as it slowly fell, lazily fell, straight down onto the bed.

William Cox jumped at it, snatched it from the blanket, and put it out with his fingers. "Got you, you bastard!" he said aloud.

Then the second match appeared. Same color and same slowness as the first. It floated down toward the bed. Olive screamed but William got that one, too. The third appeared. John Teed jumped to catch it.

A fourth. Daniel grabbed for it. It slipped past his fingers, but he caught it just before it touched the bed.

A fifth. William got that one.

A sixth. Daniel and John both scrambled for it.

Six more, then no more.

"I can't believe this is happening," Olive said. She had

tears in her eyes now. "I just can't believe this is happening to us all over again. Why?"

When they were certain there were no more matches coming, the men leaned against the wall, relaxed but alert. William said what everyone was thinking. "Suppose we don't grab the next one . . . wherever it might appear."

"Then we'll have a fire," Daniel said softly.

"It could happen anywhere," Olive said. "In the dining room or the parlor or"—and here her heart stopped for a second—"or in the boys' bedroom."

Esther let out a moan, and the tears ran down her face. Everyone heard her, but no one came to her aid. No one wiped her cheeks or comforted her. Each person's thoughts were on themselves. If there were more matches—undiscovered—if there was just *one* match that went undiscovered, they were all in danger. It wasn't just Esther anymore. It was all of them.

Daniel, as head of the household, took command. "I think we had better do some more investigating before we all lose our heads. We had better find out what this thing . . . this voice . . . has planned for us." He backed up a few feet from the foot of the bed and took an orator's stance, looking slightly ridiculous in his bare feet, suit coat and trousers, and long red underwear. "Mr. Ghost," he said aloud, "or whoever you call yourself, I'd like the answer to a question." He took a deep breath. "And I'd like the answer in the usual way. *Your* way. One knock for no, two for maybe, and three for yes." The others kept their eyes on him. "Mr. Ghost, a direct response please, sir. Do you really intend to set this house on fire?"

Bam! Bam! Bam!

"Oh, my God!" Olive felt her knees buckle, and she reached for the bedpost to help keep her steady. "Oh, my God," she said again. "My God. My God. My God." Her voice was fainter and fainter each time.

In the shock of the silence it was easy for all of them to hear the sound of rustling behind them. They turned to see Esther's skirt—the new one Jennie had given her, the new one that had come all the way from Boston—fall from its hanging peg on the back of the door. They watched, too stunned to move, as the skirt wadded itself into a ball and rolled quickly past them under the bed. Almost instantly, they could smell the smoke and see the glow of the flames. Daniel, acting on instinct, dropped to the floor, reached under the bed, and pulled out the burning garment. He threw it across the room as William emptied the pitcher of drinking water he grabbed from the bureautop.

Jennie ran, snatched up the skirt, and shook it out. They had all seen it burning; yet there wasn't even a singemark on it.

"I think," Daniel said wearily, "that we had better keep an eye out tonight. Everywhere. We don't dare go to sleep if those matches start again. Olive, you bring the boys into our bedroom and keep watch in there. William, you guard your and John's room and keep looking into the boys' bedroom as well. John, you and I will take the downstairs. You make sure there are no fires started in the kitchen and dining room. I'll take the parlor and the sewing room and the front hall. I suggest we get comfortable chairs and drink a lot of black coffee. Jennie, you stay here with Esther. She needs you."

They started out of the room, to get dressed and to take up their sentry posts in this undeclared war that had been thrust upon them.

"Oh, and one other thing," Daniel said. They stopped and looked at his grim face. "Merry Christmas!"

Friday, December 27, 1878

Christmas Day had come and gone, and so had the day after Christmas. No one had really slept, or gotten much rest. Their eyes were constantly turned toward the ceiling for the first sign of a burning match. They jumped at every little sound in the creaky wooden house and stopped suddenly to sniff at any strange odor that might indicate a fire. They had buckets of water in the corners of each room, buckets ready to be grabbed and tossed on anything they found burning.

Yet there were no more matches. No more fires. Esther had not heard the voice after that night.

This morning, after washing the breakfast dishes and putting them away, Esther was sitting at the dining-room table mending the children's socks. The table was the one place she could spread out her sewing things and still watch Olive in the kitchen. They all kept an eye on each other now. Nobody wanted to be alone in the house.

Olive moved the handle of the churn up and down, keeping the base firmly secured between her feet and knees.

This being winter, their one cow (kept in a shed in the small backyard) gave only a little milk. Olive saved the cream and churned butter only once a week. Almost everyone kept a milk cow in their backyard, and some kept chickens and ducks as well. They didn't have any chickens because Olive hated the idea of wringing the neck of something she had fed and cared for since infancy. She preferred to buy her hens already dead and, if possible, already cleaned. "Did you find Willie's other sock?" she asked Esther. "The long blue one?"

"It wasn't in his room and it wasn't in the laundry basket," the girl replied.

"I swear that child *eats* his clothing!" Olive said with a smile. "One week it's a sock and the next week a scarf. One day I'm going to hear that his closet is bare, and then so will *he* be." She laughed. "Willie's just like his pa. Daniel used to lose pieces of clothing everywhere. One time he even lost a *shoe*. Can you believe it? We went on a picnic just before we were married and he took off his shoes to walk in the grass and when we got back one of his shoes was gone. Well, he searched and I laughed, and the more I laughed, the angrier he got. He swears a goat came by and ate it, but I think he plumb forgot to put both shoes together when he took them off." She smiled remembering his red face as they rode back into town; Daniel with one shoe off and one shoe on.

"It's a good thing he works at the shoe factory," Esther said with a laugh.

Olive started to reply when she stopped suddenly, churn handle in mid-air. She held her breath. "Esther!" she said sharply, "I smell smoke. Don't you?"

The girl ran into the kitchen, stood stock still, and sniffed the air. "Yes," she said loudly, "I do."

They looked quickly around the kitchen, but everything was normal. Then they saw the thin wisps coming up from under the cellar door.

"It's down there!" Olive shouted. She pushed the churn away and jumped to open the door. A full cloud of grey smoke hit her straight on. "My God, Esther. It's down there!"

Olive grabbed for one of the emergency pails of water and hurried down the stairs, slopping the water wildly. Esther was right behind her. "There!" she shouted. "Over there!"

In the far corner of the cellar, a barrel of wood shavings was blazing fiercely. Kept to help start the cookstove fire, the shavings rose up in small bits of red flame and settled back down as glowing ashes. The fire had started to eat the rim of the barrel and was rapidly crawling up one of the wooden joists that supported the main floor of the house. The joist burnt as if it had been soaked with kerosene.

Olive took the bucket in both hands and with one swing splashed the blaze. There was a sizzling sound, then the flames rose up again, still avidly licking at the floor joist.

"We need more water!" Olive spun around and dashed up the steps, almost knocking Esther over as she stood on the staircase with her hands up to her face. "Grab that bucket in the dining room!" Olive ordered but Esther just stood there, stunned by the sight of the flames. "Come *on*!" Olive grabbed her by the arm and almost yanked her into the kitchen. "Come *on*!"

Olive, pushing Esther ahead of her now, hurried along the hallway and out the front doorway. She ran down the sidewalk, her long skirt brushing against the snow that was piled on either side of it, pushed open the gate, and shouted, "Fire! Fire!"

Esther stood in the cold, her hands still to her face.

"Fire!" Olive shouted again. "Please help! We have a fire!" She gulped for breath, searing her throat with the icy air. "Fire!"

Doors opened in houses all along the narrow street. Women appeared with buckets of water, some handing them to their husbands as the men raced toward the Teed house. In seconds there were seven men charging into Olive's basement, throwing buckets of water on the blaze. The fire didn't seem to care that it was being attacked, and it actually seemed to rise higher with each new splashing.

Two men hurried back up the stairs and grabbed the rug in the dining room, upsetting table and chairs as they pulled it off the floor and hustled it down the cellar steps. It took four men to throw the rug onto the barrel and then tip it over and away from the wall. Then as three men smothered the inferno in the barrel, three others beat at the burning floor joist with wet burlap sacks. Soon the fire was gone and only the smoke and the burnt smell remained.

One of the men stopped to talk with Olive as he was leaving. "How did it start?" he asked.

"I don't know." She shook her head. "Esther was in the dining room and I was in the kitchen and we smelled smoke.

When I opened the cellar door suddenly the house was full of smoke."

"Where are your boys?"

"They are uptown with my sister Jennie. She doesn't have to go back to work until next week, so she took them shopping."

"Well, who started the fire?"

"Who?"

"Yes. Who started it? How could a fire get started down there, all alone?"

"I don't know . . ." Her voice faltered.

"Somebody must have started it," the man insisted.

"Yes . . . I suppose you're right."

"Then who?"

"I . . . I don't know who . . ."

"Or *what*?"

"What? What do you mean, 'or what'?"

"I mean," the man said, jerking his thumb in the direction of Esther, "or *what*."

"That's all gossip." Olive was flustered.

"Maybe," the man said.

"It's not what you're thinking," Olive tried to convince him.

"Maybe."

"There's nothing supernatural going on here."

"That's what *you* say."

Saturday, December 28, 1878

The *Amherst Gazette* published a brief account of the fire. Fires were always news in town. Amherst, like all the other communities, was built of wood. Wooden houses close together, vulnerable to flames and vulnerable to high winds. It was the community nightmare that one house would catch fire and the winds from the bay would fan that fire onto the next house and then those flames would be carried by the wind to the next house and so on down the line until no houses were left standing. There had been fires like that in Amherst history—very recent history, as a matter of fact. When the neighbors had responded so quickly to Olive's cries, it wasn't out of sympathy for her but out of fear that their houses would go up in smoke if hers continued to burn.

"Did you see the story in the paper today about the Teed

house?" The woman adjusted her packages as she stopped to talk with a friend on the street corner.

"About the fire? The mysterious fire?"

"Yes. They say nobody was in the basement. Olive and Esther were upstairs, and the boys were shopping."

"I read that. Then who started the fire?"

"Who?" The woman snorted. "Who, indeed! Esther Cox's *friends*, that's who."

"She almost wrecked White's Saloon when she worked there."

"I heard that. She's a menace. Something should be done."

"I agree completely. A body isn't safe in her own home with that girl running loose."

"I think she should be sent away."

"Or arrested."

"Or put in a crazy house."

"Yes. Oh, yes, that's where she belongs. In a crazy house."

At the railroad station, two men were seated inside where it was nice and warm and where they could do nothing comfortably. "I see the Cox girl is at it again."

"Tried to burn down Daniel's house. Can you believe it?"

"After all that man has done for her."

"Took her in when nobody else would."

"She can't hold a job."

"Pretty near destroyed the Oyster Saloon."

"White was a good man to give her a job like he did. Then she broke everything."

"I heard she blames it on ghosts."

"About time she blamed it on herself. There aren't any such things as ghosts."

"She claims there are. Claims they are out to get her."

"You know what ought to go and get her?"

"What?"

"The sheriff. He ought to get her and lock her up and stop all this foolishness before somebody gets hurt."

"Yep. If she'd do that to Daniel's house, she'd do it to any one of ours."

"Ought to put her in jail."

"They used to burn people like her in olden times."

"Too bad these are modern times."

"Too bad."

Sunday, December 29, 1878

Dr. Nathan Tupper, a physician who also taught a Sunday school class, changed his lecture subject that morning to demons and spirits. The doctor had only visited the Teed home once; yet, he told the parishioners, Esther was either a Mesmerist or a fraud and that she had caused more than enough trouble in that small town.

"I suggest," he said, thumping on a Bible, "that if a rawhide whip were laid across Esther's bare shoulders by a powerful arm, the tricks of the girl would cease at once."

The devout piously nodded their heads in agreement.

Tuesday, December 31, 1878

Daniel had just settled into the large leather and porcelain barber's chair when the door opened. He glanced in the mirror and saw it was Judge Bliss. Daniel smiled to think that both he and the judge had their hair cut at the same place. He guessed he was coming up in the world after all. He didn't know the judge personally. Even though Amherst was a small town, factory workers and judges moved in different social circles. He had seen the judge at most of the civic occasions, on the bandstand, swearing in the new mayors, etc. He tipped his hat to the man when he passed him on the street, but most of Amherst did that.

So it was with great surprise that he felt the judge's hand on his shoulder. "Daniel Teed?"

"Yes." Daniel tried to sit up, but the barber was pushing him backward for the shave.

"I am James Bliss."

"I know," Daniel replied.

"Do you also know," the thin, short man said, "that I am your landlord?"

Daniel now sat up, pushing the barber and his brush backward. "My landlord?"

"Yes. I bought the house you're living in. Bought it from Joe Fillmore and his wife. Bought it on Tuesday, the tenth of this month. Have the deed right here." He whipped a folded legal paper from his inner coat pocket and handed it to Daniel. Daniel opened it by bringing his hands from under the barber's cloth, but he only glanced at it. Judge Bliss knew his law. He wasn't about to show around a phony deed. "You'll start paying me the rent tomorrow. That'll be the first of the month."

"This comes as a bit of surprise," Daniel said slowly. "I didn't know Joe Fillmore wanted to sell the place. I might have bought it if I had known."

"With what money?" the judge asked.

Daniel laughed. It was an embarrassed laugh. "With none, I guess. Anyway," and he forced a big smile, not really wanting to deal with this man when Joe Fillmore had been such a lenient landlord, "I'll have your rent on time." He paused. "You're not going to raise it, are you?"

The man shook his head. "No, but I am going to impose one condition. Something that Fillmore should have done long before this."

Daniel looked at him.

"I want your sister-in-law, Miss Esther Cox, out of my house before tomorrow morning. I want her *out.*"

"Esther?" Daniel was dumbfounded. "What has Esther done? Why her?"

"She only tried to set fire to the place, that's all. I've spent a lot of money on that property, and I don't want it destroyed. If it gets damaged, *you'll* be liable for the expenses, and I know you don't have a pot or a window to throw it out of." He looked around at the others in the shop who were listening and trying to look as if they were not. "I've been to your place of work, Mr. Teed. I know how much your salary is. You can't afford to pay for my house if it's burned to the ground."

Daniel felt something red and angry start to rise in his chest. "I really don't think that my salary is anybody's business."

"Well, I made it mine. You can't afford to replace the windows in the house, let alone the wood." He put the deed back in his pocket. "I have nothing against you. My argument is with your sister-in-law. She is dangerous to my property and to the property of all the others on the street. I have every legal right to say who can live in my property and who can't, and I don't want her there."

"But where can she go by tomorrow?" Daniel was still in shock.

"That is not my problem. It is yours. If she's not out of

there by tomorrow, you and your family will have one week to vacate the premises."

"One week? But I have two small boys and two others who board with me."

"Again, the number of children and the number of dependents you have is none of my concern. Mr. Teed, if you have any regard for the law you'll make certain everything is done as I say."

Daniel wanted to strike the man but knew what problems that would bring. "You are a very cold man, Judge Bliss. I don't know how I am going to do as you ask."

"You had better find a way, sir. I have had to learn to be cold where my property and possessions are concerned, and if being 'cold' means being practical, then you have paid me a compliment." He tugged at the top loop on his greatcoat and buttoned it. "Good day, sir," he said to Daniel. Then to the others who sat in silent fascination, "Good day, gentlemen." Then he was gone.

"Bastard!" Daniel said aloud. "That man is a real bastard, isn't he?" he said to the barber, but the barber kept his eyes averted and, for as long as Daniel had known him, never uttered a word all during the shave and the haircut.

* * *

Esther had fainted when Daniel told her she had to move. She stood in the parlor in front of him while he related what Judge Bliss had said. She didn't cry out but instead crumpled onto the carpet as if she had been struck by a bullet.

Olive hadn't had time to tell Daniel, but Esther had heard the voice of the "ghost" that morning. It had told her that she must leave the house that night or else he would set fire to the loft under the roof and burn down the house. He promised to kill everyone in the house this time.

"First she gets this from the voice," Olive said bitterly to Daniel, "and now you come home and tell her that Judge Bliss is ordering her out! Daniel, why did you agree? Why can't Esther stay? We can fight this!"

"I didn't agree or disagree," he said wearily. "I just listened to what that bastard had to say. Anyway, what is there to fight? Either Esther goes, or we all go. Even her 'ghost' wants her out of here. You and Jennie get her things packed."

"Where are you going to take her? To the edge of town and dump her in the marsh?"

"No. I walked around for a while after the barber's and ended up at White's Saloon. I told John what had happened, and he says Esther can come and live with them."

"As a what?" Olive demanded. "As a friend or as a slave?"

"As a housekeeper." Daniel was tired. "John said Esther could stay with them if she promised to clean the house and take care of the children. She wouldn't get paid, of course—"

"Of course," Olive interrupted.

"—but she would get her food and any cast-off clothing from Mrs. White."

"Aren't they afraid that Esther will burn down *their* house? They know about the falling matches and the fire in the basement."

"Well," said Daniel, "Esther will only be in the house while she works in it. She won't sleep in it. At night, there's a room in a shed that has a cot and a heatstove. The Whites had it built in case they got a hired hand."

"Well they got one now, but she's not hired. She's being put into slavery." Olive stood before Daniel, who was sitting wearily on the parlor sofa. "Daniel, I'm so blamed mad at the way things are turning out! Esther is being treated like a dog. Thrown out of her only home and into a shed. Made to work for no wages for people who don't give a damn about her. And even you, the one man who has stood by her in all this, gives up without a fight to that old crook Bliss." Olive's voice rose. "She is only eighteen years old! She's still a baby in so many ways! Now she has nobody to defend her! Not even *you*!"

Daniel opened his mouth to reply but thought better of it. What was the use? Esther—all of them—were caught in something that was not of their own making. They were all victims. It wasn't just Esther alone. They were all suffering. "Get the girl and her bags ready," he said.

"And you're not going to do anything to help her, are you? She is an innocent child, Daniel. You can't abandon her like this!"

"Olive," his voice was low but firm, "get the girl and her bags ready."

He put on his boots and coat and gloves and went out to hitch the horse to the buggy. He stayed outside until he saw the door open and Esther appear, leaning heavily on Olive's shoulder. Her face was almost hidden by her heavy scarf. Daniel couldn't tell if she had been crying or not, but he assumed she had. He took the heavy suitcase from Jennie and tossed it into the rear of the buggy.

Jennie held Esther close, hugging her but not putting any of her emotion into words.

Olive gave her sister one last long and hard hug, also in silence. Then she helped Esther raise her coat and skirt high enough so she could step up into the buggy. By the time she got settled and Olive had spread the lap robe around her legs, Daniel was sitting inside, holding the reins.

The night was clear. For the last day of the year, the skies had been decorated with stars and a bright new moon. It hadn't snowed for a few days, and so the streets were clean and the horse clipped easily along Havelock Street. When it came to Victoria Street it paused, seemed to look both ways, and then proceeded across it. It was Amherst's main street but now, so close to midnight, it was deserted. The horse clopped on past the shops on La Planche Street. When they were passing White's Oyster Saloon, Esther didn't look up. Then they passed Dale Street and were back in open country.

"Esther?" Daniel spoke her name softly. There was no reaction. She hadn't made a sound or even a movement since she got into the buggy. "Esther," he said again, "I want you to understand that I love you. It may not appear like it now, but I do. I care for you and want you to be happy."

Not the slightest reaction from the girl.

"No matter what happens, I want you to know that I am not the one who is turning you out of your home." No response. "It's not me. It's that ghost—that devilish thing—that is doing it."

Esther seemed to deflate suddenly, to crumple inwardly onto herself. "Daniel, I'm not blaming you, but dear God, it's not my fault!" She was crying softly. "I'm innocent of everything they are accusing me of. I would change it if I could, but I can't! Oh, Daniel, I can't change it! I can't!"

PART THREE

Tuesday, March 25, 1879

DUCHESS OF CLOUDESBERG (moving rapidly over to the Duke): You mean you planned it from the first?

DUKE OF CLOUDESBERG: I had trusted the truth would not be known. At least not until the armies had returned to their positions on the other side of the river.

THE KING: But that might have not been for months and if they had not been victorious, then I would not still [pause] still be in power.

DUKE OF CLOUDESBERG: That is correct. You would no longer be king and General Harubnick would have placed your son William on the throne. William would have been named but I would have been declared Regent.

PRINCE ADALBERT (going to the Duke and laying his hand on the Duke's shoulder): And as Regent you would have ruined the kingdom. You and your sons would have destroyed everything my father has worked so long to establish. You would have made a puppet of my half-brother and would have used his simple ways to enrich and to empower yourself.

DUCHESS OF CLOUDESBERG (almost swooning against the sofa): Why didn't you inform me of your plans? I, your own wife.

DUKE OF CLOUDESBERG: If I had told you of my plans, you would have informed the Queen, your sister, and she, out of loyalty and love she holds for her husband, the King, would have told him, and my desires would have been thwarted.

PRINCE ADALBERT: But they have been thwarted, sir! Your schemes have brought you to naught. Had that young priest not heard my cries and released me from the dungeon when he did, you would have been successful. But Fate was not on your side! The King, my father, has appointed me Prime Minister as well as general of all the army. I shall exile my foolish half-brother until he understands the consequences of what he almost did. And you sir, shall be stripped of your lands and castle and shall be forced to do menial labor in the public square.

DUCHESS OF CLOUDESBERG: Oh, no! Not that! The indignity of it all! (Faints.)

THE KING (embracing the Prince): My kingdom has been restored. Thanks to you.

PRINCE ADALBERT (holding up the crucifix Marian, the milkgirl, had given him while in prison): No, Father. Not thanks to *me*. Thanks be to God and that pretty peasant girl who showed me that might is not always right. The dear girl, the dear Marian, whom I love.

THE KING: And whom one day will reign beside you as your Queen. I give you permission to marry her.

PRINCE ADALBERT: You tell her, father, she has been waiting. [Marian enters from the right. The Prince rushes to hold her in his arms. The King extends his hand. She kisses his ring. Then the King embraces her as trumpets blow offstage.]

The large red curtains closed slowly, keeping the actors immobile in their final tableau as the audience heartily applauded. Even after it had completely closed the applause kept up and so, once more, the actors appeared. This time they formed a straight line across the stage, holding hands and acknowledging their due appreciation. Then they unclasped their hands, and the women walked forward and curtsied. The men walked forward and bowed. Then the curtain fell for the final time.

The Misplaced Crown had been one of the more popular presentations of the Nannery Academy of Music Company. Almost anything played well in Amherst. The townspeople were grateful for entertainment of any kind. Their wood-frame Academy of Music sat empty most of the time. While it was only a block from the Teed house, it might have been light-years away for Daniel and Olive, who rarely went to anything presented there. Jennie and her friends sometimes attended, and they were in the audience this night, peering through the darkness onto the gas-lit stage to see these wonderful creatures from another planet who called themselves actors. Jennie especially admired one young man. He didn't have the leading role (that was reserved for the pompous Mr. W.F. Burroughs), but he made a dashing impression as he strutted behind the gas footlights and spoke in round, clear, pear-shaped tones. Jennie discovered, by reading her programme, that his name was Walter Hubbell.

Hubbell was twenty-eight years old and an American from Pennsylvania. He had the kind of classic features that directors (and ladies in the audience) looked for. There was almost six feet of him with broad shoulders and a narrow waist. There was the high forehead and the wavy, jet-black hair. There were the deep-set blue eyes and the firm chin. There was also the perfect Roman nose that both he and the public admired in profile.

Walter Hubbell, at twenty-eight, was a bit of a snob. His Pennsylvania family didn't have an impressive bank account but they did have an impressive genealogical background, and it opened social doors for the Hubbells that otherwise would have remained closed. He was descended from Richard Hubbell, who came to America in 1647 and claimed to be related to the British Royal Family. Walter's great-grandfather (third in descent from the eminent immigrant) became a captain in the Revolutionary War, fighting five different conflicts alongside George Washington, including the famed Battle of Bunker Hill. Walter's father was a lawyer who also was an inventor. When the Civil War broke out, he devised a new type of shell and a better type of cannon fuse that the Northern Army used to blow up members of the Southern Army.

Instead of using his family contacts to become a businessman, Walter went on the stage. His first professional appearance (after the usual things in school) was a small part in a local company of *Uncle Tom's Cabin*. After that he toured in companies that played in large cities like Chicago and desolate areas like the Oklahoma Territory. People, starving for entertainment, would pay good money to see *Hamlet* or *Macbeth*, even in a condensed version with only a handful of actors. Being "classical" was the hallmark of a truly professional thespian, and his troupe mixed Shakespeare with Voltaire and

Jonson. *Uncle Tom's Cabin* was always a sellout, as were such modern works as *Flowers of the Forest* and *Marble Heart.*

This company had been hired in New York and consisted of American actors who obviously needed a job because they left Manhattan in a blinding snowstorm and in an unheated coastal steamer that took a full week to reach Nova Scotia. The passage had been terrible, with blocks of ice banging at the hull and snow-filled winds keeping everyone but the crew in their cabins. They pulled into Halifax on January 10 and four days later opened at the Academy of Music. By the time they set out "to tour the provinces," they had presented thirty-seven different plays.

In Amherst that night, while the others in the cast were having a drink and a late supper at the home of a social benefactor, Walter Hubbell chose to sit in his boardinghouse room and stare out the window at White's Oyster Saloon right across the street. The table by the bed was scattered with newspaper clippings. Ever since he had first read of the case in a Halifax paper, the young actor had been cutting and saving everything he could find on it. It intrigued him. He was sure it was nonsense. He told himself over and over it was fraud and delusion. There would be no validity to any of it once it was exposed to the light of investigative reason. The clippings told of objects being moved, of fires breaking out, of poundings and writings. Well, he would put it all to rest. He was the one to tackle this nonsense and show it up for the fakery it was. Tomorrow morning he would march across the street and face the girl right where she worked. He would see the things with his own eyes and he would understand immediately what kinds of stage magic she was using. It was incredible that she had flimflammed the entire population of this hick town. Unsophisticated people are always more gullible than those from progressive areas. The naïve citizens of Amherst needed an outside expert to show them how they were being tricked. For all the talk about "professional people" on the case they seemed, to him, to be nothing more than farmers who had managed to get a doctor's or a minister's license. Young Hubbell would show them all up—and if he made some money while he did it, so much the better.

Wednesday, March 26, 1879

"My dear, you missed a perfectly wonderful dinner last night!" Miss Phosa McAllister took time away from her scrambled eggs and ham to speak to Walter Hubbell as he joined the cast at the breakfast table. Even though it was not yet 8:00 A.M., the company was assembled and busy putting away the food the waiters continued to bring. They would all have preferred spending the morning in bed, but the boardinghouse rules were if you didn't get to the dining room by eight, you didn't get breakfast. "They had baked chicken and three kinds of salads and a wonderful chocolate cake," Phosa went on, "and it was buffet style so you could go back as many times as you chose."

"Phosa chose a good many times," said Miss Josie Wilmere, another female in the company. She was older and tried not to resent Phosa's young beauty, but occasionally it came to the surface.

"At least I didn't set up a tent next to the wine table!" Phosa had a smile on her face, but she didn't mean it. "It was almost necessary to get a court order to get the bottle away from Josie." She laughed and the others knew it was an exaggeration—just a little bit.

"Yes, Hubbell," said Walter Lennon, the ageing character actor, "these Canadians know how to spread a real feed, and all we had to do for it was talk at them and smile a great deal."

"The hostess had this long dining-room table and we just stood around it while the locals stared. We ate and they talked. It was quite the best of arrangements," Actor Fenwick Armstrong said, his face was still flushed under his white hair. "You really missed a feed."

"I had some reading to do," Hubbell said, and reached across Josie's plate for the platter of hot biscuits.

"Still onto that ghost stuff?" Lennon asked.

"Are you going to meet the girl today?" Phosa was intrigued but a little afraid of the entire matter. "Does she know you're in town?"

"Not yet," he replied, "but she will. As soon as the restaurant opens up, I'll go over and introduce myself. I don't want her to know that I'm coming until I get there. Don't want to give her a chance to set something up."

"I still say it's nonsense," Fenwick intoned. "You're

wasting your time. We're leaving for Moncton right after the presentation tonight."

"I know," Hubbell replied, "but a few hours today will answer a lot of questions for later." He grinned. "Anyway, what else is there to do in Amherst? In the snow."

None of them pressed him to continue. They were, frankly, a little tired of hearing about the "Great Amherst Mystery" as the press and Hubbell referred to it. They had heard the details from him (whether they wanted to or not) and had heard him expound (more than once) on why he thought it was a fraud and why he thought he could expose the girl. A couple of them privately wondered what harm the poor child was doing to others. From all reports, she was hurting herself more than anyone else involved. And they knew about Hubbell's friend Elsie. Poor Elsie! That's how they all thought of her: *poor* Elsie.

Seven years before—Hubbell had just turned twenty-one—a friend of his named Elsie had watched her mother die of pneumonia. Elsie was distraught. Elsie couldn't eat or sleep. Elsie couldn't think of anything but how lonely she was and how alone the rest of her life was going to be without her mother beside her. One day Elsie decided to visit a Spiritualist medium to see if she could make contact with her own mother. If she could just *talk* once more with her mother, get some assurance that her mother was not in pain . . . The medium told her she could arrange a séance. She was also told how much it would cost. That night, during the séance, Elsie's mother came through, faintly. Elsie was ecstatic. Could the medium do it again? The woman didn't know and couldn't promise, but if Elsie came back on another day and brought so many dollars with her, she would try. Again, Elsie's mother came in—a little stronger this time, but she didn't stay as long as Elsie would have liked. So there was another session and more dollars. Then another session and the price went up. Finally, after two months of this, Elsie's bank account was almost depleted. What could she do? She *had* to talk to her departed mother. Her mother was getting stronger every day. Elsie had to keep communicating with her; even her mother insisted on it.

Elsie's mental health grew worse as her mother's seemed to grow stronger. Finally, one day she told Hubbell what had been happening. He was appalled. He did not believe in those things. Elsie became furious with him. What did he know? How dare he tell her the medium was a fraud and it wasn't really her mother who had been coming through? How dare he even insinuate this about a woman who was doing so much to help her?

Finally she agreed. Hubbell could go with her the next time there was a séance, but he couldn't interfere. He could only sit and listen. As the medium went into trance, Elsie's mother started speaking. Yes, the voice said, sell the house if necessary. She must keep holding these sessions; Mother's health was improving because of them. Hubbell sat in the darkness listening. Then with no warning he jumped up, pushed over the table, and sent the medium toppling to the floor. As Elsie screamed, Hubbell quickly lit an oil lamp and shined it where the table had been. There, from a hole in the floor, peeped the end of a metal tube. He grabbed the tube and pulled it a few feet up from the floor. Elsie very distinctly heard a woman's voice in the room below say, "What the hell . . . ?"

When Elsie finally got over her anger, her health returned along with her common sense. She was most grateful to Hubbell and told everyone in their circle of friends what had happened. There was even a write-up about it in the newspaper, so aside from being recognized as an actor, he was also known as a "ghost-chaser." From then on, as far as he was concerned, there were no such things as ghosts, and it became his job, his duty, to debunk anything to do with spirits or mediums.

"Have some more eggs, dear?" Josie passed him the large platter. She watched as he slid two of them off onto his plate. "What are you going to do when you do meet this girl? Drive a stake through her heart?" She laughed aloud at her own joke.

"No," he said calmly, "going to put her onstage."

"Onstage?" Three actors repeated it at the same time.

"I'm not giving her a job in *our* company," manager Bill Nannery said loudly. "Don't go promising her things you can't deliver."

"Not in our company," Hubbell said. "When the tour is over in June, I plan to go around the countryside and deliver lectures on her and the evils of Spiritualism. You know, fraudulent mediums and phony psychics and the like. I'll have her on the stage with me."

"That's a good idea," Josie said. "People will pay to see her now that she's so famous and everything."

"Exactly," he replied. "I'll work up a lecture of about an hour and tell just what I've discovered. She'll be sitting right there while I talk about her fraud and her mischief. Afterward there'll be questions from the audience and *she'll* have to answer them."

"Very ingenious," Fenwick said with a drawl. "Quite clever. But what happens if she refuses to accompany you? If she doesn't want to go onstage?"

"She'll go," he said calmly. "She comes from a poor, working-class home. She needs the money. I'll give her a percentage of the profits."

"After a large amount of expenses are deducted," manager Nannery said with a laugh.

"Oh," Hubbell said, himself laughing, "a lot of expenses!"

* * *

He waited until he saw a man unlock the front door of the restaurant and then waited until another man, younger and thinner than the first, swept a path free of snow from the street to the entrance. It had snowed almost every day, and Hubbell had resigned himself to the fact that snow was one of the curses of a touring actor's life. He draped his long black wool cape over his shoulders, adjusted his wide-brimmed but low-crown black felt hat, and left the boardinghouse. He jumped a snowbank, then stepped carefully around frozen horse droppings and then onto the newly cleaned area that led to the restaurant's door. Mr. Crowe, the bartender, looked up at this first customer of the day.

Hubbell didn't order but leaned against the bar and said, "I'd like to see Esther Cox."

The man continued setting up the bar. "Do you have a telescope?"

"Telescope?"

"Yeah. Esther ain't here. She's over in St. John's." The bartender looked at him. "Who are you?"

"I'm . . . I'm a friend of Esther's."

"No, you're not. She don't have any friends anymore. Poor child." He arranged several whiskey bottles. "Anyway, she's not here. Hasn't been here since before Christmas." He looked Hubbell straight in the eye. "As any *friend* of hers would know."

Hubbell drew himself up into his own idea of dignity. "Well then, my good man, is the proprietor in? Mr. John White, I believe his name is."

"I'm not your good man," Crowe said, "and yes, White is here." He put down a towel he had just picked up. "I'll call him."

Hubbell was badly deflated and hoped it didn't show. He had planned on meeting with the Cox girl and getting all his business details worked out right away so he could start setting up his lecture tour. The troupe would be in St. John's in a week, but if Esther was staying with friends there, it would be more difficult to approach her than if she were working in a public place like the Oyster Saloon. "Damn!" he muttered aloud.

John White came out of the kitchen. He was a big man, broad-shouldered and dark-haired, so the white cloth around his body looked more like a bedsheet than an apron. He extended his hand as he approached Hubbell. "John White," he said. "What can I do for you?"

"Walter Hubbell, of the Nannery Academy of Music Company. We are playing in Amherst for two days."

"Oh, yes." White smiled. "My wife is going tonight to see you. Won't you sit down?" He motioned to a table and pulled out a chair for his visitor. It wasn't often that he had a celebrity in his place. "Have you had breakfast? A cup of coffee, perhaps?" Hubbell shook his head. "What can I do for you?" White repeated when they were both seated.

"Well," Hubbell started, "I really came in here to seek out one Miss Esther Cox, but I understand she is no longer employed by you."

"Esther? What do you want with Esther? You want to put her onstage?" White laughed.

"Exactly," Hubbell replied. "That's exactly what I want to do."

"Esther ain't no actress."

"I don't want her to act. All she has to do is sit there."

"And do what?" White was suspicious.

"Nothing. Just sit there while I talk about her and what has been happening to her."

"You mean you want to give a stage lecture about her and her ghosts, and all she has to do is sit there so folks can look at her?"

"That's right." Hubbell unfastened the top button to his cape and spread the heavy collar carefully back across his shoulders. "You see, I have been involved in this type of subject for many years. Back in '72 I did some serious investigation of Spiritualism and Spiritualist mediums and received quite a bit of renown for it. That was in the States. In Pennsylvania. You see, I had this female friend whose loss of her dear departed mother was so severe that she almost became insane. She had been going to a medium who charged her a great deal of money to bring her mother back from the grave. Each time they had a séance the mother supposedly appeared and spoke with my bereaved acquaintance. I, of course, suspected—"

"Wasn't that wonderful!" White beamed. "I'm sure it must have been great consolation to your friend."

"But you see," Hubbell tried to explain, "after serious investigation I discovered that the medium was really—"

"Bringing the mother back." White thought he was finishing Hubbell's sentence for him. "Isn't that something? You know, when all this stuff started around Esther, none of us thought there was anything to it either, but after being around her for a while we were *convinced* she had a real ghost with her. Maybe more than one. I could tell you things that happened right here in this room that would make your hair stand on end."

"You *believe* these stories about Miss Cox?"

"I sure do. I saw them happen with my own eyes. So did Crowe over there. Hey, Crowe, wasn't them wonderful things that happened when Esther was around here?" The older man nodded his head. "I had this place packed morning, afternoon, and evening with people wanting to see for themselves."

Hubbell felt he was getting light-headed. This man actually believed that the Cox girl was real! Incredible!

"That very chair you're sitting in was taken more than once and put into a kind of pyramid with other chairs and then knocked to the floor. Just look at the bangs and nicks on the legs and backs of most of these chairs. I didn't have them repainted. I wanted to keep the marks as souvenirs."

Hubbell realized he would have to change his tactics if he were to get anything out of this man.

"Esther came to live with us, you know," White said. "It was on New Year's Eve. There had been fires in the house where she lived with her sisters and brother-in-law, and the owner didn't want to have his place burned down, so he told her she'd have to move. Well, she came to live with my wife and my children, and we treated her like she was family. Had her own room in an outer shed and everything. Well, sir, one day after she had been with us for about three weeks a watch that she kept on her bedside table just rose up into the air and dashed itself against the wall. My wife was right there when it happened, she will attest to it. Matter of fact, I have it over there on the wall." He pointed to a walnut frame, and Hubbell could see it contained a shattered pocket watch and bits and pieces behind protective glass.

"Weren't you afraid Esther's 'ghosts' would do more damage?" the actor asked.

"We were prepared for it, but they never did. One day," he laughed, "and this was funny, after she had been there for about a month she was scrubbing the upstairs hall floor when—"

"Scrubbing the floor?" Hubbell thought she had been a "guest" of the Whites.

"That's right, she was down on her hands and knees scrubbing the floor when hocus-pocus, the brush vanished right out of her hand! One minute she held it, the next minute it was gone." He laughed again. "I mean *gone*. She screamed and hollered as if she was getting butchered, and my wife and daughter came running upstairs to see what it was all about. When they heard about the brush, all three got a little scared. Then whammo! The brush suddenly came out of the hall ceiling and sailed right at Esther and banged her in the head! She still had a goose egg there when I got home that night." White laughed again.

Hubbell wanted to say: "You really believe this tripe?" but he didn't. Instead he asked, "Well, if the 'ghost' could make a brush vanish, then why not a chair or a sofa? Or why not even a person? How did you know that the 'ghost' wasn't going to kidnap one of your children?"

White became serious. "Well, we talked about that but understood there wasn't too much we could do about it. Then around the end of February there was something else. . . . Poor Esther."

"What do you mean 'something else'?"

"The loud noises started. Just like when she was at the

Teed house. We live out in the country so they didn't bother the neighbors, but they did upset my wife and kids. Then the matches came. Just like in the Teed house again. They came from the ceiling and dropped on the floor and furniture. Of course, she couldn't stay with us after that."

"Of course not."

"So we had to ask her to leave. Poor Esther. My wife felt badly about it, for the girl was a good worker. You can't get decent household help anymore. And Esther seemed to like living with us. She took care of the young ones and cared for the animals and everything. She cried a great deal when we told her she had to go elsewhere. A hard worker, I was really sorry to see her leave."

"I'm sure," Hubbell agreed.

"I asked around and a friend of mine, Captain Beck, agreed to take Esther in for a while. He has a nice wife and I guess she is enjoying herself there. They have lots of parties."

"Parties?"

"The Becks are prominent, you know, him being a sea captain and all. They have been giving parties, and Esther and her 'ghosts' tell people things."

"What kind of things?"

"The date on a coin in some man's pocket. How many children a woman has. Things like that. With the rappings. That's how the ghosts communicate. With those knockings on the walls and furniture."

"So she is already in the theatrical profession," Hubbell said. "She's become a performer at the Beck home."

"Well, she won't do it for everybody. It takes too much out of her. I guess she feels she owes the captain something—after all, she doesn't have to do any work at his house. She feels obligated to show off her ghosts, even though she's still frightened of them. Are you sure you don't want some coffee?"

"No, thank you. Mr. White, do you think Esther will agree to go on tour with me? I mean, if she's frightened and all that, possibly she will refuse."

"She'll go. If I say so," White replied.

"If *you* say so?"

"I'm her legal guardian. Daniel Teed thought it would be a good idea to have somebody in the community, somebody with financial assets, to take over her affairs."

"Did Esther agree?"

"She didn't have any say in the matter. She's not twenty-one yet."

"So I *have* come to the right man to talk about this venture of mine?"

"Indeed."

"Shall I start with the details?" Hubbell asked. "I have some things written here. Dates I'd like to play and places I need to book. It all has to be set up in advance."

White put out his large hand, stopping the actor from unfolding the papers. "Just one thing before we begin to talk," he said. "Is there any money in this?"

"For Esther?"

"For me."

"If you set this up, getting the halls and the publicity, I'll give you thirty-five percent of everything I take in."

The hand stayed heavy. "Let's make if fifty percent and it's a deal."

"What about Esther's percentage?"

"We won't worry about her. She'll do as I say."

"Then it's a deal?"

White opened his hand. "It's a deal."

Monday, April 7, 1879

Mr. Walter Hubbell
Nannery Academy of Music Company
Total Abstinence Hall
Saint John's, Newfoundland

My Dear Mr. Hubbell:

I hope this letter finds you well and in good health and ready for your two months stay in Newfoundland. It is an especially fine time of the year to be there with the spring leaves and all.

I want to tell you again how much we enjoyed meeting you and having you as a guest in our home, even if it was for just a few hours before your play began. Both my small boys still marvel that they had a real actor in their midsts. I'm happy that our dear friend John White saw fit to bring you over and introduce us to you. I also want to thank you again for the two free tickets to see your performance that same evening. Mr. Teed and I truly enjoyed it. You were excellent in it. I will always remember going back of the stage to meet the others in the company and to see how the curtains and the scenery was moved. You surely showed our humble family a great deal of courtesy and concern.

My sister, Esther Cox, has returned to Amherst yesterday. She hated to leave the warm household of the Becks but they are going traveling soon and could not keep her in the house alone. She is in good health and is so very happy to be back among her family and friends.

Naturally she cannot stay here with Mr. Teed and myself (you know the reasons why) so we have placed her with the Van Amburgh family. They have a farm some two and a half miles from the center of the village. She will act as housekeeper and nanny and will have a room of her own *inside* the house.

We mentioned, but only slightly, your plan to take her on a lecture circuit. She has not replied yet saying it all depends on *them* (I assume she means her ghosts) but she does not seem averse to the suggestion. She needs to become resettled at this time so we did not press her for an answer. After all, your tour will not take place until June so we have a two month period yet. I'm quite assured there will be no problem at the time of her decision, however.

Esther passed her birthday on March 28th last while with the Becks. They gave her a party. I wished she could have been here with us on that date but it wasn't to be. She is nineteen years old! My how a lifetime flies!

I will close now and hasten to get this into the post. My sister Jennie (whom you met) sends you her regards as do I and the children and Mr. Teed. Thanks to you again for the visit and the complimentary tickets!

Sincerely,
Olive Teed
(Written by the hand of Miss
Jennie Cox)

Sunday, April 27, 1879

Mr. Walter Hubbell
Nannery Academy of Music Company
Total Abstinence Hall
Saint John's, Newfoundland

Dear Hubbell:

I wanted to get this letter off to you today, a Sunday, while the saloon is closed and I can concentrate upon what I'm writing.

I have firmed up the dates for our tour to the best of my abilities. On the thirteenth and fourteenth of June we will be in Moncton at Ruddick's Hall. It is a large place and should fit the bill perfectly. Then on the twentieth and twenty-first we will be in Chatham, New Brunswick, at the Masonic Hall. I have already sent both places five dollars as a deposit to hold the halls for us. So that's ten dollars I am already out of pocket. I have receipts. I have also been promised a reporter to write a story about our tour in each of those towns. We won't have to give the writer too much, maybe two dollars each at the most.

I thought that we'd continue north and west with the third city being Bathurst and the next one Campbellton. From there we can go to Edmundston, then Grand Falls, Fredericton and finally Saint John. As we agreed there is no sense going into Quebec Province because those Frenchies wouldn't understand what you were talking about.

Mrs. Teed tells me she has written you, so you know Esther is with the Van Amburghs. They are treating her fine, I hear. I also hear there have been no appearances by her ghosts. That makes everyone happy. Maybe the ghosts are on vacation, getting rested up for our tour. Ha. Ha.

Esther still says she doesn't know if the ghosts will permit her to go or not. Don't worry. I'll make sure they okay it.

How are you doing with those Newfoundland

women?? The land is cold but the ladies are not or have you already discovered that for yourself? Ha. Ha.

Your friend,
John White

Sunday, June 1, 1879

"Here, let me put that up there for you." Mr. Van Amburgh grabbed Esther's heavy suitcase and tossed it lightly into Daniel's buggy. Esther stood watching, one arm around Mrs. Van Amburgh and the other around her sister Olive.

"We're going to miss you, dear," Ruth Van Amburgh said. "It's almost been like having a daughter around here."

"The house is going to be empty, all right," her husband added. "You know, Olive, Esther is more than welcome here any time she wants to come. Just pack her bag and bring her back."

"Thank you, sir." Olive smiled. "You have been so wonderful to my sister. I'm sure she will never forget it. Nor will we."

"It was the least we could do." He grinned. "Besides, Esther could make the biggest and sweetest chocolate cake I ever saw! She knows I love chocolate."

"She spoiled him, that's what she did," his wife added. "Spoiled him rotten. And he loved every minute of it!"

Daniel was in the buggy now, slack reins already in his hands. "Let's get going!" he shouted.

There were more kissing on the cheeks and hugging, and when the buggy drove out of the farmyard, Esther waved until they were around a curve and the farm had vanished behind a grove of trees. Then she settled back against the buggy seat and felt the security of her sister's body next to hers. She smiled.

She had been with the Van Amburghs for a little over two months. The ghosts had not come back. She had had her own room. There had been no rappings. She had helped with the housework but only because she wanted to, not because it was expected of her. There had been no disappearing scrub brushes. She had cooked some of the meals. No bubbling buckets of water. They had sat in the evening and played card games or sang songs. There had been no matches from the ceiling. There had been nothing—nothing at all to indicate that Esther was any different from any other nineteen-year-old girl. It had been a wonderful two months!

After the first six weeks of nothing happening, Daniel had called on Judge Bliss, asking the man to permit Esther to return to the house on Princess Street. The judge wasn't that anxious to have the girl back on his property but did agree that if by June 1 there had been no manifestations at the Van Amburghs'—especially fires—she could return. The judge personally called on the farm the last week in May and asked the Van Amburghs all kinds of questions. When he heard that nothing unusual had happened in all that time, he had to assume—as most people did—that the girl had stopped her tomfoolery.

The townspeople still weren't sure. When she would come into the village on a shopping trip with the Van Amburghs, she would be pointed at and stared at. More than one mother yanked her child closer as Esther passed them in a store aisle. There would be whispers as she walked by, and once she turned to catch three elderly ladies making the sign of the cross as she passed them.

None of her school friends wanted her to visit them. She made the mistake, but only made it once, of calling unexpectedly on a girl who had been in her class. The girl kept the screen door between them, not asking Esther to come into the house. After about ten minutes on the porch, the girl's mother came to the door and coldly asked Esther to leave. She declared she didn't want her house burned to the ground.

That hurt, and she cried all the way back to the farm. The next day she was better. Her skin was a little thicker. She promised herself she would not let people upset her again. She sat at the dresser, looking in the mirror and combing her brown hair. Did all this mean that she was destined to be alone forever? To bounce from family to family? Never to have a husband or children of her own? For the first time in months she saw the image of Bob McNeal cross her mind. She smiled. He had been so handsome. He had been so sweet to her. What a wonderful husband he would have made. Then the memory of the gun, the harsh words, and the horrible way his hands felt up under her skirt. She shuddered and combed her hair even faster, hoping in that way to comb the young man and what he did to her right out of her mind.

Wednesday, June 11, 1879

"Hubbell!"

"White!"

The two men shook hands as the actor stepped from the train onto the platform at the Amherst station.

"Nice trip?"

"Excellent, thank you. Have you talked to Esther?"

"Not yet, but I don't perceive any difficulties. They are expecting us over there after the noon meal. I thought we'd eat at my restaurant and go there directly."

"Fine."

Over their food, the two men compared notes as to how the tour would be run, where it would go, and the amounts of money they should make. Both were pleased that advance sales of tickets had been quite brisk at Moncton, with over three-fourths of the large hall being sold out the first day the advertisement appeared in the local paper. It was obvious there was great interest in Esther and "The Great Amherst Mystery."

"I will take the money at the door," White said, "for you will be too busy in the stage area with Esther."

"And we'll divide the profits just as soon as we leave one town to go to another. How about Daniel Teed?" Hubbell asked. "How much is he getting for this?"

"Nothing," replied White. "He didn't ask and I didn't offer."

"And Esther? How much did you promise to give her?"

"I told her we would pay all her expenses. She's never ridden on a train before or stayed in a hotel, so she was quite excited about it. I told her she'd get it all free plus three dollars for each performance."

"Three dollars?" Hubbell was incredulous. "And she agreed to do it for that? Only three dollars?"

"I told you she was just a dumb little girl," White said with a laugh. "To her three dollars is a fortune. And to get to ride in a train and sleep in hotels, too!" He laughed again. "But she really hasn't said 'yes,' or at least her ghosts haven't said she could go. But they will."

"I thought they were gone," Hubbell said. "Didn't you write me that she wasn't bothered by them any longer?"

"At the Van Amburghs', sure, but after she got back to

Princess Street she started getting messages from them again. You know, one rap for 'no' and three raps for 'yes' and all that."

"But no fires or flying sheets?"

"Nothing. I told you, the ghosts are waiting to make their debut onstage!" He laughed again.

* * *

Esther was sitting on the parlor sofa when Walter Hubbell saw her for the first time. Even though he was a sophisticated traveler, he caught his breath for a moment when he was finally in the presence of the girl that most of Canada had been talking about.

"How do you do, sir?" She raised her hand, and Hubbell took it in his. He was surprised how grown up she looked for just nineteen, yet surprised at the little-girl quality that showed in her actions and her voice. Her dark brown hair fell fully onto her shoulders, and she was wearing a tan dress with a high collar and long sleeves that caught the sparkles of sunlight that came into the room past the red draperies. "I'm pleased to meet you," she said.

"And I you." So this was the famous Esther Cox, the girl who flimflammed a nation with her nonsense about ghosts and hauntings.

"Are you really an actor?" she said. "It must be exciting to be an actor."

"It must be more exciting to be Esther Cox." He laughed, watching the expression in her eyes. "After all, *you* are the famous one around here, not me."

"It is a fame that is ill placed," she said. "I don't do anything. Things just happen around me."

"But you are the central figure in these happenings," he said, sitting beside her. "These happenings have made you famous."

"Sir, I'd rather not be famous because of this. I'd rather just be plain old me and get back to the normal life I used to have."

Very clever, he thought, trying to get even me to believe you don't do these things deliberately. "Perhaps your life will return to normal in a while," he said aloud. "Things can't go on like this forever." In other words, you'd better do your damnedest while the locals still believe the story.

"It can't end too soon for me," she said and then sighed deeply. She looked around the room where Olive and White were watching them on the sofa. "It has upset Olive and Daniel's life too much," Esther said. "It's time it stopped."

"But it did stop when you were at the Van Amburghs'," he reminded her.

"Yes, thanks be to God, for the Van Amburghs are good people and the ghosts permitted me two months' rest. They are back now, you know."

"The ghosts?" Hubbell asked, glancing quickly at the other faces in the room to see, if he could, how much they believed of this. She nodded. "But they haven't hurt you? Or set fires or anything?"

"Not so far."

Hubbell looked again at the faces. They seemed to be taking what this girl said as gospel. Uncanny. She had done all this so cleverly that even *they* believed her!

"Bob and Mattie say it's all right," she said softly.

"Bob and Mattie?"

"My ghosts," she explained. "I talked with them this morning right after breakfast and they said it was all right to go." He looked dumbfounded. "To go on the tour. With you and Mr. White," she explained.

Again Hubbell shot a fast glance at the others. They still had those trusting expressions on their faces. He couldn't believe it. "So it's okay to go?" She nodded. "I'm glad," he said. "I suppose I should thank Bob and Mattie. Where are they?"

"Here. In this room. Bob is over by there by the window, and Mattie is by the fern stand."

Hubbell's head twisted quickly in both directions, but he didn't see any ghosts. He knew he wouldn't.

"This is something new," Olive spoke up. "Esther has only just started seeing them. She used to only hear voices, but now she sees them, too."

The actor couldn't believe it. Esther had them all buffaloed! "Why is it that *I* don't see them as well?" he asked.

"None of us can see them," Olive said. "Only Esther. I don't want to see them," she added with a shudder. "That's one thing Esther can keep for herself."

"Will they appear onstage with you?" Hubbell asked. "I want you to sit there while I talk. Will they appear and make things move?"

"What things?" Esther frowned.

"A brightly painted ball. A lit candle. A trumpet. I even

have a brass bell they can ring. If they want to," he added quickly. "I won't ask them to do anything that they don't want to do." Might as well play her game for a while.

"Don't worry," the girl laughed, "they don't do anything they don't want to do! But I'll ask them. If you want them to move things, I'll ask them when it's time. I can't guarantee that they'll do it, but I'll ask them."

"You do that," he said. They'll do it. This girl is such a clever fraud that she'll make sure things happen on that stage! She's had all this publicity and will be getting even more when the tour begins. Oh, yes, little lady, you'll do it. You'll make those candles float and that trumpet blare and probably shake the clapper out of that bell. I don't now how you'll do it. Not just yet. But I *will* know. I've had enough experience with stage magicians and Spiritualist phonies that I'll figure out how you're doing it, and then woe to you, Missy, woe to you.

"If it's all right with you, Mr. Hubbell," Olive said, breaking the silence, "will you and Mr. White come by for supper tonight? I'll make something extra special if you do."

White glanced at his watch. "I really have to get back to the restaurant. Suppose I drive you back to your hotel, Hubbell, and then pick you up at suppertime?"

Hubbell rose from the sofa. "That's a good idea and, Mrs. Teed, of course I accept your invitation. I can also use this time to go over the newspaper clippings I have and get an outline of the speech. I've got most of it written, but meeting Esther has made other things fall into place." He turned to the girl. "I truly enjoyed meeting you," he said, "and I'm looking forward to our sojourn together on the stage."

"I, too, enjoyed meeting you," she replied, "and I think they did, too."

"They?" Hubbell asked.

"Bob and Mattie. I think they like you."

"I hope so," he said, and as he walked toward the front door, a large red geranium blossom floated off and up from one of the plants in the front window and settled on the actor's shoulder. He jumped as if he had been stung by a bee.

"See?" Esther smiled. "I told you they like you."

* * *

White picked Hubbell up at his hotel and drove him in his buggy to the Teed home. "I'm still trying to figure most of this out," the young man said.

"Figure what out?"

"How she does it. These ghosts and things. And that flower flying through the air." He shook his head. "I've read up on these cases, and Esther doesn't really fit into what is considered normal."

White laughed. "I never said that girl was normal." He tugged the reins slightly, and the horse turned onto narrow Princess Street. "Whatever *it* is, it's normal."

"Normal?"

"For her. It just came on her one day. No ifs, ands, or buts. It was just there. She doesn't know why it's there, and neither do people like Carritte or a whole pewful of preachers. But it's there. Lots of people have seen it. I've seen it and you"—he laughed again—"will see it, too!"

"But I can't get up on a stage and tell people that these things are *real,*" Hubbell protested, "and not be able to explain where they come from. People won't pay good money to hear theories. They want facts."

"Nonsense." The buggy came to a halt at the picket fence. "They aren't paying their money to hear facts or anything else. They'll be paying it to see Esther and watch the things on the table move around in the air."

"But I'll have to explain where these things come from and how they got to be around Esther," Hubbell protested.

"Look, Walt, no offense intended, but folks aren't coming to see you. They're coming to see *her*. Remember that and it'll be much easier for us all."

Hubbell felt something bruise inside his body and understood it was his ego. He had intended, on this tour, to be more important than the freak he was exhibiting. He, after all, was a somewhat well-known actor. He, after all, had some renown in the States for his ability as a ghost-debunker. He, after all, hoped to establish himself as a lecturer on scientific subjects.

White seemed to answer his thoughts for him. "You want to make money with her?" Hubbell nodded yes. "Then just give a little bit of the facts and let her ghosts do the rest. They'll put on a show. Believe me."

Olive and Esther had fixed a formal dinner, much more elaborate than the coffee, bread, and cheese they usually had before retiring in the evening. Walter Hubbell pushed himself away from the table with a satisfied sigh. The conversation had been, all evening, about Esther's ghosts. He asked her questions and she answered them. He thought she used remarkable candor, and he watched closely to see how much time it took her to come up with her replies. It had always been his theory that liars had to stop to think for a moment before they made up their facts, but this girl was so clever at it that she breezily said the first things that came to mind. Of course, he reasoned, she has been telling these stories for almost ten months now, so she should have them down pretty pat.

After the dishes had been cleared away and the kitchen put back in order, White asked Esther if she was able to give a demonstration of what her ghosts could do. "I think Walt would like to see some of the stuff."

She looked at the actor, then at Daniel and Olive.

"I . . . I haven't done anything with it for such a long time. The Van Amburghs didn't ask for any of it . . . but I suppose if Olive and Daniel don't mind . . ." She was so happy to be permitted to live in the house again and didn't want to do anything that would jeopardize it. If Judge Bliss heard that she was giving demonstrations on his property . . .

"Fine with me," Daniel said. "Why don't we sit around the dining-room table again. It'd be easier that way."

Hubbell chose a chair that was directly opposite the girl. He wanted to be able to observe her every move. "Why don't you bring in another lamp?" he suggested, and Jennie took the parlor lamp and put it on the buffet. It shone on Esther's face, and Hubbell could see every movement, every expression.

"What shall we ask them?" Esther said aloud.

"Why don't we just find out if they are here," Hubbell said.

Esther took a deep breath. "Is anyone here?" They waited. "Is anyone here?" she repeated. Another silence. "Bob? Bob, are you here?"

Bam! Bam! Bam!

Hubbell's eyes widened. Both of Esther's hands were on the table.

"Is that you, Bob?"

Bam! Bam! Bam!

Hubbell couldn't see any movement on Esther's part. Not even the slightest swaying of her body or rustling of her dress.

If she were kicking the underside of the table to produce those sounds, she was doing it very cleverly.

"Is he alone?" Olive asked.

Bam!

"Is Mattie with you?" she asked. Bam! Bam! Bam! "That's nice," Esther said. "Good evening, Mattie. How are you? Are you fine?" Bam! Bam! Bam! Esther smiled. "Mattie, we have a friend here tonight with us. A new friend, named Mr. Walter Hubbell. You gave him a flower this afternoon."

There was a scratching sound across the top of the table. It came around Hubbell's hands as they lay flat on the tabletop. He thought he could feel the air move near his fingers. Now, how did the girl do that? He would go along with her charade. "Hello, Mattie," he said. "How are you?" No answer.

"You have to ask her a question that can be answered with a 'yes' or a 'no,'" Olive said.

"Okay. Mattie, are you dead?" Bam! Bam! Bam! "Mattie, may I ask another question?" It was time to get to the bottom of this. "Mattie, is my mother also dead?" Bam! Hubbell looked at the others around the table. "That's correct. My mother is still alive. Mattie, what is my mother's first name? I know you don't know it. Nobody here knows it. Is it Mary Ann?" Bam! "Is it Louisa Mae?" Bam! "Is it Flora?" Bam! "That's good, Mattie. Is it Elizabeth Catherine?" Bam! Bam! Bam!

"Is that correct, Mr. Hubbell?" Jennie asked. "Is your mother's name Elizabeth Catherine?"

He nodded, not at all sure what was taking place here. "Yes, that's her name."

"You see," said John White, "I told you it would be interesting!"

"Ask her another question," Esther said, "but be sure it can be answered by a 'yes' or a 'no.'"

Hubbell thought for a moment. "Mattie, I have a pocket watch that was given to me by my grandfather. There is a registered number engraved on the inside of the case. Can you give me the number?" Bam! Bam! Bam!

"She can't do that by a 'yes' or a 'no' answer," Esther spoke up.

"Maybe she can determine the number by knocking so many times for each digit." Hubbell was sure he had Esther now. Here was something she hadn't rehearsed. There was no possible way she could have taken his watch from his vest pocket, opened it, and memorized the number. "Instead of one knock for the negative and three knocks for the positive, Mattie or Bob—I don't care which—I want you to give me the correct number of raps for each digit. What I mean is, if there is a four, then give me four raps. Like that." Now he had her. He had changed the rules right in the middle of her game. Let's see her get out of this one.

There was a pause of at least half a minute while everyone sat looking at Esther's face. She had closed her eyes. Hubbell didn't know if it was in concentration or embarrassment.

Then the first raps came. Bam! Bam! Bam!

Everyone looked at Hubbell.

Then seven raps in a row. Then two. A pause. Three more raps. Another pause, and eight rappings in rapid succession. Then it was quiet.

Hubbell reached for his pocket watch, took it out, and read the numbers aloud. "Three, seven, two, three, eight." Jennie applauded delightedly. "That's amazing!" The actor exclaimed. "Simply amazing."

"What'd I tell you?" White said, beaming. "Is she good or not? Can't you just see her onstage?"

Hubbell smiled. "Yes, I can," he said, grinning directly at Esther. "You'll be a sensation."

Back in his hotel room that night, Walter Hubbell tossed and turned on the large feather mattress. He had tried to sleep, but sleep wouldn't come. How did she do those tricks? He had been watching her hands. They hadn't moved. Her body didn't jerk when the raps were heard. How did she know his mother's name? He hadn't told it to anyone. It hadn't been in any newspaper article about the theatre company. He punched the pillow and tried to keep his eyes closed. And the watch! The numbers on his god-damned watch! How did she do that? He'd have to find out. If he was going to debunk her—to show her up for the charlatan she was—he would have to know exactly how she worked her tricks. He slid out of bed and rummaged in his suitcase bringing out a metal flask that was filled with Bourbon. He raised the flask to the moon. "However she does it, it means money in my pocket," he said aloud. "A lot of money. I'll drink to that." He tipped the flask and took a long, full swig of the brown whiskey and wiped his mouth with his nightshirt sleeve. "Esther Cox, you and I and your ghosts are going to have a long and profitable relationship. Long for you and profitable for me."

Thursday, June 12, 1879

Aside from everyone in the Teed household there were friends, neighbors, and the curious crowding the train station platform to say good-bye to Esther. Word had spread quickly that the girl was off to make her fame and fortune and was a real celebrity. They heard she was going to be gone for two months. How wonderful! Olive, Jennie, and Daniel would miss her. The neighbors would breathe easier. She was taking her ghosts (thank God!), and Amherst would be put on the map. Other towns converged on their railway stations to wave to local athletes or politicians or theatre stars. Amherst had a celebrity other towns didn't have. They had a crazy one with ghosts. Maybe they should be proud of her. Maybe.

The ride to Moncton took an hour and twenty-five minutes. Esther sat beside the window, marveling at the scenery along the way. An occasional farmhouse. A plowed field. A group of barefoot children waving at the engineer and waiting to wave at the man in the caboose. Expanses of marsh grasses and clumps of dense, never-cleared forests. John White sat next to her, and Hubbell was across the aisle, writing his lecture. He thought he had it almost finished, but the events around the dining-room table last night had left gaping holes in his theories and his thinking.

The lecture was—deliberately—very general. While he had specifics on what she did, he didn't have any on *how* she did it. He planned to open with a dissertation on the growth of Spiritualism over the past thirty years, when the Fox Sisters started hoodwinking everyone with their spirit raps, then bring it up to date with tales of other phony mediums. Then he would give his personal experience with the medium who tried to take his friend's money to hear her mother's voice. Then he would tell Esther's story, starting with the rustling noise in the mattress, through the flying bedcovers, the writing on the wall, the fire in the basement, the lit matches, and right up to the present.

All this time, while he stood at a podium to one side of the stage, Esther would be sitting in the center of the stage. There would be a chair for her and a low table right beside her. On this table would be placed lightweight objects that she could easily manipulate. There was a silver bugle she could blow. There was a candle she could light and float in the air. There was a silver bell she could ring, and other small but visible objects.

Hubbell looked up from his writing and studied the girl as she stared intently out the train window. She knew what she was getting into. She knew what was expected of her. She was going to have the adventure of her life and get paid for it as well. When the time came, she would perform. Both he and White were sure of it. She might appear to be the innocent young bumpkin, but she knew what was expected of her. It would be one helluva stage show.

They checked into the American House on Wesley Street in Moncton, each getting a room of their own. There were two reporters waiting for them in the lobby, and after Esther had unpacked and refreshed herself, she and the two men traveling with her came to the lobby to answer questions. They were the usual questions: Were these ghosts for real? Was she frightened of them? Were they from Heaven or Hell? Did they do horrible things to her? Were they still trying to destroy the house she lived in? Were these ghosts *really* real?

As the reporters folded their notebooks and started to leave, one of them gasped. A large rocking chair—with nobody in it or near it—began to rock rapidly by itself.

White looked at Hubbell and both men grinned. What a tour this was going to be!

Friday, June 13, 1879

Ruddick's Hall was filled to capacity at least ten minutes before the show was to begin. It pleased John White greatly to inform latecomers that there were no seats available, so he began selling tickets for the next night's performance.

Esther was nervous. Hubbell placed her in the chair and carefully arranged the small objects on the table beside her. It was low, so everyone in the audience could see the objects atop it.

"Is my hair all right?" she asked for the fifth time. She had been nervously combing it for the past half hour.

"It's perfect," he said. "It looks just fine."

"Did you say you wanted my feet to show, or not? I mean,

do you want my dress to cover my shoes, or do you want the tips to show?" She fussed with the hem of her skirt.

"It doesn't matter," he said. "However you want it."

"Well, show them or hide them? I don't know."

He made the decision. "Hide them."

She smiled. "Thank you."

They could hear the audience calming down. The talking had stopped, and a few people coughed. Hubbell went behind the podium and stood there, straightening his notes. Esther smiled at him, put up a hand to smooth her hair, then tugged the side of her skirt to make sure it was covering her shoes.

The curtain opened.

The quiet of the audience turned into a buzzing, like bees returning to a hive.

"That's her."

"She's Esther Cox."

"She looks so young!"

"Pretty dress."

"Poor thing!"

Walter Hubbell cleared his throat and waited for the buzzing to stop. The gas lamps along the walls of the theatre had been turned down, and the ones that lined the stage were turned up. Hubbell and Esther were bathed in warm tones from the flames.

"My Canadian friends, my name is Walter Hubbell. I will be your lecturer for this evening, hoping to elucidate and illustrate the mystery of the world beyond. I have dealt for years with the so-called supernatural. I have seen many things that have left others bewildered. Yet this young lady, this mere child sitting here—in person—on this stage with me has had the strangest experiences of anyone I have ever encountered. I plan, during the course of this evening, to explain what has been happening to her and around her and through her." He swept an arm in her direction. "Ladies and gentlemen, may I present Miss Esther Cox."

Applause.

"I told you that's who she was."

"She looks older than nineteen."

"Look at her hair. Nice color."

"Hope she doesn't do anything too scary."

"Poor thing."

Hubbell waited until the applause had stopped. Esther had flushed at all the sudden attention. No one had ever applauded her before. She felt her face burning beet red and hoped the extra face paint Walt had insisted she wear hid her uneasiness.

"You will notice that beside Miss Cox there is a table. On that table there are several objects. All are light and easily portable. None are attached to wires or special mechanical devices such as those used by stage magicians. During my discourse on the merits—pro and con—of spirit communications, it is possible that some or perhaps all of these objects will rise from their position on the table and float through the air."

A few loud gasps from the audience.

"Of course, I cannot promise this will happen. I do not control the force. Miss Cox herself controls the force and only Miss Cox. During my lecture, I would advise you to listen to me, but keep your gaze attentively fixed on Miss Cox and the table alongside her. Is there anyone in the audience, either male or female, who would be so kind as to come up onto the stage and examine the objects in question? Someone to act as your representative to verify my statements and guarantee to the others gathered here this evening that these objects in question are not attached to wires and cannot be manipulated by mechanical means?" His eyes scanned the group. "Anyone at all. Please."

A large man in the third row got up from his seat and, using the stairs at the side of the platform, came onto the stage. He looked carefully at each item on the table. "Do you agree, sir, that there is nothing untoward about any of these items?"

The man nodded his head yes. As he started for the side steps, he halted and came back to Esther. He walked around her chair, feeling the air for wires or anything else. Then he smiled and patted her on the head. Esther blushed again. As he left, the audience laughed and applauded.

Hubbell started his lecture. "As far back as the days of the ancient Greeks and Romans—nay, as far back as the earliest Egyptian pharaohs—there has been great public curiosity in the world regarding ghosts and spirits. In the temples of that great ruler Amenhotep, ghosts and spirits were prayed to, given golden ornaments, and served food in gem-encrusted bowls. In Babylonia, where the priests of their abominable pagan religion held absolute sway, ghosts and spirits were appeased with songs and libations of human blood. It is said that Phoenician sailors, before embarking on their perilous sea journeys, would . . ."

As Hubbell droned on, all eyes were on Esther. She sat perfectly still, trying to breathe as little as she could so as not to appear nervous. Her feet remained together and hidden under her skirt. Her hands remained clasped in her lap. And the objects on the table remained exactly where they had been placed.

A half hour went by. Hubbell was up to early England and tales of ghosts in Henry VIII's castle. He tried to keep his eyes on his notes but kept glancing at the table beside Esther. When is she going to start moving things? he wondered. She knew what was expected of her.

The second half hour was almost over. He was now giving the sequence of events that had happened to Esther. Most of the audience was familiar with the story—had read it in the local newspaper—so he embroidered it just a bit. After all, this was a *dramatic* demonstration.

Nothing happened. Nothing moved. Esther fidgeted a couple of times, becoming tired sitting in the same position. Her throat was dry, and she had started to perspire from the warmth of the lights and the warmth of the June evening. She could see that Walt was glancing more and more often in her direction. She knew he was waiting—wanting—something that was on the table to get up and move. She saw the look of desperation in his eyes. "Bob," she said in a whisper, trying not to move her mouth, "Bob and Mattie, do something! Make that bell ring. Light the candle. Anything!" She silently commanded. "Please!"

Everything remained motionless on the table.

"It would appear that these manifestations," Hubbell carried on, "had been the work of some satanic force that had, uninvited and on its own volition, arrived in the village of Amherst to create trouble. It would also appear that . . ."

Another couple got up and left. Hubbell didn't know how many walkouts that made. He had stopped counting after fifteen people had gone. There were murmurings from some who remained. Many were talking among themselves. To his chagrin, few seemed to be listening to what he had to say. Why didn't that blasted girl *do* something? Was she trying to make him look like a jackass?

He glanced to his right; someone was trying to attract his

attention in the wings. He turned and looked. It was John White. He had his two hands together, one atop the other, and began moving them up and down as if he were pulling the curtain. Hubbell nodded.

"And so, ladies and gentlemen, that concludes our lecture for the evening. Thank you and good night."

White rang the curtain down quickly. There were scattered applause and several catcalls.

On White's suggestion, they waited until everyone in the hall had gone and the streets were clear. Then he brought a horse and buggy around to the stage door and drove them back to their hotel.

"What happened?" Hubbell demanded. "Esther, you didn't do a thing!"

"I'm sorry," she said.

"Sorry? You can't just be 'sorry.' All those people paid good money to see you do things, and all you did was sit there!"

She had tears in her eyes. She knew he was going to be angry with her. "You told me not to move," she said softly. "You told me just to sit there and look at the audience while you were speaking. That's what I did. Just as you told me."

"Well, I expected some kind of movement from the *table*," he said. "That's why I put those things there, so you could move them. That's why the people paid money to see you. So they could see you move things!"

"Walt," John White said, "I don't think you should blame Esther. It just happened."

"Happened?" His voice rose. "What happened? *Nothing* happened! I stood there like an idiot talking about ancient Greece and ghosts, and nothing happened. You can't have a spectacle if nothing happens."

"I asked them," the girl replied. "I asked both Bob and Mattie to make things move, but they didn't do it."

"Wonderful," Hubbell said sarcastically. "Well, ask them again tomorrow night, will you? Better yet, don't ask them. Tell them. Tell them you need some action around the table. Can you do that?"

"I'll try," she said in a little girl's voice. "I can't make any promises they'll do it, but I'll try."

He wanted to grab her and shake her and remind her that she was expected to perform. After all, she had done her tricks for farmers and yokels for free. Why the hell couldn't she do it when she was getting paid for it? Why did she deliberately do that to him tonight? Why was she being so stubborn? A few more nights like this and they'd have to start giving the money back.

"Maybe Esther was just too nervous," White said. "Sitting there in front of all those strangers and all. Isn't there anything you can do to make it easier for her? Maybe if she didn't have to look at those people she'd be more relaxed."

"You mean perhaps the crowd stopped her?" Hubbell considered this. "A type of stage fright?" That was possible. Even the best actors forgot their lines when they had stage fright. Magicians often fumbled their tricks when they were nervous. Maybe that was the reason tonight was a failure—the girl was too frightened to perform. "If that's the case," he said, "then tomorrow night I'll give you a feather fan to hold. It will give you something to do with your hands, and if you get embarrassed or nervous, bring it up to your face. Hide behind it if you want to."

"That ought to do it," White said.

"I hope so," Hubbell answered. "For everybody's sake, I hope so."

Esther said nothing more, and when they reached the hotel, she went straight to her room. If either White or Hubbell had cared to listen, they could have stood outside her door and heard her crying.

Saturday, June 14, 1879

The next night Ruddick's Hall was only three-quarters full. Many reserved tickets were not picked up at the box office. White thought the crowd was rowdier than the night before. Word had circulated that the Cox girl had done nothing but sit there.

Hubbell gave her the fan. It was rather large and made of white feathers. She could shield her entire face with it if she chose. She did. Several times. Hubbell gave the same lecture. Nothing happened. The crowd became upset earlier than the night before. There were even a few shouted demands while Hubbell was speaking. The objects sat on the table. Hubbell became uneasy. Esther hid her face with the fan, afraid she might start crying in front of all these people. Finally White pulled the curtain, twenty minutes earlier than the night before.

"Here," he said, shoving a canvas bag at Walt, "these are tonight's receipts. You get out first and take the early train to Chatham. There's one leaving in about ten minutes. You can make it."

"I wasn't going to go till mid-week," he said.

"You'd better go *now*," White insisted. "Esther and I will stay on here and keep the lid on things. We'll bring your valise to Chatham."

"But I can't go without you two. It'll look like I'm running out."

"It'll look like a funeral if you stay!" White shoved the money bag inside Hubbell's vest. "Now take this cash and get the hell out of here!"

The actor caught the next train out of town.

Wednesday, June 18, 1879

The *Moncton Dispatch*, front page:

> Miss Esther Cox arrived here in care of friends, on Friday afternoon last, and a detailed account of the manifestations and working of the mystery was given in Ruddick's Hall, on Friday and Saturday evening. On Sunday, Miss Cox essayed to attend service at the Baptist Church, but during the first singing, the ghost, which had been quiet for some days, again manifested itself by knocking, apparently on the floor of the pew in front. When told to stop by Miss Cox, it would cease the noise for a moment, but then it would break out worse than ever. Throughout the prayer it continued; and when the organ began for the second singing, the noise became so distinct and disturbing that Miss Cox and party were forced to leave the Church.
>
> Upon reaching the house on Wesley Street, where they were stopping, the ghost seemed to enter into Miss Cox and she was sick and insensible until morning. Lying on the bed, she seemed for a time in great pain, her chest heaving as though in a rapid succession of hiccoughs and her body and limbs being very much swollen. A medical gentleman of

this town, who saw her at the time, stated that the symptoms were as those of a functionist heart disease, probably caused by nervous excitement. The heart was beating at an exceeding rapid rate, and her lungs seemed gorged with blood, so that a portion was forced into her stomach, causing the patient to vomit blood afterwards. A sound could be distinctly heard in the region of the heart, resembling the shaking of water in a muffled bottle, supposed to be caused by the blood in a cavity, being shaken by the violent hiccough motion of the body. As to the cause of the affection, that is the mystery.

Toward morning, Miss Cox relapsed into a state of somnolence and late in the day awoke, seeming entirely recovered. She states, however, that on Monday afternoon, while sitting near the window of a room on the ground floor, a fan dropped out of the window; she went outside to recover it, and on returning a chair from the opposite side of the room was found upside down near the door, as though it had attempted to follow her out of the room. No one else witnessed the occurrence.

Again, while writing, the ghost took possession of the pen, and wrote in a different hand altogether other and entirely different words from what were intended; in fact, it wrote itself, the young lady being able to look in another direction and not show the least interest in what the pen was writing. A gentleman who was present at the time, asked the ghost its name, when it wrote in reply, "Mattie Fisher" and stated that she had gone to the red schoolhouse on the hill in Upper Stewaicke, before Miss Cox did but left when she went. Miss Cox did not know this Mattie Fisher, but it seemed that a girl of that name, now dead, had attended previously.

Monday night, Miss Cox was again attacked and held under the power of the ghost, much the same as the night previous. A representative of the *Dispatch* called on Esther Cox yesterday afternoon, but she not being under the power of course, no manifestations could be seen. The lady appeared quite pleasant and affable, and looked well. She considers her trouble to be a ghost and is more perplexed than anyone else. She says she cannot tell, by any premonitory symptoms, when the manifestations are to commence, is becoming rather frightened concerning it and is very easily annoyed and excited by any noise, except that which she herself may cause. If the ghost is willing, Miss Cox will leave for Chatham by train today.

Friday, June 20, 1879

"She really was sick, Walt." John White watched Hubbell's face as he read the article in the *Moncton Dispatch*. "Awfully sick. Just like it says there, we had to call a doctor and, of course, the old fool didn't know what was happening, but he gave her a sedative that seemed to calm her down."

"But what about Sunday? In church? Is this true? Did she do things that disrupted the service?"

"There were knockings on the floor, and once a hymnbook came out of the pocket in back of a pew and hit the wall. I don't know why the reporter didn't put that in his piece. Finally, the preacher asked us to leave." White shook his head. "It was mighty embarrassing. Poor Esther was almost in hysterics on the way back to the hotel."

"That happened on Sunday morning." Hubbell's voice rose. "Why couldn't she have done that Saturday night? Huh? Why did she wait until the next morning to do what we wanted her to do the night before? Really, John, I can't understand why she's not cooperating with us. It's almost as if she wants to ruin the tour! Doesn't she understand that if we don't have a show onstage we aren't giving the public what they're paying for?" He tossed the newspaper into a corner of the hotel room. "I don't want to be mean with her, but she *must* understand that she has to do *something* while I'm speaking. She can't just *sit* there. Where is she now?"

"In her room, just down the hall. She said she was tired and was going to rest up a bit. She was sick, Walt," White repeated. "I thought we might have to cancel the shows here in Chatham."

"We *will* have to cancel them if she doesn't hold up her share," he said angrily.

"It's not that she's not trying," White said, defending her.

"Well, what is it, then?"

"It looks like her ghosts don't want to do it."

"Her *ghosts*? Oh, please, John, I don't want to hear any of that ghost nonsense! Esther doesn't have any more ghosts around her than I do. Or you do. Or President Hayes does! I'm tired of hearing about the ghosts and tired of her acting like Goody Two-Shoes!"

White sat down heavily on the edge of Hubbell's bed. "Are you telling me," he said slowly, "that you don't believe in Esther's ghosts?"

"Of course I don't. And neither should you. You're a grown man, for God's sake."

"You don't believe?" White was incredulous. "After all you've seen?"

"I haven't *seen* anything," Hubbell said. "I've read a lot of stories and heard a lot of rumors, but I really haven't *seen* anything. Sure there were the rappings that night at Daniel's house and the reading of the numbers on my watch, but that's all."

"How about your mother's name and the rocking chair in the lobby in Moncton?"

"The first was a good guess and the second one could have been the wind."

White took out his handkerchief and wiped his brow. "I really am surprised to hear this. I thought you believed in her as I do."

"Well, I don't. I only believe what I can see, and I haven't *seen* anything at all." He picked up the newspaper and waved it at White. "Why is it that things like this happen—this damned church thing—when I'm not around?" He didn't give the man time to answer. "I'll tell you why. Because she knows I'm on to her tricks and she knows it wouldn't take me but a minute to figure her out once she started with me. That's why."

"But all the things *I've* seen, the things that happened at my home."

"Mesmerism, self-induced delusions. You wanted to believe them. It was good for your business."

"And you *don't* want to believe them," White stated.

"No, I don't," the actor said. "I want to unmask them. I want to show the public what a fraud that sweet and innocent little girl really is."

White got up from the bed and walked toward the door. He stopped and turned back to Hubbell. White's face was ashen. "Look," he said, almost not moving his lips, "if I had known your true feelings, I would never have gone along with you on this damned tour thing. You hoodwinked me, and you're trying to hoodwink Esther. I'll admit I took advantage of her when she worked in my restaurant, but I never *used* her, not in the blatant way you're doing. Esther deserves better than that. She deserves better than you! I'll go along with the rest of this tour because I promised you I would, but I'll also be along to make sure you treat Esther fairly. If you don't, God help your soul." He slammed the door behind him.

Hubbell walked down the hotel corridor and knocked at Esther's door. When she opened it, he could see how pale she was. "I have to talk with you," he said. There was anger in his voice, but he tried to not let her see it. He went into the room and closed the door. She took a chair by the dresser.

"We are going to have another lecture tonight," he said.

"I know," she replied.

"I can't have it turn into a fiasco like it did in Moncton." He stared at her face. "Do you understand me?"

She nodded.

"Tonight you must give the audience some manifestations of what your so-called spirits can do. You *must* make things on that table move. Do you understand me? Do you understand what I'm saying to you?" He felt his voice rising, and he brought it back in control. "We have to make a damned good showing tonight. Not just because the house is sold out but also because the stories about the shows in Moncton have started circulating here. People are paying good money, and they want something for that money." She didn't say anything. "Do you understand me? You *must* produce some manifestations tonight. You must!"

She started to say something when the noise started. They both looked toward the dresser. There, atop the hotel dresser, her two perfume bottles were jumping up and down. Then her bottle of sleeping pills began to jiggle and move in and around her comb and brush set. A necklace of black beads rose up on one end and slithered like a snake ready to strike.

Hubbell took several steps backward, away from the inanimate objects that had suddenly come to life. Then he grinned. "Will you do that tonight?" His voice rose. "Will you make things dance like that tonight?" The perfume bottles acted as if they were waltzing with each other. The pill bottle hopped up on the hair-brush handle and spun crazily. The bead necklace rose straight into the air, hovered for a moment, and jumped into Esther's lap.

"That's what I want!" He was shouting now. He grabbed her hand and shook it. "I don't know how you do it, and at this moment I don't care. It can be your secret. Just do that tonight. You promise?" He laughed and stared at the lively bottles. "You promise?"

* * *

Everyone who had purchased or had reserved a ticket showed up that night at the Masonic Hall. There was an excitement in the air that was helped along by three members of the Chatham Baptist church marching outside with signs warning that the Devil would be on that stage that night.

The crowd had heard of the strange things that happened to Esther in Moncton: the hotel-room furniture and the disruption of the Sunday service. They had all heard of what had happened in Amherst. They all knew the stories, and now they wanted to see this phenomenon for themselves. There were people in the audience, farmers and sod cutters, who had never gone to anything presented at the Masonic Hall. But tonight they were there. It would be something to see. It would be something to tell their grandchildren.

There was a hush and then a thunderous applause when Hubbell introduced Esther sitting calmly. The objects on the table sat mutely, catching the sparkle of the footlight gas lamps. White had turned away the last patron and taped a "sold-out" sign on the front doors. He stood in the back of the auditorium, praying that Esther would vindicate herself—if not to the audience, then at least to Walt.

"As far back as the days of the ancient Greeks and Romans—nay, as far back as the earliest Egyptian pharaohs—there has been great public curiosity in the world regarding ghosts and spirits. In the temples of that great ruler Amenhotep, ghosts and spirits were prayed to, given golden ornaments, and served food in gem-encrusted bowls. In Babylonia, where the priests . . ." Hubbell intoned his prepared lecture, his eyes pleased with not an empty seat. Attention, as usual, was centered on the teenage girl in the chair. The one with the white feather fan to her face. He knew he could have been reciting "The Three Little Pigs" backward, for all they cared. He didn't mind that. His ego would take a back seat when the money was counted.

"Inscriptions in old parchment volumes speak of unsuspected horrors awaiting those humans who . . ." He talked on, glancing occasionally at Esther. There was nothing so far. But there would be. She had promised him there would be.

"On the pyramids of the Aztecs, hearts were rendered from breathing, living bodies to appease the spirits of . . ." The large clock on the wall showed him he had been talking for almost twenty-five minutes. When was she going to start her part of the act? She knew what the audience wanted, he told himself, she knew why they paid to see her. She was probably waiting for the right dramatic moment. Wait till these yokels see that trumpet float or hear that bell ring! He had put a bouquet of cut flowers in a large vase on the floor. Wait until those flowers started rising up out of that container and landed in the laps of those in the front rows! "Most of the conquistadors, of course, wanted nothing to do with such pagan beliefs and so the temples were destroyed and the priests killed. But that did not eliminate the Aztec need for a belief in those figures of the nether-world who could appear at . . ." What in *hell* was she waiting for? Christmas? Get those damned things in the air! He could feel the mood of the crowd turning on him, just as it had done that second night in Moncton. He faced her and gave a grand gesture with his arm: "Miss Cox," he said in his actor's mellifluous voice, "you may commence the demonstrations at any time."

There was applause at this, and someone shouted: "Get on with it!" More applause after that and quite a bit of laughter.

"It was not until modern times—just a few years ago, actually—that the mystery that later became known as Spiritualism began to grow. It happened to three small girls, sisters all, named Fox who resided in a humble farmhouse in . . ." Is she *never* going to do it? Jesus Christ! What the hell is she just sitting there for? He had to keep smiling as he looked at her. He didn't want the public to know how upset he was getting. She had promised. He wanted to go over and slap that face that was partially hidden by that damned fan! Just one quick backhand and maybe she would do what she had been told. "Of course, there were those gullible enough to believe that the knocking heard in the presence of the Fox Sisters were produced by ghosts, but the investigative eye soon revealed that . . ."

"Young man!" a voice came out of the audience.

Hubbell stopped talking, surprised by the interruption, and stared into the darkened theatre.

"Young man, beware!" An elderly gentleman with white hair and beard waved a cane above his head. "We do not take lightly to charlatans here! Beware!"

Loud applause, followed by laughter, whistles, and catcalls.

"The investigators of the Fox Sisters soon proved that these girls were producing these sounds by . . ." Hubbell struggled to continue.

"We don't care about the Fox Sisters," someone shouted. "When is Esther going to do her stuff?"

"Come on, girlie, let's see something!"

A woman called out: "I knew she was a phony!"

John White moved quickly through the semi-darkness from the back of the theatre along one side of the auditorium. There was a doorway there that led backstage. He wanted to make it through that doorway before it was too late.

"Shut up, Hubbell! We didn't come to hear you!"

"Just like in Moncton. All talk and nothing to show for it!"

"In Moncton, they skipped town with the money!"

Three men in the center of the audience jumped up. "Well, they ain't going to do that here!" One of them spotted John White. "There's the ticket-seller! Somebody grab him!"

White dashed for the door, put his hand on the knob, but other hands spun him around. Instinctively, he lashed out with one of his big fists and sent the closest assailant falling back into the others. There was stunned silence while a woman screamed. It gave White just enough time to get through the doorway, throwing the bolt, and run backstage.

The elderly stage manager had pulled the curtain, the heavy asbestos fire curtain, just as soon as the catcalls reached their height. he had seen acts like this one before. He had heard about the fiasco in Moncton and had been ready for this from the moment Hubbell started talking. "In there!" he shouted and pointed to an open doorway behind a fire hose. He grabbed Hubbell's arm and shoved him in the direction of the doorway. "Come on, Miss," he said to Esther, "get in there quick!"

Esther looked at him, dazed and uncomprehending what was taking place around her. One second she had been sitting by the table, another second Hubbell had been dragging her across the stage as the curtain came crashing down in front of her. Now this old man was tugging at her and pointing. She felt her legs rise in the air, then heard John White's sturdy voice in her ear as he picked her up and carried her. "We've got to get out of here!" he said.

The stage manager slammed the door shut and rearranged the hose in front of it. The mob surged around the edges of the fire curtain and onto the stage.

"Where are they?"

"They've got my money!"

"Where'd they go?"

"He can't hit my brother and get away with it!"

They stopped and stared at the stage manager. He pointed, wordlessly, to an open side doorway.

"Come on!"

"They went out this way!"

"They think we're some kind of idiots!"

"He can't hit *my* brother!"

Inside the stuffy wardrobe room, Hubbell shakily lit a wall candle. "What are we going to do?" he asked.

"Do?" White said. "We're going to get out of here." He looked at Esther. "Are you all right?" She nodded. "Are you sure?" She nodded again.

Hubbell grabbed her arm. "You promised! Why the hell didn't you do something? You promised me!"

White's large hand removed Hubbell's from Esther's arm. "Leave her alone, Walt. Just leave her alone. The girl's in no condition."

"Well, neither am I. I'm in no condition to put up with her nonsense! Look at this mess we're in. All because of her. It's her fault!"

"It's nobody's fault," White said. "It's the ghosts' fault. They just didn't want to cooperate."

"Oh, Christ, don't start with that stuff again. It's Esther's fault and you know it. She knows it, too." He looked around the small room. "Now what do we do?"

The door opened and the bald dome of the stage manager appeared. "It's all right. They've gone. They think you left from the side doorway. Here, let me help you." He grabbed a wooden box and shoved it against the back wall. Then he stood on it and undoing a latch, swung open a small window. "You first," he said to White. "You can help the others."

"Out that window?" Hubbell was affronted. "I'm not going out that thing! In all my years in the theatre, I've never had to do such a thing as that."

"Have you ever had a screaming mob after your rear end?" the old man asked.

"Of course not."

"Then you'll use this window. Get your rear end out of here."

White climbed atop the box. Hubbell grabbed him by the pant leg. "Where's the money bag?" he asked.

White reached into his vest, loosened his belt, and tossed a flat canvas bag at the actor. "Here. You take it. Put it in your trousers. After I get out, wait a few minutes, and then take Esther back to the hotel."

"We can go together," Hubbell protested.

"No. The mob will be looking for me. They'll think I have the money. I'll go to the left as soon as I get out and attract their attention. You take Esther to the right and get her back to the hotel as soon as possible."

Hubbell shook his head. "I don't think that's a very good plan."

"Oh, for Christ's sake, Walt, will you just shut up and do as you're told. *Your* plans got us into this mess!" He raised himself toward the window, then his legs and shoes disappeared.

"Wait about five minutes," the stage manager said.

Hubbell was more than willing to wait that amount of time. He didn't look at Esther, didn't want to see her face. If she was crying, at least it wasn't very loud. The minutes dragged on; there was no noise from the street.

"Okay," said the old man, and Hubbell lifted himself by his elbows onto the window ledge and fell a few feet into the soft grass. It was pitch black on that side of the theatre. He stood and waited until he saw Esther's head, then braced himself as she slid out and into his arms. She pulled away quickly from his touch. He patted his trouser front to make sure the cash bag was still there. "Let's go," he whispered.

They hugged the dark side of the building, making no noise as they neared the sidewalk and the street. Hubbell edged his way to the corner of the wall and peered into the lamp-lit darkness. "It's safe," he whispered again. "Come on."

They were on the sidewalk now, walking away from the theatre, walking quickly in the direction of their hotel. Esther had started to cry. She tried to stifle the sobs, but she couldn't stop the tears that coursed down her cheeks. Hubbell was determined not to notice. Let her cry.

"Two blocks to go," he said softly when they reached the first street corner. They hurried across the dirt roadway, and Esther almost stumbled as her shoe hit a rock.

There was another rock and then another and suddenly they both understood that the rocks were being thrown at them. From behind the trees, hidden in the darkness of the residential street, a dozen men and boys came running, throwing rocks, screaming, shouting, and swearing.

One man took careful aim, pulled back his arm, and like a professional athlete, threw a baseball-size stone. It headed straight for Esther's body. In the dim light, the crowd could see the rock's projection. It was going fast, it was gaining speed, it would hit her just below her right shoulder.

The rock got a hand's distance from her. It stopped. It dropped straight to the ground.

A gasp. Another stone was hurled. This one smaller than the other, but aimed with the same precision. Its target: Hubbell's head. It was going right for the target. It was a few inches from the target. It stopped. It dropped straight down onto the sidewalk.

A gasp. Another stone. It, too, seemed to meet an invisible wall, hover in the air for an instant, then drop straight to the ground.

A young boy threw a handful of gravel. It flew at Esther, and she put her hands to her face. The small stones charged at her, stopped suddenly, and scattered harmlessly straight down to the ground.

"This'll get one of them bastards!" a deep voice shouted, and a red brick, with pieces of white cement that had just a moment ago held it in place, came sailing through the air at Esther and Hubbell.

They silently watched it heading for them. It was coming at a low angle. No need to duck; it would hit them anyhow, someplace. Esther didn't bother hiding her face. She was resigned to the pain that would soon be hers. The brick sped; everyone, even the attackers, held their breath. Hubbell could smell the cement particles, the brick was now so close. Then it stopped in mid-air. Just stopped. It waited for a second. It fell straight to the earth, breaking in half on impact.

The mob didn't talk, didn't move. It stood dumbfounded

at what it had just seen. This would be something to tell for years at the local saloon, but right now there was complete silence.

That's when the horse and buggy noisily pulled up beside Esther. "Get in!" a voice commanded. They looked up to see John White sitting beside the driver. "Get in!" he ordered again. Hubbell jumped up into the buggy and pulled the girl with him. "I got your clothes from the hotel," he said. "I paid the bill. There's a train leaving for Amherst in twenty minutes. We're going to be on it. The cabbie is going to go down side streets and alleyways until it's time. We'll get on the train at the very last minute. We're going to get the hell out of this town." He turned to look at Esther. "We're going home," he said softly. "It's all over now."

"Thank God," she gasped between her sudden sobs, "thank God!"

Saturday, June 21, 1879

Olive was in the kitchen trying to get her two sons to eat their breakfast when she heard the door open. She took a deep breath and put her hand to her heart. She was not expecting anyone, and both Daniel and Jennie had gone to work. (The two boarders, afraid of what would happen if Esther came back to live there, had moved out, renting a small house on the other side of town.) Olive heard the footsteps coming down the hall; then she looked up in surprise and with pleasure at the face before her. "Esther!"

"Oh, Olive!" The young girl ran and hugged her sister. "Oh, Olive! It's so good to be home! It was terrible, just terrible."

"Hello . . ." Walter Hubbell stuck his face around the doorway and tipped his hat.

"Mr. Hubbell!" the older woman exclaimed. "How are you?" Then a pause. "What are you doing here?" She held her sister out at arm's length. "What are *both* of you doing here? You're supposed to be in Chatham."

Then Esther started talking. It was a torrent of words and gestures and a voice almost in tears as she gave a brief—but thorough—rundown on what had happened. Hubbell stood, his hat in one hand and his suitcase in another, waiting for her to tell the part where he had yelled at her, had accused her, had grabbed her—but Esther never said one negative word about him or his actions. As far as she was concerned, it was all the fault of her non-cooperative ghosts. "And I don't really care," she laughed and hugged Olive again. "All that's important is that I'm home again. Here with you and Daniel and the boys."

"And John White," Olive asked, "where is he? Did he return to Amherst with you?"

"Oh, yes," Hubbell answered for Esther. "He came back. He's here but he doesn't want anything to do with me anymore. He says he's going to stick with his restaurant. He doesn't want any part of 'the terrible power,' as he calls it."

"Was he angry with you?" Olive asked the girl.

"No," she shook her head, "but he was angry with Mr. Hubbell. He thought I had been mistreated. He thought Mr. Hubbell had taken advantage of me."

"Do you think I did?" he asked her.

"No. There were a couple of times," she smiled, "when you were cross with me, but that was only because my ghosts didn't respond as you had hoped. It was natural. I understand now. I didn't at the time, but I do now."

Olive started clearing off the breakfast dishes. "Well, John White will just have to come to his senses about it all. Give him some time. He is a good person but"—and she laughed—"it must have surely annoyed him that he didn't make all the money he had hoped to make. Anyway," she wiped her hands on her apron, "it's over and you two haven't had breakfast yet. Esther, why don't you put your things up in your room and change your clothes and come down and help me fix some food for you both. You will stay to breakfast, Mr. Hubbell?"

"Well . . ." he set his suitcase on the floor. "I will, of course, yes, but I would also like to stay a little longer. If I may. Like stay for six weeks. Till the end of July."

"Here in Amherst?" Olive was surprised.

"Here in Amherst and here in this house, if it can be arranged and it's all right with you and Mr. Teed. I know your boarders have gone and you have a spare room to rent. Your sign is still on the door. I don't have to be in New York until August, and I'd like to stay and watch Esther's ghosts for myself. Here. In this house."

Esther shot a quick look at Olive. "Well, I'm sure it's perfectly fine with me," the older woman said. "Of course, Daniel will have to be consulted, but I don't see why he shouldn't . . ." She stopped and looked at him. "To watch Esther's ghosts? Here? In this house?"

"Exactly."

"Why?"

"As a writer. I am certain there is material here for a series of articles for American newspapers on Esther's 'friends,' and it would be most convenient for me to observe them here, firsthand. And, as I say, I haven't any theatrical commitments until the fall."

"But all you saw of my ghosts on the tour were the things jiggling on the dresser," Esther protested slightly. "John White said you didn't believe in them." She hadn't told him she knew.

"But everyone else has seen them," he replied, smiling. "I believe there is *something* there. I don't know if it is a ghost or not, but there is some reason that these things happen. I did see the things move on your hotel dresser, and I still don't know how it was done." He had decided on the train trip back to Amherst that if he couldn't make any money with a tour he ought to be able to make some money with newspaper articles. He thought about it all the way back to Amherst. It had been a quiet trip. Esther sat with John White, sleeping on White's shoulder and ignoring Walt.

"I certainly hope your plans don't turn out the way you wish them," Olive said flatly. "I don't wish you any unfortunate luck, but I sincerely hope that *nothing* happens in this house to give you the *slightest* bit of proof of Esther's ghosts. None of us wants the manifestations to commence again. *None of us!*"

The actor went into the dining room and put his suitcase on the floor. It was the perfect case for traveling. Imitation leather (that wouldn't scuff) brasslike hinges (that wouldn't tarnish) and a quite modern strap with a built-in pocket that held his umbrella (so he wouldn't lose it). He turned to walk back into the kitchen when he heard a movement behind him. Turning rapidly, he saw his umbrella wiggling its way from under the strap. It pulled itself free, rose into the air, pointed itself in his direction, and charged quickly. He ducked just as the black cotton missile sailed past his head.

"Did . . . did you see . . . see that?" he managed to sputter as Esther crossed the kitchen on the way to the dining room, carrying a large bowl of fresh fruit.

"What?" she asked.

"My umbrella!" he exclaimed. "It came right at me and . . . look out!" he yelled, grabbing Esther's arm and pushing her against the wall. One more second and she would have been stabbed by the large carving knife that was now quivering in the far wall. "My God!" He staggered back against the dining-room table. "Did you see . . . ? My God!"

He peered into the kitchen. Olive wasn't there. He knew she had gone upstairs with the boys. There was no one downstairs but himself and Esther. She couldn't have thrown the umbrella because she had been in the kitchen. She couldn't have thrown the knife because her hands were full.

Esther was pale but not shaken by the incident. She shrugged as if to say, "I warned you," but instead she said, "Why don't you go sit in the parlor. I'll call you when breakfast is on the table."

With a hand that he tried hard to control, Hubbell picked up his suitcase and carried it to the parlor. The umbrella lay on the floor of the dining room. There was no way he was going to pick that thing up. He collapsed into a small chair, hoping his heart would stop beating so rapidly. He took a deep breath, then watched it start toward him.

The heavy armchair, largest of the sofa set pieces, raised up on two back legs and skidded across the floor taking carpet, side table, and all with it. Hubbell yelled, raised his legs, and the large chair smacked straight into the one he was sitting on, sending him crashing to the floor.

Esther came running to the doorway. It was difficult to tell if she had a slight smile on her lips or not.

He jumped up, trying to retain some modicum of demeanor. "I . . ." he stuttered. "I think I'll walk around the block. Just for a while. Until breakfast is ready." He didn't wait for her answer but hurried to the door and got out of the house as quickly as possible.

He shoved his hands in his trouser pockets. That way nobody would see how they were shaking. He headed down Princess Street toward Church Street. He was muttering to himself. "I really don't understand this. I mean, I surely don't. I was all alone with that umbrella. There was no way she could have thrown it at me. I *saw* it, for Christ's sake. It wasn't as if I imagined it. I saw the thing. Whizz! And the knife. The damned knife sailed right for her head. She could have been killed! How did she manage that? She couldn't have managed that. I was right there. She was coming into the dining room. I was going out. I saw her. She had that bowl of fruit in her hands. The knife was behind her. Behind her! God damn, it was *behind* her. Coming out of nowhere. Olive and the youngsters were upstairs. That cursed blade came from *behind* her. No way she could have thrown it and picked up the bowl and then turned around and walked toward me in time to be in *front* of the knife so that I would have time to yank her out of the way. . . ." He stopped at the corner, picked up an imaginary knife from an imaginary counter, threw it, picked up an unseen bowl, turned quickly, walked fast, and twisted to one side. Old Mother Burns, out sweeping her sidewalk, watched in astonishment, then wondered who the young man could be who was drunk so early in the day. "No, it couldn't have happened like that," he reasoned aloud. "She couldn't have thrown it herself. And that damned chair! That damned thing just came at me like a wagonload of potatoes, crashing and knocking me over! I could have been killed! It's a wonder I wasn't killed. I could have been. Yes, indeed, I just could have been." He stopped, wrinkled his brow, and cocked his head to one side. He was thinking. "Do I really want to go back there? To stay there? Is it necessary to *be* there to write about it?" He got to Victoria Street and turned right. In front of Greenfield's store, he paused and saw his reflection in the window. "If you were going to write about snakes," he asked his image, "would you have to live in their pit?" He shook his head. "This is more important than snakes," he replied to himself, and two ladies hearing the word "snakes" jumped to one side and raised their skirts. "This could be the most important thing you were ever involved with, Hubbell," he said. "Nobody will believe you, of course. People will think you're as daft as a dodo if you admit you believe in it at all. Yet, if you write about it, you must come to *some* conclusion. You have to state *why* you came to that conclusion if you are to be believed at all." He smiled as he reached the corner of Havelock Street. He turned right. It felt good. "Yes. So what if they don't believe me? So what? It's skin off their nose, not mine. I'll write what I see and what I hear and what others tell me they have seen, and if people don't want to believe me, then it's their decision. Not mine. If people don't want to believe in Esther's ghosts, they don't have to. As long as they buy my book, that's all I care about. My *book*." He stopped just before making the turn back onto Princess Street. He could see the yellow cottage from the corner. "A book! I'll make the articles into a *book*! What a great idea! I'll have a book and then I'll go on the lecture circuit and people will pay to hear my speech and pay to buy my book! Hot damn! Hubbell," he said out loud, "you just stepped in it, all the way up to your chin!"

He opened the door to the house and walked down the hallway. As he passed the entrance to the parlor, there was a clamorous commotion as all the chairs in the room began moving around the floor and toppling noisily over onto their backs. They slammed up and down and bumped against each other and rose up on one or two legs, only to crash into the next one and then clatter to the floor. As all this racket was going on, Hubbell saw his valise skid across the room, hit the wall, and then skid across to smash against the other wall. He jumped back quickly as the valise sailed up into the air and headed straight at him. The case hit the doorjamb and fell with a thud at his feet.

Olive handed him a cup of coffee. "You know," she said, "I don't think they like you."

Monday, June 23, 1879

Sunday came and went, as it always did in the Teed home, without incident. Esther's ghosts let her alone on Sunday, except when she went to church. They obviously didn't like going to church and resented her taking them there. The girl found it easier just to stay home and read a few verses from the Bible rather than upset entire congregations.

Walter Hubbell had had no trouble convincing Daniel to rent him the empty bedroom. Hubbell paid the price that the two boarders had paid, and as he would eat for only one boarder, Daniel felt far ahead in the deal. Jennie was pleased that the handsome young actor was staying with them. She didn't imagine any romantic entanglements (after all, he would be going back to his own country in just six weeks), but he would be someone exciting to go places with. Her tailor shop would be having its annual summer outing, and she hoped Walt would escort her. Oh, how it would make the other girls in town green! There were concerts once a week in the downtown park, and Walt had already told her how he liked good music. She supposed she did, too. Olive was reconciled to the idea because he would be in the house with Esther all the time. If he was going to write about her, he would have to observe her. She was comforted that no matter what calamity the ghosts decided to dump on her sister, there would be a man there to rescue her immediately. Also, the young American was funny. He knew a great many stories and could tell them for hours. Olive needed to laugh. The two small boys—Willie, now six, and George, just turned two—seemed to like Walt. He would sit them on his lap and make them laugh. He admitted he would have liked a wife and children of his own, but the life of a traveling actor didn't permit it. Eventually he would settle down. He felt an obligation to the Hubbell family to marry and carry on the illustrious line that had first come to America in 1647.

Esther wasn't sure if she was pleased or not having Hubbell living under the same roof. She had been the only one in her family to see him under stress, to see how he could change from nice to nasty when things didn't go his way. She had been upset by the way he treated her on that ill-fated tour but, she reasoned, she had not been properly prepared for it. If she had known in advance that he had expected her to move things right there in front of everybody, she wouldn't have agreed. But Olive and Daniel had thought it was a good idea and so did John White, so it had seemed the thing to do. Hubbell didn't understand her ghosts, didn't even believe in them. It's no wonder they refused to co-operate with him. They would make a believer out of him before he left Amherst, of that she was certain. They had already started with the umbrella and the knife and the furniture. She had seen the puzzled expressions on his face as he tried to interpret—logically—what was going on. There was no "logic" to any of this. When he understood *that,* perhaps he would understand the ghosts. Perhaps he would understand *her.*

"Good morning," he said as he came into the dining room. "Beautiful day, isn't it?"

"It is that, Mr. Hubbell," Olive agreed. "June is one of the fairest months in Nova Scotia. Not cold nor hot but just right."

"Just like Goldilock's porridge," he laughed.

"Exactly." She quickly straightened the tablecloth before he sat down. The others had already eaten. Daniel and Jennie had gone to work. The actor preferred rising a little later so he could have the table to himself and not have to be part of the morning conversation. He hated small talk. He had to speak so much of it from the stage. "I have some of her porridge for you this morning," Olive said, laughing. "And some coffee and some biscuits. You so liked my corn-flour biscuits yesterday that I made a new batch today. Just for you."

"Now, Mrs. Teed, you didn't have to do that." He smiled in appreciation. "But I'm glad you did. They are delicious."

Olive felt a surge of pleasure. Nobody ever complimented her on her cooking anymore. She put it on the table, they ate it, and they left. Daniel, when they were first married, used to praise her roasts and her baked goods, but now he just wiped his mouth and went to work. It was real good to have someone around who appreciated her many hours in that small kitchen.

"Good morning." Esther came in with the pot of fresh black coffee.

"Morning," he said and smiled. She was wearing her long brown hair pinned up today, exposing her ears and the back of her neck. It was a pretty neck, he noticed. He always noticed the parts of a girl's body that were left uncovered. He appreciated a comely neck and small wrists and hands. Occasionally a girl would give him the glimpse of an ankle. Not bare, of course, but neatly encased in a tight-fitting stocking. Some of the more daring girls in New York and Philadelphia had taken to wearing stockings in colors that contrasted completely with their outfits. Many older folks condemned the fashion, but Walter and other young bucks enjoyed the glimpse of a bright red ankle suddenly appearing from under a jet-black skirt. He glanced down at Esther's ankles, but her long brown cotton dress kept them hidden. All he could see were the pointed toes of her side-button shoes.

Esther poured him a cup of coffee. He reached for the sugar bowl, removed the lid, and set it on the table just long enough to get a spoonful of sugar. He reached to put back the lid, but it slid away from his touch and fell to the floor. Sighing, he bent over to pick it up, but it was gone. He put his hand on the thin carpet under his chair and searched for the lid. He couldn't feel it, couldn't see it anywhere.

"Esther." He called her in from the kitchen. "I just dropped the sugar lid. Will you get it for me?"

She walked to the other side of the table, bent down, then looked up at him. "I don't see it," she said.

"It fell right there," he replied. "I heard it drop, but I couldn't find it."

"Nor can I. Olive!" she called. "Come here a minute, will

you?" When her sister entered the room, Esther said: "Mr. Hubbell dropped the sugar lid, but I can't seem to locate it."

"Well, it *has* to be there." Olive knelt beside Esther. She looked carefully, then straightened up. "It's not here," she said in a low voice.

"It *has* to be." Walt pushed his chair away from the table and got down on his knees. "Did you look way under the table?" He could see that there was nothing there. "Well, I'll be a monkey's uncle!" He came from underneath and stood with his hands on his hips. "Where could it have gone?"

Esther drew in her breath, noisily. "Look." She pointed to the ceiling. All three saw the lid emerge slowly from the wallpaper that covered the entire ceiling directly over the table. Then the lid fell, slowly, as if it were a feather. Just before it reached the table, Hubbell grabbed it. It was solid and slightly warm. "Well, I'll be . . ."

"What's going on?" Olive looked at Esther. "What are they doing?"

The girl shrugged. "That's the first time they've ever done *that*." Her eyes grew wide. "Or that." Now she pointed to the table.

The knife, fork, and spoon that Hubbell was about to use slid quickly across the cloth and fell to the floor. Olive reached to pick them up and they slid away from her grasp. Hubbell ran after the fork, poised his foot to step on it, and it skittered away to safety under the buffet.

That's when the chairs fell over. All six of them clattered and banged on the floor. The rug—a scatter rug Olive had made years ago—slithered and bunched itself and straightened and then managed to free itself from under the table and the fallen chairs. It gathered itself up neatly and rolled to a quiet spot against the wall.

"Well, I never!" Olive said and started to pick up one of the chairs. It was rudely yanked from her hand and tossed onto another chair. Yet another chair rose up and crashed into the pile, then a fourth chair spun on back legs to reach the others. Olive screamed as the heavy table tipped sideways, spilling the dishes and the coffee and her fresh biscuits all over the floor. She grabbed Esther and pulled her out of the way. Hubbell was determined to remain in the room to "investigate" all this commotion. He bent over to examine a chair when a cloud of fine white dust rose out of nowhere. It floated across the room and showered everything with minute powdery particles. Hubbell began to cough, then sneeze, then retreated to the safety of the parlor.

"What is it?" he shouted, but there was no one there. Olive and Esther had run outside and were standing in the street, holding each other in fear. He thought it would be wise to join them. He ran across the parlor to the door that led to the hall when something red whizzed past his face. He put up both arms to ward off the blow, but it settled on the carpet in front of him. He looked down. It was one of Jennie's geraniums, still in its large clay pot.

"You could have killed me!" he shouted at the flower, then took three large steps toward the hallway when he stopped short and quickly retreated several steps into the parlor.

In front of him, just a menacing foot away, floated a wooden bucket filled with water. It remained at eye level, as he backed still farther into the room. He recognized that bucket. It was one Olive kept by the door for well water. it had been empty the last time he saw it, and now it was full and was threatening to dump its contents all over him.

"Now, don't," he pleaded. "Please don't do that." He stepped backward a few more feet. "Just hold off. I haven't done anything to you." The bucket swung back and tilted slightly. He could see the splashing water pointed directly at him. "Come on," he pleaded, "this is my best suit! Now, now . . . please don't do what you're thinking of doing."

The bucket tilted still farther, seemed to go backward, and then the water was tossed. It came straight for Hubbell and his best suit and his horrified expression, but as it got inches from it, it rose like a fountain in the park, went over his head, and splashed down to water the geranium neatly on the floor behind him. Then the bucket floated around him and settled calmly beside the flower pot.

When they saw him dash out to join them, they were, at first, frightened by his appearance and then amused by it. There he stood, in the middle of the street, his face and clothing covered with fine white dust and his eyes as big as saucers. Esther was the first to laugh. Olive tried to hold hers, but she finally gave in. They laughed as he brushed, and then he started laughing. Anyone passing would have had all three of them locked in the looney bin.

"Ladies," he said as the tears clotted in the dust on his cheeks, "I am a skeptic no longer!"

* * *

The activities of the afternoon pretty well paralleled those of the morning. While the young actor sat on the parlor sofa making notes on what had been happening, two empty bottles came out of the kitchen closet and sailed for his head. He ducked and they collided directly over him, showering him with chunks of glass.

Later, still in the parlor, he and Esther were talking. She was busy knitting a scarf when the knitting needles jumped out of her hands and tried to jab him in the chest.

The baby, George, came into the room, eating a piece of chocolate cake. He let out a howl as the cake was yanked from his hands and thrown at Hubbell. It splattered against his vest. Esther got the boy another piece of cake and that calmed him down, but only until that piece was tossed at Hubbell. Then a third piece was aimed at the actor. In spite of George's protests, he wasn't given a fourth piece.

A short time later, the baby was sitting on Esther's lap as she told him a story. The child gave a cry as all the buttons on his shirt were undone, then the shirt fell to the floor. Then his trousers were yanked over his shoes and tossed on the floor. Then his diaper was unpinned and flung at Hubbell. The shoes—the ones with the copper toes that Daniel insisted he wear if he were going to learn to walk properly—were untied. They came at Hubbell. He ducked the right one, but the left one hit him squarely on the side of the head. He had a bump for two days.

Jennie came running downstairs later that evening shouting that the newspaper she had been reading in the bedroom had been taken from her hands, rolled into a tube, and set afire. The window was open, so she tossed it onto the front lawn.

After that, the chairs in the parlor gathered together and formed a pyramid.

Then a bottom chair was yanked away, and they all clattered to the floor.

While Hubbell delightedly took notes about all these happenings, Esther became more distraught with each one. She was unable to eat her supper and complained of a headache.

"Why don't you go up to bed, then," Olive suggested. "Jennie and I can clear the table."

"It's just that I wish all this wasn't happening," the girl said. "It's all happening again. Some of the things have never happened before."

"It must be for my benefit," Hubbell said. "They know I'm writing all this down, and they want to show off."

"Let's hope they don't get too carried away," Daniel added. "I don't want old Judge Bliss to send Esther away again. I do trust, Walt," he said, "that you'll be very discreet while you're here and not tell anyone in town of these new manifestations. It could get us evicted if that old man thinks the ghosts have returned to his house."

"Of course," the actor promised. "I won't tell a soul. Let them read about it in my book," he said and laughed.

"Esther," Jennie said, "just go upstairs and get into bed. You've had a long day. You look pale."

"Yes," said Olive, "you don't have any blush on your cheeks."

As if to remedy that problem, there was a loud slapping sound and the girl staggered against a wall. Tears came instantly to her eyes, and everyone could see the mark of a hand imprinted in red on her cheek.

"He hit me," she cried. "He actually hit—" Slap! Her other cheek instantly glowed crimson, left by the imprint of long fingers. "Ow!" she shouted. "That hurt!"

Slap! The marks appeared on the left side of her neck. She put her hands up to her face, but some force yanked them way and then slap! the redness rushed across her nose and mouth.

"Now, wait a minute!" Daniel jumped up from the table and grabbed Esther. "You leave her be!" he shouted. "Don't you dare touch her! You bastard! Hit me, if you dare!" He braced to receive the next blow himself, but none came.

Olive put her arm around her sister and helped the near-hysterical girl up the stairs.

"This is the first time this has happened," Jennie said. "He's hit her before, but he's never been *this* cruel."

"Who? Who are you calling 'he'?"

"Bob Nickle. That's what he said his name was. Bob Nickle."

"He told Esther that?"

"That and the fact that he died when he was sixty years old. He had been a blacksmith by trade."

"He knows he's dead?" Hubbell reached for his note pad and pencil. "I mean, he actually told her that he knew he was dead?" Jennie nodded yes. "That's quite unusual. Often they don't know they're dead."

"What?" Daniel had been lighting his pipe in an effort to calm himself. "Don't know that they're dead? That's kind of ridiculous."

"According to the Spiritualists, some people die and don't know it. So they don't go to Heaven, or wherever the soul goes when the body dies; they just hang around the earth. That's where ghosts come from."

"You believe that?"

"I don't know." Hubbell shook his head. "I don't know what to believe anymore. Yesterday I didn't believe in any of this. After all the things that have happened today—all the things I've *seen*—my beliefs are all mixed up. I just don't know what is real and what isn't anymore. I'm confused, really confused."

"That's the trouble with thinking you know it all." Daniel drew in a puff of smoke. "It's always been my understanding that people who claim to know it all really don't know nothin'. They confuse the issues and everyone that's around them."

Hubbell busied himself with his notes. He didn't dare look up—he didn't want Daniel and Jennie to see the embarrassed glow on his face.

Tuesday, June 24, 1879

"Good morning," Olive smiled as Walter Hubbell sat down at the dining-room table. "Sleep well?"

"Yes, I did, thank you. Did you?" She nodded. "How is Esther? Did she get over her headache?"

"She did, but she didn't sleep at all, she says. There are some strange marks on her hands and neck, looks like pinpricks or something. As if she had been stuck with needles."

"Was there any blood?"

"No, no blood at all, just the pain in the night and when she lit the lamp, she saw the indentations. Odd. Very odd."

"Where is she now? Still in bed?"

"Right here, Mr. Hubbell." Esther came into the room

from the kitchen carrying a fresh pot of hot black coffee. "Good morning." She filled his cup and placed the sugar bowl closer to him. He glanced down and saw the small red marks on her hand. "The biscuits are about ready, Olive," she said. Both women went back into the kitchen.

Walt took a deep breath, drawing in the aroma of the fresh coffee. Pleased with life in general and himself in particular, he took the lid from the sugar bowl, set it aside, then put two heaping teaspoonsful in his cup. His hand went out to where he had placed the lid. It was gone. Again. "Olive! Esther! They're doing it again this morning!"

They hurried into the dining room, Olive wiping her hands on her apron. "What's wrong?" she asked. "Is anything wrong?"

"The sugar bowl lid," he said. "They've taken it again."

"Oh, no." Esther knelt on the floor looking for it under the table, praying she would find it. "It's not here," she said. "They've got it."

"I was hoping they wouldn't do that today," Olive stated flatly. "I really was."

"So was I," Esther replied. "Yesterday was enough to last a long time."

Hubbell shrugged and stirred his coffee, keeping one eye on the silverware and both feet firmly planted on the floor. If they were going to turn the chairs over today, they'd have to do it with him in one of them.

Back in the kitchen, Olive arranged the plate of fresh biscuits while Esther went toward the pantry for a jar of jam. She heard the noise—a whirring sound—and looked up to see the sugar bowl lid come sailing out of a broken glass pane over the pantry door. Olive heard the noise at the same time and both watched in awe as the porcelain top sailed through the kitchen, around the door, into the dining room, and landed with a thud on the carpet near the table.

"Thank you," Hubbell said reaching down, picking it up, and placing it on the bowl. "Please don't do things like that anymore." His voice was level and calm. "It really does. . . help anyone's digestion, you know." Esther brought in the biscuits and jam. "Please inform your friends that I don't appreciate nor find amusing their antics while I am trying to have breakfast." The girl stared at him, sure he had gone a little crazy. "They do not frighten me," he said, "they only show their own childish lack of manners." He glanced at her and winked. She understood and smiled. "If they are adult, be they spirit or corporeal, they should act adult. They will never be taken seriously if their comportment continues to be so juvenile." Another wink at Esther.

"Don't do anything to make them angry," she told him.

"Angry? Educated adults don't get angry. Obstreperous, ignorant children do."

"They are all supposed to be adults," she agreed loudly, going along with his new tack. "Of course, I agree they should act like adults." She hoped she had conviction in her voice.

"Making sugar bowl lids vanish and throwing tables and chairs to the floor are acts of juvenile vandalism." The actor used his best rounded tones. "Certainly your friends, these discarnate entities, prefer to be considered intelligent and not untutored emotionals."

Bam! Bam! Bam! Three loud raps on the dining-room wall.

Hubbell spread half a biscuit with jam. "What does that mean?" he asked. "Three hits. Does that mean 'yes' you know how to behave in civilized company?"

Bam! Bam! Bam!

"Does that mean you are prepared to call off your destructive ways?"

Bam! Bam! Bam!

"And to cooperate with Miss Cox and myself in mutual understanding and for the good of science?"

Bam! Bam! Bam!

"Very good. That's better." He could see Esther visibly relax at this. Olive stood in the doorway, watching. Hubbell took a small note pad and a pencil from his coat pocket. "First I'll need a name. Your name. Are you Bob Nickle?" Bam! "You're not. Very well. Are you a male ghost?" Three raps. "Very good. Are you a friend of Bob Nickle's?" Two knocks.

"What's that mean?" he asked Esther.

"Maybe. Two raps means 'maybe.'"

"So sometimes you're a friend and sometimes you're not a friend. Correct?" Three raps. "Does Bob Nickle do things you don't approve of?" Three more raps, a bit louder this time.

"I know who it is," Esther said. "It's Peter Teed. He's a great-uncle of Daniel's."

Olive spoke up. "Esther, how on earth can you know that?"

"He came to me once, one afternoon at Mrs. Snowden's. He said I needed some protection and as a distant relative he'd look after me."

"I don't recall Daniel ever talking about an Uncle Peter," Olive frowned and shook her head. "Are you certain?"

"Oh, yes, he said he was Daniel's great-uncle and that he had died many years before Daniel was born. In a barn fire. Daniel never knew him."

"I'll have to ask Daniel," Olive said. Bam! Bam! Bam! "Oh," she smiled. "You want me to ask him about you?" Bam! Bam! Bam!

"Uncle Peter is a good ghost," Esther explained. "He doesn't like it when Bob and the others throw things or break things. He tries to stop things before they hurt people. He's not big like Daniel is, but short and a little bit thin. He's got snow-white hair but no beard. Uncle Peter's got the smoothest little face!"

"You act as if you'd seen him," Hubbell said.

"Oh, I did. He sat down, at Mrs. Snowden's, and we had a long chat. I like him. I wish the others were as nice to be around."

"The others?" Hubbell was trying to write and talk at the same time. "There are *others*?"

"Of course. There's Mattie Fisher—she's the one that gave you the flower the other day—and there's her sister Mary. Mary is older than Mattie and not as much fun. Mary is about thirty-five. I guess Mattie is twenty-something."

"You've seen these ghosts, too?" Hubbell was incredulous.

"Oh, yes. I see Mattie a lot. She has hair about the color of mine and she wears the *oddest* dress. It's a kind of purple color and wraps around her like a robe and goes all the way to the floor. She likes to sit in the front window upstairs and watch people in the street. The other day, when the egg lady came by, I looked up and saw her hanging out the window. She was making funny faces at the egg lady. Good thing she couldn't see Mattie or she would have had a heart attack and fallen on top of her eggs! It was really funny!" She laughed, and Olive smiled.

"And this ghost sits there? In the window? All day?"

"No, not all day. Just sometimes. She's quite pretty. That purple material she wears looks real nice on her."

"Is she in the window now?" Hubbell pushed his chair back. "Show me," he said.

"Oh, she's not there," Esther said matter-of-factly, "she's here. There in the corner. Next to the buffet."

Hubbell and Olive looked rapidly at the buffet but couldn't see a thing.

"I can't make her out," he said. "Ask her to do something."

Esther hesitated. "I don't like to ask."

"Go ahead," he urged, "ask her to show us she's there."

Esther was about to make the request when her eyes grew wide. Olive and Walt stared at her as the girl's gaze followed the unseen entity across the room. As Esther was looking directly at Hubbell, he felt something press against his lips and felt something muss his hair. His face turned beet red.

Esther was embarrassed for him. "That's probably the first time," she giggled, "that you've ever been kissed by a ghost." She laughed aloud.

"I could *feel* her," he stammered, "I could feel her lips. I knew it was a *hand* that was in my hair. I could feel the fingers! That was fantastic. Absolutely unbelievable." He touched his lips with his own fingers, trying to reproduce the sensation, but it wasn't there. "Amazing. Simply amazing."

"Mary would never have done that," Esther explained. "Just Mattie. She's the wild one. She's gone now." Esther looked around the room.

"Mattie's gone?" He looked, too, but didn't see anyone. "Too bad. I kind of liked that." He laughed and blushed again.

"It's a habit very easy to get into," Olive smiled.

"The other two girls wouldn't do that, either," Esther continued. "Both Jane Nickle and Eliza McNeal act like ladies."

"McNeal?" Olive's voice rose. "McNeal? The same last name as Bob McNeal? The young man you were sweet on last year?" This was the first time she had heard her sister mention that name since the rainy night in the buggy.

Esther nodded. She didn't seem upset by it. "It's his sister. She died several years ago. She was just a schoolgirl then."

"His *sister*? Did Bob tell you he had a sister in spirit?"

"Oh, no. Of course not. We never discussed things like that. I wasn't interested in those things way back then. No, he never told me. She did. She told me she was his sister."

Walt had never heard the story of Bob McNeal so didn't

know what they were talking about. "You say the other female ghost is surnamed Nickle? Like Bob Nickle, the destructive masculine ghost?" The girl nodded. "Is it his sister, too?"

"I don't know. I never asked. It's either his wife or his sister. From the way he acts when he is around me, I'd guess it's his sister. A wife wouldn't stand for some of the things he says and does when he's with me."

Hubbell raised an eyebrow. "Oh?" This was all new material. "What do you mean?"

Esther began to stammer, looking first to Olive for help then to her invisible friends around the room. "Nothing," she said. "I don't mean a thing. I've said too much as it is." She gathered her full skirt in her hands and ran from the room.

Walt watched her go. "Do you know what she's talking about?" he asked Olive.

"Yes."

"Will you tell me?"

"No."

"Oh. Why?"

"It's not something a lady discusses."

"Oh." He paused. "Will Daniel tell me?"

"I doubt it."

"But he knows."

"He knows. He is a gentleman. There are some things even a gentleman refuses to disclose."

"It's that bad."

"It's that *horrible*."

* * *

"It'll be ready in a few more minutes," Olive said to her husband. The steak, Daniel's lunch, was spattering in the frying pan. Esther was slicing tomatoes as the teakettle began to whistle on the stove. The actor stood in the doorway between the kitchen and the dining room, just watching.

Olive reached automatically to the shelf above the cookstove, then stopped, puzzled. "Where's the salt crock? Esther, do you have the salt?" The girl shook her head no. "Well if that isn't the oddest . . ." Olive stood looking at the empty space on the shelf. "It's always right there. Are you positive you don't have it over there?"

"No," the girl replied. "It was there on the shelf the last time I saw it."

"Whoa!" they heard Hubbell shout and they looked to see

the large earthenware crock come around the corner from the pantry, heading directly for his face. He ducked, and the crock sailed into the dining room and plopped itself loudly on the table.

Daniel, who had been washing his hands at the kitchen pump, dried them quickly on his trousers. "Oh, no," he said. "They're not starting that again, are they."

"They took the sugar bowl lid this morning," his wife told him.

"And I got a kiss," Hubbell added.

"A kiss?"

"Yes, from a lady ghost named Mattie. She kissed me smack on the lips and I could *feel* her lips. And she mussed my hair. I could feel her fingers. It was amazing." He smiled, then frowned. "I still don't know what to make of it, though."

"Don't make anything," Esther spoke up, "just observe. Perhaps if nobody reacts, they'll go away."

"If they don't burn down the house first," Daniel said glumly.

Olive gave her husband a gentle shove toward the dining room. "Now, I won't hear any depressing talk about fires," she said. "Don't give those ghosts any ideas. Get in there and sit yourself down. The food's almost ready."

She turned back to the stove. That's when she screamed and jumped backward, almost falling into Daniel's arms.

They all saw it happen. First the frying pan, still hot and smoking with the steak in it, raised itself off the stove. Right afterward, the boiling teakettle rose in the air beside it. Then the two red-hot utensils, kettle right alongside pan, floated through the kitchen, through the open back doorway and settled calmly on the stone steps outside.

"Don't give them any ideas?" Daniel said loudly to his wife. "They've just stolen my meal!"

The steak was retrieved and divided between the two men. Daniel ate glumly in silence, while Hubbell chewed the well-traveled filet and brought his notes up to date.

Daniel, still in silence, rose from the table and went out into the backyard to smoke his pipe before returning to work. No sooner had the women cleared the dishes than the table was tipped quickly to one side and then over onto its top, its round, carved legs in the air like a stranded turtle.

Olive and Hubbell righted it. "Don't tell Daniel about this," she whispered. "He gets upset over these things."

"I can see why," Walt answered. "It's all very puzzling. I recall once when I was in Philadelphia—" But he never had a chance to tell his story because Olive let out a yell and with both hands pushed him off balance and knocked him to the floor. His head just missed hitting the edge of the buffet. He stared at her in astonishment, then saw two butcher knives whizz across the dining room and heard the thuds as they embedded themselves in the wall. If he had been standing, they would have hit him rather than the wall. "I *know*," he said, sitting up slowly, "Daniel gets upset over these things."

About an hour later, when a box of rags in the pantry burst into flame, all Olive could think of was how glad she was that Daniel had returned to work.

* * *

Walt had spread his notebook and writing papers on the parlor table. Olive and Esther had taken the two boys and gone shopping. He was alone in the house. He had started his research only the day before, but already his notes had grown. Using the rapping methods Esther had shown him, he was busy conversing with the ghosts—on his own. It was a slow process of asking the wrong questions and getting one rap or hitting on the right questions and getting three raps. When he needed to spell a name or get a specific time or date, he would go letter by letter or number by number.

"Mattie Fisher died, aged twenty-one years;" he wrote, "had been dead twelve years; said 'she was in hell,' and that her sister, Mary Fisher, was in the house with her yesterday, who had been dead three years and was nineteen years old when she died."

He had asked the sisters: "Are you in heaven?" One rap. "Are you in hell?" Three raps. "Have you seen the Devil?" Bam! Bam! Bam! so loudly that the pictures on the wall were shaken crooked. Walt wanted to get up and run but he reminded himself he was doing serious scientific research. Scientists never ran.

"Is that you, Bob Nickle?" he asked. "Did you make those appallingly loud knockings?"

Bam! Bam! Bam!

"The ringleader," Hubbell said with the firmest voice he could find. "Glad to meet you. Are you glad to meet me?"

Bam!

"Oh. Well, never mind. I refuse to be insulted by the likes of you. I'd like to ask you some questions. I'm writing a book. About you and Esther. Your full name is Bob Nickle?" Three raps. "And you are dead?" Three raps. "Esther told me you were sixty years old when you died. Is that correct?" Three raps, very loud ones that shook the room again. "Please don't pound so loudly," Hubbell requested. "I'm not deaf. Just slight knockings will suffice. You're going to upset the whole street if you continue like that. Now, you were a blacksmith by trade?" One rap. "A farmer?" One rap. "A fisherman?" One very loud rap. "Well, I'm sorry, but this process takes too long. I wish you'd come up with another method. Were you a factory worker?" One rap. "In metals?" One rap. "In clothing?" Three raps. "Good, we're getting somewhere. In a shirt factory?" One rap. "A shoe factory?" Three very quick raps. "Good. Here in Amherst?" One rap. "In America?" Now one very loud and very definite, almost angry, rap was heard. "I'm sorry," Hubbell apologized. "I don't know why I assumed you were an American. I didn't mean to offend you. You're Canadian?" Three raps. "Fine. Did you know Esther or Daniel or anyone in the family before you died?" One rap. "Why are you picking on Esther, then? I mean, with all the others out there, why bother with her?" No answer. "You are making her life an inferno. Do you realize that?" No answer. "Don't you care that you are upsetting the young woman and making it impossible for her to lead a normal life?" Three raps. "Oh, so you do care?" One rap. "You don't care?" Three raps. "You really don't care that you are destroying her?" One rap. "That's a fine thing! An innocent girl, almost a child, and you make her very existence miserable. You must be ashamed of yourself." No answer. "All right, I'll make it into a question. Are you ashamed of yourself?" One rap. "You're not?" One rap. "Well, you should be. I can't imagine what pleasure you derive from all this. She's never done a thing to you." Hubbell stopped his one-sided conversation just long enough to become angry. "And while I have you here, why didn't you co-operate when Esther was onstage? Why didn't you make things move so others could see that you were real? You made her so ashamed. Don't you care that you made her ashamed?" One rap. "You don't?" One rap. "And you made Mr. White ashamed, too. And myself! I had to climb out a backstage window in the dark and run from a stone-throwing mob! Thanks to you. Yes, thanks to you." Walt sat back in his chair, feeling better now that he had finally told off the person who had ruined his tour. "Now, I'm going to be in this house for a while," he said, "and I expect some co-operation. I don't want any more knives tossed at me or tables upturned or sugar bowl lids disappearing. I want you to behave youself. Do you hear me?" No answer. The actor's voice rose. 'Do you hear me? I will not countenance any more of those childish acts! If I am to investigate this case, *I* must be in charge. Do you hear me?" Three small raps, very faint and timid. "That's better. That's what I'm after." He straightened his tie and assumed his air of authority. "You promise to act like an adult?" Three raps. "Yes?" Three raps. "Fine. I'm delighted. You promise to help me in this investigation?" Three light raps. "To answer my questions?" Three more. "To help me come to the truth of this case?" Three more. "And you'll leave Esther alone? You'll stop harassing her and sticking pins in her and frightening her? No response. "Do you promise?" No answer. "I'm serious." He was almost shouting now. "I'm serious. I want you to leave the girl alone. Do you promise?" Still no answer. "If you don't leave her alone, you'll kill her. Do you know that?" Silence. "Do you know that?" Hubbell waited but again there was not the faintest reply. "Are you still here? Are you listening to me?" Three faint knocking sounds. He was elated. He felt as if he had tamed a wild animal, had dominated a beast and the beast was his. "Then you'll leave the girl alone?" No reply. "You must answer me!" he shouted. "If you don't leave her alone, you'll kill her. Is that what you want? Do you want to kill her?"

Bam! Bam! Bam! Three resounding blows came from the wall, shaking the small frame house.

"You *do*! That's what you want! You want to *kill* her!"

Bam! Bam! Bam! The chair's turned over, the pictures fell from the walls, the carpet on which Hubbell was standing moved from under his feet. Flower pots rose in the air, the draperies were yanked open and closed, open and closed. Hubbell's notebooks and loose papers fluttered into the air and rained down on his head.

"My God!" the man yelled. "You *do* want to kill her."

Bam! Bam! Bam!

* * *

Walt said nothing to anyone about his "conversation" with the ghost named Bob Nickle. By the time the women came home from shopping, he had straightened up the parlor and put his papers in his bedroom. He wanted to talk about his success in communicating with the spirits but, as he mentally reviewed it, it made him sound as if he were losing his mind. A week ago he had denied that any such thing as a Bob Nickle existed. On Saturday, he had seen things that made him wonder. Now today, Tuesday, he had been talking with ghosts, asking questions, and writing down their answers. Back in "civilization" he prided himself on his skepticism and his powers of deduction. Now in this backwater hamlet, he was confused—and slightly frightened—by manifestations he could not explain. He couldn't even tell anyone about this afternoon. Not even anyone in the Teed home. It was too impossible. It made him appear to have lost his wits. It took him from a position of outside investigator to that of just another believer. If he was to remain above it all, to keep an open and free investigative mind, he didn't dare admit to anyone that what he had seen really happened. He didn't even dare admit it to himself.

Wednesday, June 25, 1879

That night, by lamplight in his bedroom, Hubbell wrote:

> On Wednesday, June 25th, the ghosts threw knives, other articles about the house and at us all. Since I had cursed them in the strongest kind of language, they were rather reserved in their actions toward us; but I supposed they would break out again, and they did. They set fire to the window curtain in the pantry and stuck pins into all parts of Esther's person. They moved the trapdoor which opened into the loft under the roof, and we, fearing that demon, Bob, would start a fire, kept water in readiness all day. Esther and I walked into the parlor in the afternoon; and just after we had gone about two feet from the door toward the flower stand we both saw, at the same instant, a chair thrown over; and while we were looking at it, it was placed on its feet again. Esther informed me that Mattie, the ghost, talked with her during the day; but I could neither hear nor see the

ghost, although I had Esther point out the exact spot on the floor where she said Mattie stood, and listened for the faintest whisper.

It was really strange, he thought as he wiped his pen point, that he could almost hear the voice of the dead girl named Mattie. Each time Esther stopped talking, he would strain to hear the ghost's reply. He thought he *did* hear words like "tired" and "dead" and once the phrase "going into Heaven," but he couldn't be sure. When he repeated the words to Esther, she said that was exactly what the spirit had said. He wanted to believe her, and at the same time he didn't. It would be so much easier to explain away if he remained convinced that Esther was bluffing at times.

But then there was that kiss. . . .

Thursday, June 26, 1879

"Here and here and right here, too." Jennie pulled up the long sleeves of her dress and showed Walt the places on her skin.

"Look at this mark." Esther opened the top button on her blouse. There was and "X," starting to scab over, scratched at her collarbone.

"It went on for about twenty minutes," the older girl said. "He woke us up by pulling the covers off both our beds, then he grabbed our nightgowns."

"He ripped the hem on mine," Esther added.

"I didn't have a chance to turn up the lamp until it was all over," Jennie continued, "but I could feel his hands all over my body." She shuddered. "It was horrible! It was the first time he's ever touched me. I hated it!"

"I have marks on my shoulders and on my legs, too." Esther blushed. She knew Walt wanted to see them, but proper modesty kept her from showing him any part of her person that was covered by clothing. She didn't add that Jennie had the scratch marks on her stomach and thighs. Nor did she dare mention that she had what looked like teeth marks around the nipple of each breast. "I cried," Esther said. "It hurt."

"We heard you," Daniel spoke up. Olive nodded but didn't say anything. They had come to an agreement with the girls: They would not go running into their bedroom unless they asked for help. In this warm weather, both girls wore light cotton nightclothes, and to have Daniel or Walt—Heaven forbid—see them so lightly clad would have been unthinkable. Daniel and Olive had had two children, but he was a proper gentleman: He had never seen his wife completely naked. Ladies never showed themselves to their husbands, and the husbands, if they were gentlemen, never wanted to see them that way.

"I thought I heard something," Hubbell said, "but you didn't make a great deal of noise."

Jennie shook her head. "I couldn't. I tried to call out but it felt as if he had his hand over my mouth. Even when he was torturing Esther I couldn't open my mouth to cry out."

"Perhaps there was more than one of them," Olive suggested.

"Well, one *had* to be Bob Nickle," Esther said. "I know his touch. The only other male ghost is Peter Teed. And he would never do a thing like that."

Daniel turned slightly red. "A Teed? Impossible." Walt had asked him if he knew anything about a great-uncle named Peter, and Daniel had said his father sometimes talked about a Peter Teed who had died in a barn fire. It had been years ago, long before Daniel was born. No, he hadn't told Olive about it. It just wasn't that important, and no, he had never mentioned it to Esther. Ever.

"Are you well enough to go to work?" Olive asked Jennie while pouring her another cup of coffee.

"Oh, yes, just a little tired, that's all. Fortunately, they didn't scratch my hands or face. If they had, I could never show myself at the shop."

"I'm sorry, Jennie." Esther looked at her older sister.

"It isn't your fault."

"Yes, it is. If you hadn't been in the bedroom with me, they would never have attacked you." She started to cry.

"It's all right," Jennie said soothingly and put her arm around her sister. "Don't let it bother you. There's been no real harm done."

"But why would Bob and Peter do that to *you*? I'm the one they're after."

"I don't think it was Uncle Pete!" Daniel said rather loudly. "It had to be another man."

"There isn't another man," Esther insisted. "The only men are Bob and Peter."

"Maybe it was a woman," Hubbell suggested. "Maybe a woman had her hands on your bodies and did those things."

"A *woman*?" Olive was shocked. "Mr. Hubbell, sir, that would be *unthinkable*." All of them looked at him as if he had suddenly passed wind.

* * *

They were in the parlor that afternoon. Walt was interviewing Esther while she darned the boys' socks. Olive made sure the children were always out of sight and sound when Hubbell was taking notes.

"And that's all you remember about it?" he asked.

"It's the best I can recall," she said. "I was in terrible pain and the room was full of people when suddenly there was this scratching sound on the wall. It must have taken at least two minutes for the ghost to write those words." She shuddered. "I still can't get myself to say them."

"Esther Cox, you are mine to kill!" Walt said them for her.

"Exactly. You've seen them upstairs. Olive wanted to plaster over them the next day, but Dr. Carritte wanted them to remain. For scientific study, or some such reason." She sighed. "I really wish they had erased them. I hate going into that room now."

"It doesn't bother me," he said a bit too loudly. They had rented him that room. When the two boarders moved out, Olive put her sons in their room. Esther and Jennie had already been moved to the front bedroom where the boys had slept. That bedroom—with the terrible writing—had remained empty until the actor asked to rent it. He had never noticed anything in that room. Olive had hung a curtain over the writing. If she couldn't get rid of it completely, at least she could hide it. "It doesn't bother me at all," he repeated.

"Well, it did me," the girl said. "I hated that wall and hated that room. It got so that I tried to stay awake all night rather than go to sleep. Dr. Carritte gave me a sleeping potion that helped—sometimes. You haven't met him yet. The doctor, I mean."

"Not yet, but I plan to just as soon as I have more of the story written down. He was instrumental in it all."

"He was," she agreed, "but he didn't do anything. Nothing that helped. He tried, but he told me that there was nothing medical science could do about it. Can you imagine? With all the books and knowledge about medicine, they *still* can't do anything to help me? And these are supposed to be modern times!"

"Did I understand correctly that the local minister tried to do an exorcism on you?"

"Tried to do a what?"

"An exorcism. That's when a priest or preacher tries to drive out a demon. They used to do it a lot in the Middle Ages."

She looked at him. "They tried nothing." Her voice was flat and tired. "Nothing! They came and looked. Two of them. Reverend Temple even brought his wife, but they didn't try to get rid of the ghosts. They just came to gawk." She passed the needle and thread one last time over the darning egg and bit off the thread, tying the loose ends quickly into a small knot. She laughed. "It was really comical. To see them run. The preacher and his wife, I mean. When they heard the knockings and saw the writing appear on the pantry wall, they almost fell over each other trying to get out the front door." She snickered. "I suppose I shouldn't think it was funny, but it managed to keep a lot of nosy biddies out of here. You know, there was a time in the beginning when perfect strangers came to the front door and wanted to be let in. There would be crowds of people blocking the street, just standing there looking and pointing. More than once someone called the police and had them dispersed. Sometimes Daniel and Jennie had to push their way through just to get into their own house."

"So they started going to White's place. They could see you there."

"That was a little later, when Mr. White was kind enough to offer me work. I really didn't do a very good job." She looked at him, a little embarrassed. "I thought I could handle it—and I did for a while— but it just got to be too much. Chairs falling over all the time. Dishes and mugs breaking. That oven door banging and then flying around the kitchen. It was when they stuck me with the knife that I had had enough. I just couldn't go back there. Bob told me they didn't like that place. He said Mr. White was just using me. He wasn't, of course," she said with a smile, "he is a good man and his wife is a dear, but Bob and the others didn't want me there and they kept after me till I quit. It all stopped over there. Nothing happened after I left. I'm sure Mr. White was glad nothing kept going on."

Walt nodded but knew better. "That knife in the restaurant," he said, "was that the first time the ghosts ever hurt you?"

"Where there was blood, yes." She didn't want to mention the attacks in bed.

"Until last night? When they scratched your skin and Jennie's skin?"

Esther nodded. "There was that one time before, just last week, when they stuck pins in me. I showed you the marks on my hand." He nodded. "That was it. They've thrown things and I've ducked but never anything that physically hit me."

He was busy writing. "Why do they hate you?"

"Oh, they don't hate me. I think they like me. I really do."

"Like you?" He looked at her. "They threaten to kill you and stick you with pins and knives and you think they *like* you?"

"It's just their way." She shrugged. "The only way they have to show me they are with me."

"They talk to you," he said. "That should show you."

"They do, but others can't hear them. Or see them. I think they do those physical things to prove to other people that they are there. If it hadn't been for the chairs and the writings and all the other things, I'm sure I would have been locked in the boobie hatch long ago. Who would have taken my word? Nobody. I'd just be a looney girl who imagined things. Nobody would have taken my ghosts seriously. Now they do. People see things with their eyes they can't explain. If they believe one thing—because they've witnessed it personally—then they'll believe other things." She reached for another sock. "I wish they'd go away, but at least they haven't made me look too much like a fool. People feel sorry for me now."

"Is that what you want? You want people to feel sorry for you?"

"No. I don't want their pity. I just want their understanding."

"Understanding?"

"Yes. That this terrible thing that has happened to me can

happen to anybody. I'm not unique. I'm not special. I'm just a girl who has something terrible happening to her. Some folks have accidents. I have ghosts."

"Have they given you any indication how long they plan to stay with—"

"Ow! That hurts!" She jumped up, knocking the basket of socks onto the floor. "It hurts!" she yelled at him. "It hurts!"

Hubbell turned white. He stared. There were needles, dozens of them, sticking out of her skin. They were all over her face, her neck, and her ears. They were on top of her hands, in the palms of her hands, and in her wrists. They were everywhere there was exposed skin. She stood before him, shaking her hands that bristled with a forest of silver needles, and shouted. "Get them off me! Please, Mr. Hubbell, get them off me!"

* * *

There had been no blood. Walt had yelled for Olive, and she came running. Together they pulled out the needles and put them in a dish on the parlor table. Hubbell wanted to count them, but after he had washed his hands and returned to the parlor, they had vanished. Esther, terribly upset, had taken a swallow of the doctor's calming medicine and had gone to her room. Olive took her a tray at suppertime, but she refused to eat. When she came back downstairs, Olive reported that there were no marks on the girl, no signs of the dozens of needles that had driven themselves into every inch of unprotected skin.

Walt thought the family was a little cool toward him that evening. They didn't say so, but he got the impression that he was to blame for what happened to Esther. All these manifestations had started up again after he moved in and begun his research. Things around the house—and in Esther's life—had been quiet before he came to Princess Street.

He wanted to tell them that he was merely a scientific observer, that he was not the cause of the phenomena, merely their recorder. But they hadn't asked him, hadn't come right out and blamed him, either. He didn't want to defend himself until he had been accused. That would probably come. Perhaps Daniel would ask him to leave. That would be terrible, especially if he hadn't completed his note-taking. He felt sorry for the girl but delighted at the same time. The more bizarre the event, the better his book would read. And what a lecture this would make back in the States! He didn't need her with him next time. Once the newspaper articles and the book were published, he would be famous, a national figure. Folks would come from miles around to hear him tell of Esther Cox! And gladly pay for the privilege.

He finished pulling off his socks, then hung his trousers on a peg in the wall. He scratched himself under the lightweight summer long johns he wore. They would be coming off in two days. Saturday he would take a bath, and then he'd change his underwear for a clean pair.

He got on the bed—not under the covers, because it was warm that night—reached out, and turned down the lamp wick. He sighed. He scratched again. It felt good to be free of those heavy woolen and cotton clothes. They were so hot in the summer and yet so needed in the winter.

Yes, it would be a good book. Maybe even put a portrait engraving of himself right after the title page. He would have to get one drawn when he was back in New York. A profile, preferably. Authors always looked better in profile. At least *he* looked better in profile. He tried, when onstage, to give the audience as much profile as possible. His roman nose was one of his best features. He had many good features, but the nose was the best.

Yes, and he scratched again, it would be a definite step up the ladder. This book, the fame from it, the lectures he would give, the money he would make. And the best part? It would all be true. No, that wouldn't be the *best* part: The best part would be that all the money from the book and the lectures would be his. He wouldn't have to share it with anyone. Not even Esther. She had never asked for a dime from the book. He was ready to concede a small percentage of the profits to her should she have asked. Or if Daniel and Olive had asked. But they didn't. They never acted as if they expected anything from it at all. It would be good for Esther and the Teeds, however. It would make them famous. Not that they wanted fame. Actually, they wanted nothing more than just to be left alone, for the world to go away, to go back to the quiet days on Princess Street before the ghosts made their appearance. Well, that was too bad. They were in the public domain now, and they would have to get used to the idea. Esther had been in all the local papers and written up as far away as Halifax. She was well known in eastern Canada. She'd be even better known when his book came out. It would make her famous and make him rich. Nothing wrong with that arrangement at all. He smiled and scratched again. If he could live with being rich, she ought to be able to live with being famous.

It was in the middle of that pleasant thought when he felt the bed move.

He opened his eyes in the dark and waited. The movement came again. It wasn't as if the bed were being pushed, more like someone getting onto the bed from the other side. It was a double bed, the one the two boarders had shared, and there was room for another person. The mattress squirmed a bit. Could it be Jennie? He threw that thought—no matter how pleasant—out of his mind. The bedroom door had been locked from inside. He had turned the key and set the hook. Jennie could not have come in without him knowing it.

The bed moved again. He held his breath. Then he slowly slid his left hand across the bedspread, inching it toward the other side of the mattress, to where someone must be lying. The fingers crept as far as his arm could go. They touched nothing. He picked up his hand and set it down in spots within his reach. The fingers touched the bedspread. Nothing else. Certainly no body.

The bed moved again. He drew his hand back quickly, putting it to his chest. The springs creaked. His eyes were wide open now. He hadn't moved, yet the springs had groaned. Then something cold touched his face. He jerked his head to one side, but the touch remained. He almost shouted in panic, but no, he had to keep his calm. He was a scientific investigator. He must remain collected. He must not have any fears.

The touch came again. This time it was softer. It started at his hairline and moved lightly down his left cheek and then to his neck and then across his shoulder, finally stopping at his hand that lay trembling on his chest. Then the touch encircled his hand and he could feel fingers. Fingers?

He sat up. The fingers pushed him back down. He sat up again. Again he was pushed back, harder this time. He held his breath, tensed his muscles, and waited. The fingers went back to the clenched fist on his chest. Carefully but forcefully, they pried open his fist and slipped into his sweating palm. They were long fingers. And they were female. And they were cold. Cold as ice.

Then something nibbled at his earlobe. Tiny little bites that frightened him yet gave him pleasure. Something cold licked at his ear, then cold lips whispered something. He couldn't make out the words.

The hand in his hand then undid itself, got out of his grip, and slid toward the top button of his long johns. The button flipped out of the buttonhole. Then the second button popped free. Then the third. He could feel the hand popping ivory buttons free. Soon none of them was trapped in the holes, and the newest sensation was a hand sliding itself under the cloth and across his warm chest. The hand was icy and almost stung his nipples as it caressed them.

"Cold," he murmured, "cold."

There was a pause. The hand raised up, then came softly back down on his exposed skin. It was warm now, suddenly warmer and suddenly more enjoyable. The nibbling at the earlobe came again, this time warm, and the tongue was almost hot. He writhed atop the bedspread, enjoying what was happening. Not understanding what was happening, but certainly enjoying it.

He brought his right hand up to caress the body beside him. It felt only air. He ran his hand quicker, right where he could feel the body pressing against his. Nothing. Not even the warmth. Wherever her body touched his body, he could feel it. Where they failed to touch, there was nothing at all.

Then the lips. The warm lips landed lightly on his. The same touch as before but with a brand-new meaning. He didn't know whether to be frightened, to escape, or to give in. He could sense his own warmness and the swelling down between his legs, pushing up at the crotch of the long johns. She must have sensed it, too, because the caressing hand slid rapidly from his chest down to his groin. The fingers rubbed, then caressed, then squeezed. He thought he was going to go to the ceiling. Right through the blackness of the night, through the plaster, through the roof, and float dazedly over Princess Street. If she kept that up, this narrow street that had already seen so much would see a whole lot more.

He managed to find his voice. "Mattie?" he whispered. "Mattie, is that you?"

Instead of the answer given as three loud raps, it came as three quick squeezes on his erection.

"Hello again," he whispered. "Oh, yes, hello again!"

Friday, June 27, 1879

About the night just past, Hubbell recorded little, except to say of Mattie: "I carried on a most interesting conversation with her, asking a great many questions which were answered by knocks."

* * *

This day's activity was as varied as on any previous day. As he wrote in his notebook:

> The knocks commenced in my room in the morning before I was up. I began to think the ghosts would follow me when I left the house. At breakfast, the same sugar bowl lid disappeared at eight o'clock, and in fifteen minutes fell from under the dining room sofa. This was the third time it had disappeared and returned in a mysterious manner.
>
> A trumpet was heard in the house all day. The sound came from within the atmosphere—I can give no other description of its effect on our sense of hearing. It was evidently a small trumpet, judging from its tone and was at times very close to the ears of all. I asked who was blowing it, and was told Bob. I requested him to let it fall into the room and he said he would do so. That night, he let the trumpet fall, I picked it up and still have it in my possession. It is composed of metal either lead or pewter—and is about three inches long. I could never ascertain where he obtained it, nor could I find an owner for it, nor one like it in any of the Amherst stores. He must have stolen it from somewhere, for he and Mattie were both continually stealing small articles, and after keeping them for days and sometimes weeks, would suddenly let them fall, out of the air, upon the floor. This we saw, time after time.

That same evening the *Amherst Gazette* published the following news item:

Esther Cox

The manifestations in the presence of this young lady have recently been of a very lively character. She is now staying at Mrs. Teed's.

The case has lately been watched closely by Mr. Walter Hubbell, who has seen similar phenomena, and had determined to spend some time in its investigation. He has frequently caught bogus "mediums" in their deceptions, and considers that Miss Cox could easily deceive him if she were inclined to do so. He informs me that he had heard knocks at times very loud, and that these have denoted the dates on coins in his pocket, time of day, etc.; that on different days the heavy cover of a stone-china sugar bowl disappeared from the breakfast table, and afterwards dropped from the air in the room; that when he asked for matches for lighting his pipe, they dropped in front of him on several different occasions; that chairs, tables, and a lounge were upset, and various articles were thrown from ten to thirty feet.

Daniel handed the newspaper to the young actor. "I really don't like this, you know," Daniel said. "I trusted you to keep us out of the press." Hubbell shrugged. "We want people in this town to forget about Esther's ghosts," Daniel continued. "I assumed you would be enough of a gentleman not to bandy about everything that was happening here."

"I didn't expect the newspaper to publish it," Walt answered. "It was just in conversation over a beer. I mean, he wasn't interviewing me or anything."

"Well, you should know better than to tell things to a reporter that you don't want published. Especially in this town, where nothing ever happens and so *everything* is news."

"I *am* a visitor here," Hubbell said, "and a well-known actor and so, I guess, people are naturally curious about what I'm doing. They know I'm boarding here. The whole town knows I'm boarding here."

"They do now," Daniel said crisply.

"And they know about Esther's tour and they're anxious to know the latest details. That's news."

"That's gossip." Daniel was trying to keep his voice level.

"Gossip becomes news when it's printed," Walt replied.

"Almost everything in a newspaper is gossip or rumor or innuendo. I can't help that. That's the nature of the business."

"Well, your gossip-turned-news caused old man Bliss to visit me at the factory today," Daniel said. "Again. He said he had read the article and he had been hearing stories about 'things happening' in his house. He wanted to know what *things* had been going on in here. He especially wanted to know about fires. He doesn't want this place to go up in smoke, and neither do I. I told him as much."

"There was nothing about fires in the paper," Hubbell said, defending himself. "I could have told them about the curtain in the pantry catching fire, but I didn't. I've been especially careful about not mentioning that incident."

"But you did tell about matches falling to light your pipe!" Daniel's voice was much louder now. Olive and Esther could hear it even out in the kitchen. He grabbed the paper back from Hubbell and read aloud: ". . . that when he asked for matches for lighting his pipe, they dropped in front of him on several different occasions . . ."

Walt shrugged again. "I didn't say they were *lit* when they fell. I just said they fell. That's all. It doesn't have anything there about them being *lit.*"

"It's the same thing!" Daniel shouted. "A match is a match, and matches start fires. One match can start a fire that would burn this house to the ground, and you have them dropping all over the place! That's what old man Bliss was concerned about, and that's what I'm upset about. He can throw us all out of here tonight if he thinks we're a danger to his precious house! Don't you understand that?"

"I guess so." The actor's voice was low.

"Well, I hope so!" Daniel threw down the newspaper and walked from the room.

Walt picked up the paper and carried it upstairs to his bedroom. He reread the article and smiled as he tucked it away with his other research on Esther. He needed that article. He needed something printed that would prove he had really spent time in Amherst and that he had been personally involved in the case. It was one thing to tell people what he'd been doing, but it was a whole other thing to have proof. And he had it now. The *Gazette* linked his name with Esther's, established his personal experiences in the Teed house, and made him appear to be a professional spirit investigator. And the paper had the day and the month and the year neatly printed at the top of the page. He smiled again as he buckled his briefcase. The ghosts weren't going to burn this house. That was absurd. And what if they did? It was an old pile of sticks, anyway.

Saturday, June 28, 1879

"I have so many chores to do today." Esther kept sweeping the parlor rug, not looking at Walt. "Olive wants me to go marketing with her later, and the windows need washing something fierce."

"It won't take long," he coaxed. "It's just an experiment. You'll see."

Esther didn't want any more experiments. She didn't appreciate that article in the paper yesterday and was afraid that every little thing that happened in the privacy of her home would be printed for all the world to see. Daniel had been upset. It wasn't like him to shout—not at the children, not at Olive. But he had raised his voice at the American and, as far as she could see, the American wasn't contrite at all. Here he was, the very next day, wanting her to do an experiment. "What kind of an experiment?" she asked.

"You just sit quietly here in the parlor—or anyplace you choose—and concentrate on a certain item. I'll put it on a table in front of you and you stare at it and will it to move."

"*Will* it? What do you mean?"

"You stare at it and tell it, silently with just your mind, to move. You mentally command it."

"And then what?"

"And then we'll see what it does and how far it goes and all that. I'll take notes."

"Oh." She started sweeping again. "That's all?" she said, looking up.

"That's all. It's just an experiment. Nothing more."

She sighed and leaned the broom against the wall. "Where do you want me?"

"Anyplace you choose. Here in the parlor or in the dining room or kitchen. Anywhere."

"The parlor's fine. Here?" She sat on the sofa.

"Fine. That's good. Now just let me move this little table in front of you. Like that. That's straight in front of you, right?" She nodded yes. "Now let me put the . . . it should be something unbreakable . . . photo album on the table." He grabbed it and placed it in the center of the table. "Good. Very good. Now all you have to do is stare at it and mentally command it to rise into the air." He sat on a nearby chair, settling his notebook on his lap.

Esther stared at the album. Her large grey-blue eyes were fixed on the red velvet volume. Hubbell kept his body rigid, his attention squarely on the book. The mantelpiece clock ticked loudly. Soon drops of perspiration appeared on the girl's forehead. She wanted to brush them away but instead kept her gaze fixed on the book.

"Are you commanding it to rise?" he asked in a soft voice.

She nodded yes. Her eyes remained on the book. The sweat glistened. The clock ticked.

"Are you sure you're telling it to rise?"

"Yes," she said between clenched teeth.

"Well, it's not doing it."

"That's not my fault," she said, trying not to move her lips "I'm staring at it."

Hubbell stared at it as well, willing it to rise. He wanted that book—that damned book—to do something. But it just sat there. Like a load of lead. Esther continued to perspire. The clock continued to tick. "All right," he said, "I guess it won't work because it's paper. Maybe your mind can't will paper." He stood up and looked around the room. "What else can we use? An object that's made of something else besides paper."

"How about the queen?" she asked. "That bust of Queen Victoria on the table in the corner. It's made of china. It should be easy to lift."

"Excellent!" He hurried to the corner, grabbed the image of the unsmiling woman, and put it on the table where the photo album had been. "I know this works," he said as he sat down. "I read about it in a Spiritualist magazine. The medium concentrated and the object rose from the table."

"I'll start now." She wrinkled her brow and gave her full attention to the head and shoulders of the china queen. It had never been one of her favorite bits of bric-a-brac in Olive's parlor. She thought Victoria was too bossy and, if the latest engravings in the ladies' magazines were correct, was getting fat. It had been too bad when Victoria's husband died, however. Esther thought he had been handsome and dashing. She stared at the bust. The woman with the crown stared back.

Walt looked at his pocket watch and then at Esther. She

was doing everything he had told her to do, but the figurine wasn't moving. It should be by now. It should have moved at least a few inches one way or another. What was the matter? These experiments had worked for other serious investigators. Why not for him? "Are you're sure you're *really* willing it?" he asked.

"I want it to fly to the ceiling!" she said, still trying to keep her lips from moving. "I'm concentrating. I'm concentrating."

The clock ticked. Esther's face became bathed in sweat. A housefly buzzed past and landed on her hand. She didn't flinch. She was intent on making that ugly piece of cheap china fly around the room. God knows, other things had taken off as if they had a life of their own, so why wasn't this thing doing it?

"I don't think you're thinking hard enough," Hubbell said. "Think harder!"

She wanted to shout, "How do you know how hard I'm thinking?" but she didn't. She was getting tired. She had been sitting like this for at least five minutes, and if anyone had come in and caught her, they would have thought she'd gone mad. Maybe she had. Maybe all this had made her looney. Maybe the gossips in town were correct: Esther Cox was crazy. Esther Cox should be locked up. At least, she thought with satisfaction, if I were locked up I wouldn't be expected to do silly stunts like this one.

"It doesn't seem to be working," Hubbell said. "You might as well stop."

"Good." Esther blinked, shook her head a couple of times and took a handkerchief from her apron pocket. Her brow was soaked with sweat. "I tried, Mr. Hubbell, I truly did."

"I'm sure you did," he said. "Obviously, your talents do not lie in the direction of making inanimate objects move. At least, when you want them to." He followed her into the kitchen and watched as she bathed her face in cool water from a bucket on the sideboard. "It's as if things you *want* to move *won't* and the things you *don't* want to move *will*. Things like chairs and tables and flower pots jump all over the place, but only when you don't want them to. Like the screwdriver there on the shelf above the stove. If you didn't want it to move, it would probably be all over the place."

At that, the screwdriver rose up, hesitated, came directly for Walt, and stabbed him in the forehead. Esther tried not to laugh as she put the bandage on him.

Wednesday, July 2, 1879

"I'd like to try something else today. If you don't mind."

The girl was taking his breakfast dishes into the kitchen. She stopped, turned around, and looked at him. "Must you?"

"It's another experiment. I read about it in a book."

"What do I have to move?"

Walt fingered the spot on his forehead that had scabbed over. "Nothing," he replied. "I don't need any more proof about your moving things. No, this one has to do with sending energy from your body into another person. You send it and the other person receives it."

"Who is the other person going to be?"

"Me."

He placed two of the parlor chairs facing one another. He had her sit in one and he in the other. Their knees almost touched, but not quite. He took both her hands in his. "Now you take a deep breath and I'll take a deep breath and then you mentally send me electrical energy. See it coming down your arms and out your hands into my hands. I'll mentally picture it coming into my hands, up my arms, and into my body. It should fill me with force and vitality."

"Force and vitality," she repeated. "Down my arms, out my hands, and into your hands. That's what I'm supposed to imagine?"

"Not imagine. Actually feel! Try to see the energy with your mind's eye. Just see it and then send it into my body. It should make me alive and tingling all over. Are you ready?"

"Ready."

"All right. Start."

Esther took a deep breath, held it a second, released it, and imagined lightning bolts coming down her arms, out through her hands, and into Mr. Hubbell's hands. She put all the mental effort she could behind it, and thought she actually could feel this dynamic charge race through her body.

He could sense it. Could feel it. The surge came into the palms of his hands and moved up his arms! What a wonderful sensation! What a power charge! What a success!

Then he yawned.

She relaxed her grip. "What's wrong?"

He yawned again. "I don't know. I feel so sleepy all of a sudden."

"Do you want me to continue?"

"No." He yawned again. "I'm sorry. I should have covered my mouth. I am really terribly sleepy."

"All you all right?"

"Oh, yes. Don't know what hit me. I slept well last night." He yawned again. "Excuse me. Terribly bad manners." Another yawn. "I think," he said getting up from the chair, "I think I'll just go upstairs and lie down for a bit. I really do feel terribly sleepy, I don't know what . . ." He stumbled to the staircase and made it slowly to his bedroom. When he awoke, dinner and supper had both been served and the dishes cleared away and washed. Olive had knocked several times on his door but couldn't rouse him. When he finally was able to focus his eyes, his watch told him he had slept for twelve hours. He resolved never to try *that* experiment again.

Tuesday, July 8, 1879

Little things had happened around the house for the past few days, and Hubbell noted them all.

He and Esther and Jennie had been in the parlor when the ghosts began bringing things to them. Things like fresh eggs from the kitchen, hairpins from their bedroom, spools of cotton thread from Olive's sewing basket, and even a shaving brush from his closed leather traveling kit.

At another time, a heavy paperweight rose from its place on the parlor table and chased him around the room.

Olive put freshly cut flowers in a vase, put them on the dining-room table, and when she returned they had been replaced by weeds and broken sticks.

Daniel sat reading the paper, wearing his slippers, and his right foot began to itch. He removed the slipper, scratched his foot, and when he went to put the slipper back on, it was gone. They looked all over for it. The next morning, it was found in the bread-box.

Monday morning, Hubbell had heard Esther and Olive whispering. When he asked them what the secret was, Esther shyly told him that Mattie was wearing her black and white striped stockings and wouldn't take them off. They had been in her bureau drawer and she had seen the ghost put them on. Hubbell was astonished that the women would even allude to the stockings, let alone tell him such a story. After he overcame his embarrassment, he commanded Mattie, in a very loud voice, to "take off Esther's stockings instantly! It was an infamous thing to do!" In a minute a pair of black and white stockings fell out of the air onto the floor. Esther and Olive (and later Jennie as well) swore that they were the very stockings that Esther wore.

On this Tuesday morning, the postman brought a letter for Daniel. It was from a friend who had heard about Esther and her ghosts, and he had a sure-fire way for her to rid herself of them once and for all.

First she was to copy, on slips of paper, the third verse of the second chapter of Habakkuk. Then she was to go away and stay away long enough for Olive to paste one of these slips of paper on every door and window. The theory was that when she left the house she would take her ghosts with her. When she came back, the ghosts would see the biblical quotation on every entrance to the house and would be too frightened to come in with her.

Daniel thought it sounded like a good idea. Olive and Jennie weren't so sure, but they were ready to try anything once. Hubbell didn't think it would work, but why not give it a chance? After all, the things he thought would work hadn't, so maybe this thing would. Esther didn't comment, but she knew it was all foolishness.

So she copied, in her slow, large scrawl: "For the vision is yet for an appointed time, but at the end it shall speak, and not lie: though it tarry, wait for it; because it will surely come, it will not tarry."

"I don't know what this has to do with frightening my ghosts," Esther said with a scowl as she wrote. "It doesn't make any sense to me."

"Nor me," Olive replied. "But ours is not to reason why, ours is but to—"

"Yes, I know. I'm doing it so I won't die."

"We have to give it a chance, darling."

Esther sighed. "I suppose so," and went back to her writing.

Hubbell insisted she make a big production out of leaving the house. They dressed her in her traveling clothes, made her take a small suitcase and even her knitting. Olive hugged her several times, said good-bye at least half a dozen times, and stood on the porch waving as she trudged up the street and around the corner.

"Do you think they're gone?" Olive asked Walt.

"I don't know. If they saw everything that was happening, they are bound to think she's left home. All we can do is hope."

Olive quickly pasted the biblical quotation on each of the windows and both the front and back doors. When she finished, she poured herself and Hubbell a glass of lemonade each. "Oh, I hope this works. I really do."

Esther, all dressed up and carrying an empty suitcase and her cloth bag of knitting, didn't know where to walk or how much time to kill before the slips of paper started working. She sat in the downtown park for a while, stood and watched men putting up a brick wall, and walked to the edge of town, sat on her suitcase, turned around, and walked back. She decided, before going home, to stop in and see Reverend Temple. Maybe he could help—this time.

"So that's what we did," she explained. "I wrote out sixteen slips of paper with that verse and got dressed up and left." She looked at him anxiously. "What do you think? Will it work?"

"Well, it just might. You are dealing with words from the Holy Book. Those words are powerful. All words in the Holy Book are powerful. They are God's words, and He would not have chosen them for His book if they were not powerful. Stranger things have happened." He had taken out his Bible when Esther told him which chapter and verse she had copied, and after he'd read it, he couldn't understand what it had to do with anything, either. But he didn't tell her that. All he said was: "Most interesting. Quite spiritual. Hmmm. Yes."

"I really want this to work," she said. "I'm so tired of it all. The flying things and the missing things and the experiments."

"Experiments? What experiments? Is Dr. Carritte conducting some new tests?"

She shook her head. "Not Dr. Carritte. The American fellow. Mr. Hubbell, the actor."

"Oh. I thought it was something scientific."

"It is," she said, trying to sound positive about it all. "Mr. Hubbell has done this sort of work before. Down in the States. He has read a great deal and he takes notes while the experiments are going on. He plans to put them all in a book. When it's over."

"When what's over?"

"The ghosts. When they go away and stop bothering me."

She smiled. "That's when it'll be over. When the ghosts aren't around me anymore."

"Do you think that will be soon?" He hadn't been anywhere near the house on Princess Street since early October—over nine months ago—when Reverend Clay had had his hat pulled down over his eyes. After that, Reverend Temple told everyone it was for "the good of the parish" that he didn't visit her again. He might bring a spirit back with him, and that would be terrible for the church.

"I hope it will be soon," she said. "Olive and Daniel have been so good about it all. I'm really lucky to have such an understanding family."

"And you think this American is helping you?" He hadn't been able to do a damned thing to help her. "I mean, is there any noticeable improvement?"

"Well, Mattie listens to him," the girl said brightly. "That's an improvement. Before, she just did as she pleased, but not now when Mr. Hubbell talks to her, she pays attention."

"'Mattie'? I don't remember any Mattie."

She laughed. "Mattie is one of the ghosts. A lady ghost."

"They have *names* now?"

"Oh, yes, thanks to Mr. Hubbell, they've given us all their names."

"All? How many are there?" Maybe the Cox girl *was* a little strange after all.

"Six. There's Bob Nickle, of course. He's the oldest one and the loudest. I think you met him."

The preacher nodded. He had sure met somebody!

"The other man ghost is named Peter. Peter Teed he used to be when he was alive. He was a great-uncle of Daniel's. Isn't that odd?" He nodded again. "Then there are four girls: Jane, who is either Bob's sister or his wife, and Eliza, who used to be the sister of a boy I was sweet on who lived right here in Amherst. She's dead now, too. Then there's Mary and Mattie Fisher. Mary is the quiet one. Mattie is the noisy one. She put on some of my clothes the other day and wouldn't take them off until Mr. Hubbell ordered her to." He nodded again. No doubt about it, the girl was going mad. "Mattie hangs out the upstairs window and waves at people."

His eyes opened wide. "And do they wave back?"

"Oh, no, they can't see her. They don't wave back."

"That's good." He wondered how many other crazies there were over on Princess Street.

"I have to confess," the girl said, lowering her voice, "I kind of like Mattie. She's spunky and funny. She tells me things sometimes that make me laugh." Then she frowned. "I don't like the others, though. Especially Bob Nickle. I don't like him at all. He hurts me. He does things to me that hurt me." She shook her head. "I don't care for him one little bit."

"Then these—" he paused to choose his words carefully—"these people, these ghosts, are very real to you?"

"Oh, yes. I see them and hear them and talk with them. They're as real to me as you are. They're that real"—she paused and looked at the floor—"real to *me*, at any rate."

He squirmed in his chair. "Are there any of your . . . friends here now? In my office?" He thought she would be surprised by the question, but she wasn't.

"No," she said slowly, looking around the room. "Not at the moment."

"That's good." He was about to say something else when he stopped and looked at her. "Would you tell me if there was a ghost in here? You wouldn't keep it from me, would you?"

Now she was surprised by his question. "Why, of course I'd tell you, Reverend Temple. I wouldn't lie."

He visibly relaxed. "I knew you wouldn't."

"That's been the problem all along," she said. "People think I'm lying about my ghosts. I'm not. I'm really not. I see them and I talk to them, and they talk to me. I don't lie. My mother, who is in Heaven, taught me it was a sin to tell a lie. Olive says the same thing. I never lied before. Why do people think I'm lying now? It bothers me, it really does, that folks think I tell lies." She started searching in the pockets of her dress. There was a handkerchief in there somewhere, and she expected tears to start soon. "I have always been a good girl. Haven't I? You know that. I've always been *good*. I've done nothing to be ashamed of. I've done nothing that I have to lie about." Her eyes filled with water. "Yet everybody thinks I'm a terrible person in league with the Devil or something. I'm not! I'm good. Real good. I don't like it when people point their fingers at me and accuse me of being crazy!" She found the handkerchief and began to blot her cheeks.

"No one ever thought you were crazy," he said soothingly. "Distraught. Unusual, perhaps. But not crazy." He wondered how he could get her out of his office. "It's just that folks don't understand these things, and when they don't understand, they imagine. Folks imagine all sorts of foolish ideas." Maybe if he got up slowly and walked toward the door, she would follow. "I'm sure this has grown on you and upset you to the place where you are really not seeing it in the proper perspective." He had to do it slowly. He didn't want to upset *whatever* might be around her. "Why don't you take this little Bible and keep it with you." Oh, yes, that was a good idea! He handed her one from a stack of New Testaments he kept as gifts to parishioners. "You take this book. It's a powerful book, and it will protect you." He rose from his chair and handed her the Bible. She took it with the hand that wasn't holding the hankie. "You take it with you. When you go. Now that you're going. You take it and you put it under your pillow at night and it will help you. It will keep the evil spirits from bothering you." She looked up at him, gratitude and tears intermixed. "That's better. Now you just get back on home"—he took her arm and helped her to her feet—"and you put this book under your pillow." He managed to steer her toward the door. "It'll help." He opened the door. "I'll pray for you," he said, patting her on the shoulder. She was on the other side of the door now, clutching the Bible and her knitting and the empty suitcase.

"Thank you, Reverend Temple. Thank you so much." The tears were in her voice now.

"Not at all," he said, slowly closing the door. "That's what I'm here for. I'm here to help. Good-bye." His smile was cut off by the closing of the door. He listened for the sound of her feet down the wooden steps to the street. When he couldn't hear her any longer, he relaxed and took a deep breath. "Good God," he said aloud, "that girl's daffy as a jaybird!"

Olive and Walt watched her open the fence gate, close it, and start up the path toward the door. Her face was solemn, and she kept her gaze on the ground. Suddenly she fell, just collapsed onto the lawn. Until they could gather their wits about them, she lay on the grass like a large wounded blackbird, knitting, Bible, and suitcase thrown in three different directions.

Olive, still screaming her name, was the first to reach her. When Walt turned her over, they saw the gash in her forehead and the blood that was pouring down over her eyes and mouth. She made no sound, but Olive was moaning as they carried her into the house and then into the kitchen.

"Put her in a chair," the woman ordered, "and then put her feet up on another chair. That's good. Oh, my God. Look at that wound! You hold her head back. Like that, yes, just like that, hold it back so the blood runs the other way. I'll get a cloth and some water."

"It was this thing." Walt reached in his pocket and took out a bone. It was dry and dirty and old. "It looks like a beefsteak bone," he said. "This sharp edge here, right here—see, it has blood on it."

"That's been in the yard," Olive replied hurriedly. "I saw a dog with it this morning, and I was going to go out later and throw it in the trash." She started wiping at the still bleeding wound. "They hit her with it. Those damned ghosts of hers hit her with it." Hubbell had never heard her swear before. A real lady never said "damn." "Why don't those damned things leave her alone?"

He stood watching, helplessly. "They probably didn't like the Bible verse on the windows when they came back. I'll bet that's why they did it."

"Well, it's unfair." Olive had stopped the blood; now she was wiping her sister's face and hair. "She's just a child. An innocent child!"

"They have it in for her. For some reason. I wish I knew why."

"We all wish we knew why, Mr. Hubbell. Get me a clean basin of water, will you? We all wish we knew why. If we knew that, we would know a lot of things."

He emptied out the red-stained water and poured fresh water into the bowl. As he walked back toward the still unconscious girl, the butcher knife whizzed past his arm. It stopped just inches short of Esther's neck, poised. Then it turned, the cutting edge gleaming and the point of the knife making an indentation in her skin.

"Damn you!" Olive grabbed the knife handle and threw it far across the room. "Damn you!" she screamed.

The knife lay on the kitchen floor for a second, then rose up and headed back toward Esther's throat. This time Hubbell grabbed it—he thought he could feel other fingers as he did so—and he ran with it to the back door. He opened the door, threw the knife outside, and slammed the door shut.

"It's not fair," Olive said loudly. She wasn't crying; she was too angry to cry. "It's just not fair!" She washed Esther's face with the cold water. "Damn all their souls into Hell!" she said loudly. "They are supposed to be in Hell. Why don't they stay there? Why do they have to torment my little sister? Why?" She looked at Hubbell, but he didn't have an answer. For her sake and for Esther's, he wished he had.

The girl stirred and opened her eyes. She struggled to get up, but Olive held her back. "Take it easy, darling. Just don't excite yourself. Everything's all right. It's all right."

Esther put her hand to her forehead and then looked at her bloody fingers. She closed her eyes and sighed deeply. "I felt something . . . it hurt for just a moment. . . ."

"Don't you mind," Olive soothed her. "It's over now. It's all over."

"Perhaps we should get her up to her room," Hubbell suggested. "She needs to lie down."

"Can you?" Olive asked her. "Can you get up? We'll help you up the stairs."

Esther opened her eyes and gave them a half smile. Walt gently took her feet and swung them from the chair seat to the floor. Olive put the wet cloth back on the wound and kept it there as Esther managed to get into standing position. Then with Walt on one side and Olive on the other, they helped her to the staircase.

Halfway up, the scissors gleamed. They just floated in the air, handles pointed up, the sharp ends pointing down at Esther. Her eyes grew wide. "It's Mattie!" she cried out. "Look out! Mattie has the scissors!"

Hubbell almost fell over backward as Esther jerked her body out of the way. The sharp points of the scissors missed her neck by inches, burying themselves in the baseboard at the bottom of the stairs.

"Son-of-a-bitch!" he exclaimed.

"Mr. Hubbell, sir!" Olive shouted.

He reddened. "I'm sorry," he mumbled. "I apologize." He kept staring at the scissors. "It was such a surprise." He could feel his own body shaking. If those things had hit Esther, they would be sticking out of her neck now instead of the woodwork.

They continued up the stairs, Esther, with her eyes half closed, leaning heavily on the other two. They went up a few more steps when Hubbell saw the fork. Like the scissors, it seemed to float in the air, pointed at the girl.

"Oh, no," he exclaimed. "Look!"

Esther opened her eyes. "It's Mattie. Now she has a fork in her hand! Mattie, why? I thought you were my friend!" She started to cry.

The dinner fork came at the girl. Both Walt and Olive tried to grab it, but the invisible hand that held it veered around their reach and the fork stabbed Esther in the head. It pulled back and managed to stab her again before Walt could grab it and throw it down the stairs.

"Son-of-a-bitch!" Olive said loudly. Then she glared at the American, defying him to make a comment. "Son-of-a-bitch!"

Sunday, July 13, 1879

"If you ask me," said Daniel, "I think it's a foolish idea."

"They didn't ask you." Olive poured him a second cup of coffee.

"Well, they should have. I am the boss in this house."

She smiled. He might be the boss, but she had all the responsibility with the children and Esther. "Hubbell feels he needs it for his investigation."

Daniel made a face. "Uh-huh. Hubbell. It would be interesting to see if he really knows what he's doing. All we have is his word that he's done this sort of thing before. We never checked up on him, you know."

"How could we? Amherst is a million miles from New York and Philadelphia."

"It's not that far," he said.

"It feels like it is sometimes," she said. She pushed the sugar bowl toward him. "Walt says that he should see for himself what the ghosts do or do not do in a church. And it's been days since there has been anything at all. Here in the house, I mean. Since they hit her with the steak bone and stabbed her with the fork, things have been very quiet. Perhaps they've gone from her."

"Wouldn't that be a blessing."

"It would indeed."

"But I doubt it." Daniel stirred his coffee. "It's a pattern with them. They do things for a stretch of time and then they let up. It's almost as if they play their tricks and then stand back to watch *our* reaction." He put the spoon down and looked at his wife. "I've been thinking. It seems to me that your friend Hubbell—"

"My friend Hubbell?"

"*Our* friend Hubbell, our houseguest and boarder, has been responsible for bringing a great deal of this mischief about. Before he came here and started his so-called scientific investigations, the ghosts were not violent. They lifted a flower pot or made water boil, but they didn't *hurt* the girl. They didn't stab her and make her bleed." He shook his head. "No, it's almost as if they are doing it to show Hubbell that they really exist and are in charge of things around here. It's as if he is the . . . what's the word I want?"

"Catalyst."

"That's it. That he's the catalyst for all this and Esther is suffering because of him. And now"—he buttered a slice of toast—"he's taking her to Sunday morning services to disrupt everything at church. I don't like it. Not one bit."

"It'll be over soon," she replied. "He's going back to New York the first week of August. That's just a little over a fortnight."

"Good."

"Yes, you can say 'good,' but we'll have to find another boarder. His room will be empty."

"We'll find somebody. I'll put a notice up at the factory."

"And you'll find somebody who is willing to pay to live in a house with six ghosts? I doubt it." She poured herself a second cup of coffee. "I doubt it very much."

"Don't you worry about it," he replied. "You just leave it to me. That's my responsibility. I am the boss here."

"Oh, yes, dear," she patted his hand, "that's true. You *are* the boss."

He looked at her quickly, wondering if he really heard a note of sarcasm in her voice.

* * *

Walt and Esther had the entire pew to themselves. The Bronson family had already been sitting there when they arrived, and they slid down to make room for them. When Mrs. Bronson saw who it was, they kept sliding until they had slid across the aisle into another pew entirely.

Several people came down the aisle, saw Esther, and kept on going. The pew in front of them remained vacant, too. Folks filed in behind them, but nobody sat in front of them or beside them. Reverend Temple watched the shuffle for seats from his perch on the platform near the altar. He had thought it was just going to be one more Sunday until he saw Esther and that actor come in. He hoped the actor would keep his charge in tow. He had no intention of having his service disrupted. Things were going smoothly in his church. Crazy people were not welcome.

Esther wore her Sunday best: a deep purple dress that went from her neck to her toes. She had on a matching summerweight bonnet, held on with purple ties under her chin. Hubbell had on his best black suit, the one with a buttoned-up vest and a buttoned-up jacket. His white stiff shirt collar barely showed above the black coat. His red and white polka-dot tie was the only note of color in his entire outfit.

The choir, up front behind the preacher, did the opening hymn. Most of them sang looking straight at Esther. If anything was going to happen, they had a wonderful vantage point to view it. To their disappointment, they got through the song without incident.

A deacon read the church news: things that had taken place and things that were going to take place for the church members.

A child read an interminably long poem about blessings at summertime.

Another deacon read three verses from St. Mark.

A large lady, with many ruffles that accentuated her already enormous bust, sang a hymn about climbing to the sky.

Reverend Temple, as all could see, visibly relaxed. It was obvious that this was going to be just one more Sunday service.

After the lady with the bust and all the ruffles finished singing, the preacher rose to his place in the pulpit. "My sermon, this morning, is on the many ways we should be thankful to God. How many of us thank Him as often as we should?" He paused and gazed over his parishioners. "How many of us just take for granted what He has blessed us with?" Another pause. Another gaze. "How many of us, even when the day is done and we have come to a time for relaxing and contemplating, still do not give Him our praise and thanks?" The pause, the gaze. "If we do not give thanks to the Creator, then are we, through our omission and our negligence, in reality giving thanks to Satan? To Satan, who is always there to take credit for whatever the Holy Spirit has done?

Bam!

Reverend Temple stopped short, staring in the direction of the noise. Esther turned beet red. There had been a knock on the back of her pew. The sound had come from where that girl was sitting. He decided to continue.

"What kind of thankful children are we if we do not give the proper due to the Holy Father?

Bam!

All heads turned to stare. There was nothing to be seen but the overdressed American and the red-faced local girl.

"Miss Cox," the minister said in a level voice, "I must ask you not to interrupt the service." Esther put her hands to her face. "This is a temple of the Lord. This is not the dwelling place of Satan."

Bam! Bam!

Some people sitting in the back stood up to get a better view. A few members, in the pew directly behind Esther, slid away from her.

The minister tried to control himself. "If your satanic friends—"

Bam! Bam!

"—think they can interrupt the words of the Lord—"

Bam! Bam!

"—in His own home, they are mistaken. We do not cotton to Satan here and we—"

Bam! Bam! Bam! This time the knocks were louder and seemed to come from under the floor near the altar.

"I really must insist that you desist from these games!" He was shouting now. "This is a house of worship! It is not a center of destruction!"

Bam! The knock came on the side of the altar. The minister jumped back. Bam! The knock came just inches from where he was standing.

"This is not a circus, Miss Cox, this is a—"

Everyone gasped. They could all see it. It was a hymnal, and it rose from a pocket in the very last pew and sailed in the air above the heads of the parishioners. Several women screamed, and a lot of people ducked their heads. Esther was mortified. Hubbell was delighted.

The minister was too slow. The book hit him on the side of

the head, knocking his spectacles sideways and leaving them dangling from one ear.

The choir was impressed:

"Did you see that?"

"Right through the air!"

"Higher than a man could carry it!"

"Poor preacher."

"Yeah." Then a giggle.

Reverend Temple hastily adjusted his glasses. He pointed a finger at Esther. "That kind of conduct cannot be permitted! This is a house of the Lord."

"Watch it, Reverend!" someone shouted. "Here comes another one!"

A second hymnal sailed the length of the sanctuary, aimed at the minister. This time he ducked, and the book hit the lady with all the ruffles. She let out a howl.

"I won't have this!" The man of God was screaming now. Screaming at Esther but keeping his attention out for any other book that might be flying his way. "I cannot have this! I must ask you to leave! You and your actor friend! This is *not* a theatre, sir! This is a place of worship!"

That's when the small stool, where sinners sat in shame before the congregation, jumped into the air. It rose to the rafters, pointed one end down, and then like a hawk aiming for a rodent, sped straight for the minister. Amid the noise of the collision, the thud of the body falling to the floor, the screams of the ladies, and the shouts of the men, Esther and Walt hurried up the aisle and out the doorway.

"Maybe," he said to her as they ran down the street toward home, "maybe that wasn't such a good idea after all."

Wednesday, July 16, 1879

It was Jennie who awakened them by pounding on the door. "Daniel! Olive! Come quick! It's Esther! I think she's dying!"

Daniel tumbled out of bed, struggled into his trousers, and not bothering with a suitcoat over his underwear, hurried into the girls' bedroom. Olive, wearing a light wrapper, was already there.

Jennie held the lamp. Esther was on the bed, her limbs horribly swollen, her skin stretched red.

"Oh, my God!" Daniel exclaimed. "Not this again! Please, God, not this again!"

The girl's face was as big and smooth as a full moon. Her large blue eyes, now small and half shut amid the puffed-up features, were filled with fear. Her breasts were swollen like melons; her belly as if she were nine months pregnant; her arms, legs, hands, and feet like hams. The lightweight summer nightdress stretched itself to almost bursting at the seams. There was a heat rising from her, a heat that could be felt by those at the foot of the bed. She struggled to speak, but the mouth was stretched so tightly, she couldn't form her words.

"What is it?" Hubbell ran into the room. "I'm sorry for the intrusion," he said, "but I heard the . . ." He stared at Esther. "Good God!"

Olive probably should have told him that he couldn't see Esther in bed, wearing only her nightgown, but she forgot propriety. Her little sister was suffering. Her health was more important than what people would think. "This has happened before," she told him. "Not recently, but it has happened before. It hurts her so, and it's so unfair!"

"Now, don't cry," Daniel ordered. "We don't need your tears."

"I'm not crying! She is! Do something!"

"What?" He raised his hands in an empty gesture. "What can I do?"

"Go and get the doctor," his wife replied. "Run and get the doctor. Tell him what's happening, and bring him back with you." He looked at her and then back at Esther. "*Now*, Daniel!" Olive barked. "Go now!"

Daniel, almost relieved to be able to leave the room, hurried down the stairs and out the front doorway.

Hubbell went closer to the bed. Stunned, he could see the grotesque features and the swollen limbs. "She's hot," he said. They nodded. He reached out and lightly touched her hand. "Very hot. She's got a terrible fever. What is it?"

Jennie and Olive shook their heads. "Don't know," the younger girl said. "She had this before, before you came. She gets in terrible pain. She can't control it."

Esther writhed atop the sheets, her young body filling the full-size bed. She stared at them, tried to make her lips and tongue work, tried to beg them to help her. Her swollen skin felt like it was going to split at any moment, split and tumble out her muscles and her blood and even her bones. The heat was incredible. It washed across her in waves, like the sun burning into the mud flats outside town. She was able to make out the figures standing around the bed. Why did they just *stand* there? Why didn't they *do* something? Why didn't they take care of her pain? Why didn't they kill her and take her out of her misery? She tried to say Olive's name, tried to make her swollen lips respond to the thoughts she was sending them. But they refused to obey, refused to form, refused to stop their incredible aching.

"Put another sheet over her," Olive told Jennie. "We can't have the doctor seeing her like this."

Walt was still in shock. He stared at the girl. He had never even heard of such a thing as he was seeing. "But why?" he asked aloud.

"Why?" Olive looked at him. "Why? Don't ask us, Mr. Hubbell. You are supposed to be the expert. Suppose you tell *us*. *Why* have these demons taken her over like this? *Why* can't you solve this mystery and then leave us all alone?"

"Olive!" Jennie put her hand on her sister's shoulder. "Olive, it's not *his* fault."

"Then whose? Whose?" she demanded. "God damn it, I demand to know whose?"

The laugh came from the body on the bed. It was deep and rough and very masculine. "Mine!" the voice said. Esther's lips still did not move. "Mine! It's my doing!"

Jennie screamed and clutched Olive. Walt began to shout: "Who are you? Who are you that's doing this dreadful thing?"

"Bob. That's me."

"Bob Nickle?" Walt shouted again.

"No, you fool. McNeal."

He looked at the two women. Neither of them spoke. "McNeal? Who is McNeal?" They shook their heads. He turned to the girl on the bed. "Who is Bob McNeal?" he demanded. "Why are you doing this?"

"He sent us," the voice growled. "We came from *him*!" Again the deep laugh.

Walt looked at the women. "I don't understand. Who is Bob McNeal?" he asked again, and again, they shook their heads.

Then Esther cried out. She had control of her mouth then, and her eyes and then her hands and feet as the swelling went down, receded as if someone had pulled the plug and let out all the water from a tub. In less than a minute, her body was reduced to normal size and the heat was gone. She reached toward Olive; then Esther's arm fell back and she was unconscious.

Olive kept putting a cloth dipped in cool water on Esther's forehead. She sat on the edge of the bed, touching her arms and hands, murmuring words of comfort.

Jennie had gone down to boil some water. She knew the doctor would want some when he got there. Walt followed her to the kitchen.

"Who is Bob McNeal?" he asked. "I never heard of him."

Jennie shook her head. "I really can't tell you," she said. "It's Esther's business. If she wants you to know, she'll tell you. I can't. I'm sorry."

"But it is someone she knew? Is he dead?"

Jennie didn't look at him as she waited for the water to boil. "Yes," she finally replied, "it's someone she knew."

"And he died."

"I don't know. He might be dead. If he is, we never heard about it."

"Was he a friend? A school chum, or what?" Hubbell was insistent. "I mean, where did she meet him? Was he a cousin or something?"

"I said I couldn't tell you," Jennie replied. "It's Esther's business. Not mine."

"But Jennie, if I'm supposed to help Esther, I have to know all the facts. I can't see the whole picture if there are pieces missing." He leaned against the doorjamb and folded his arms. "Tell me, who is this Bob McNeal?"

"He was a boy who lived in Amherst. He doesn't live here any longer. Esther was sweet on him for a while. That's all." She lifted the lid of the teakettle, wondering how much longer the water would take. "That's all."

"She was sweet on somebody who sounds like that?" He shuddered, remembering the voice that came out of Esther's unmoving lips.

"He didn't sound like that. Not when we knew him. He had a nice voice," Jennie said. "And he was nice-looking, too. Real nice-looking. All the girls thought so."

"And Esther was stuck on him." She nodded yes. "Were they going to be married?"

"It never got that far."

"How far did it get?"

She whirled on him. "Really, Mr. Hubbell, you ask very embarassing questions! You'll have to get your answers from Esther. Not from me."

He tried a little psychology. "So it went *that* far."

"No! My sister is a good girl! He wanted her to. He tried to force her, but she wouldn't."

"Doesn't sound very innocent to me." He didn't have to wait long for her reaction.

"My sister is an innocent girl! Bob had a gun. He threatened to shoot her if she didn't do what he wanted. He would have shot her, but someone came by and frightened him. So he drove her home, in the pouring rain. She thought she was in love with him. She never saw him after that night."

"Where'd he go?"

"Nobody knows. He left his job and left Amherst and never came back."

"Is he dead?"

"Mr. Hubbell, I am a Christian woman and try to keep Christian thoughts, but if Bob McNeal is the cause of all my sister's troubles, then I hope to God that, yes, he *is* dead!" She pushed past him, taking a basin of fresh water up the stairs. She stopped and turned. "If he is not dead, then God help him if anyone in this house should meet him on the street. We would gladly kill him!"

Walt was still leaning against the kitchen doorjamb, trying to put all this into perspective, when Daniel returned with Dr. Carritte. There was another man with them, an Arthur Davison, who worked for the county courts. Daniel stopped briefly to introduce the American, then all three hurried up to Esther's room. Hubbell followed.

"She's still asleep," Olive told the doctor. "It was just like the other time. She swelled up real big, her skin got real hot, and then suddenly she deflated and fell asleep."

"Daniel told me some of that coming over," he said. He sat on the edge of the bed, opened his bag, and took out a stethoscope. After listening for a minute or so, he pronounced her heartbeat regular and her pulse normal. "I was afraid she was dying," he said. "It's a good thing she's as strong and healthy as she is. Someone weaker might not be able to take it."

"Whatever it was has passed," Olive said. "Do you have

something you can give her, Doctor? Something so it won't come back?"

"I wish I did," he answered. "I surely wish I did."

"She said Bob McNeal's name," Olive told her husband. "In a low and terrible voice. It wasn't her voice at all."

"Bob McNeal?" Mr. Davidson spoke up. "Whatever happened to him? Didn't he used to work with you at the shoe factory?"

Daniel nodded. "He did. But he doesn't anymore. Hasn't since last August. Almost a year ago."

"Why would she mention *his* name?" Davison asked. "Sick and all, the way she is."

Hubbell saw Daniel color slightly. "I really don't know, sir," he said. "I don't see the connection." He looked quickly at Olive and Jennie. Their faces were blank.

"Strange," said Davison.

"Very," said Hubbell.

The doctor got up and walked to where Daniel and Olive were standing. "I'd like a word with you two, in private, if I could." They nodded and followed him from the room. He stopped at the top of the stairs and ran his hands along the shining wood of the bannister. He took a deep breath and tried to sound professional. "I'm very concerned about Esther. And about the two of you. If she keeps having these things, it might kill her. I don't seem to be able to do anything. I don't know any more now about what ails her than I knew ten months ago. And she's gotten worse."

"Worse? How can you say that?" Olive asked.

"Not so much physically as mentally. Oh, yes, I know that attacks like this one tonight are rare, but what about all the other things that happen to her, around her? The lighted matches that fall from nowhere. The poundings on the walls. The other day in church. What about those things?"

"They really don't *hurt* anybody," Daniel said.

"No, but they hurt Esther. They hurt her inside. I don't know too much about the mind, but I do know it can affect the body. All these things *have* to affect her physically. And that's not good. It may just pile up in there and one day it'll snap like India rubber and you all could be hurt. Esther will hurt herself, but she might hurt all of you first." He paused and looked at them in the darkened hallway. The only light was coming from the oil lamp in Esther's room. "She might hurt all of you *first*," he repeated.

"Are you saying Esther is dangerous?" Olive didn't want to believe what she had heard.

"Possibly," he replied. "Unstable people can be very dangerous—suddenly."

"You're saying she's crazy," Olive said.

"Not crazy. Not yet. Only possibly."

In the silence, his words sunk in quickly. "You think we should have her committed," Daniel finally said the words. "Put her away. In some crazy house."

"It might be a precaution. It might become necessary."

"But she's my sister." Olive felt herself on the verge of tears. "I can't do that to my sister."

"She may be your sister," the doctor replied, "but have you forgotten you have two children? Two small children under the same roof with her? Have you thought of them?"

Olive swayed and leaned back into Daniel's firm embrace. "I never thought it would come to this," she said in a small voice. "Not Esther. Esther never harmed anyone. Not my Esther." She fought to control the tears that she knew were just at the rim of her eyelids. "Not my little sister. We're all she's got. We could never lock her up."

"You might have to. She is becoming dangerous to herself and to others around her. It's not a case of what you want to do, it's a case of what's best for the girl."

"Do you think she's crazy?" Daniel asked.

The doctor shook his head. "I don't know. I really don't know. She would have to be examined by mental doctors. I'm only a physical doctor. I work with the body, and everything I've done so far has been useless. Perhaps a mental doctor would be better for her. I just don't know." He smiled. "I'm sorry there is so little I can do for her. So little."

"Where would she be put?" Olive asked. "Is there a place around here?"

"There is in Halifax. I think we could get her in there. Once she's there, at least, she'd have continual care. The staff would be there around the clock. Here, with only you and Jennie to care for her, there is no way she can be properly treated." He touched Olive lightly on the shoulder. "I'm sorry, my dear. Please believe how sorry I am."

They walked to the bedside. Hubbell, Jennie, and Mr. Davison were there, watching the sleeping girl.

"I asked Arthur here," Dr. Carritte said, "to come along tonight so he could see her condition. He's at the courthouse. He can help you when the time comes."

Olive nodded.

"When the time comes for what?" Jennie asked.

"If Esther gets worse," Daniel said.

Hubbell looked at them, trying to read what was on their minds. "Why do you need a clerk of the court?" he asked.

"For the legal papers," the doctor replied. "He knows which ones to fill out."

"She needs competent medical help," the actor insisted, "not a lawyer! Just look at her."

"My dear sir," said the doctor, "if she doesn't get help of some kind, she will only need the services of an undertaker." He went to the bed and checked the girl's pulse. "We've gone as far as we can go with her in Amherst. She needs other care . . . somewhere else."

"You'll send her away?" Jennie's voice rose.

"If necessary," the doctor replied.

"To a hospital?"

"Of sorts."

"To a *mental* hospital?" Hubbell asked. "To a crazy house?"

"If necessary."

"Who decides?" the actor asked.

"Another medical man. A mental doctor."

"She's not crazy."

"Sir, you are not a doctor."

"No, but I have watched her and studied her. A person is judged crazy by what happens *inside* them. Esther's manifestations have all happened *outside*. Outside her body. Not in her mind. Flying chairs and loud poundings and floating sugar bowl lids are *outside* things."

"You are not a doctor"—this from Arthur Davison.

"No, I'm not. But I've been around long enough to know when somebody is doing something and when somebody is having things done to them. Esther is on the getting end of all this, not the giving end." Walt was angry. Angry with small minds and quick solutions. "I came here to prove that this girl was a fraud. I was sure I could uncover her hoax. Well, she is not a fraud. She is real. What happens around here is real. What happens *to* her is real. There is no stage trick that could make her body swell up like it did tonight. There were no mirrors on the stairs to make it look like the scissors were floating. She didn't have time to rig up the whole damned church to make those hymnbooks fly! She doesn't need locks and keys, she needs understanding. For Christ sake, can't anyone in this burg understand that? At least *try* to understand that?"

Olive reached out and put her hand on Hubbell's shoulder. "You've changed," she said. "I'm glad. Thank you."

"Mr. Teed, good evening and please excuse my coming right in." They turned, startled at the new voice. Judge Bliss stood in the bedroom doorway. "I knocked, but everyone was up here. The front door was ajar." He paused. "I came to see for myself."

"See what?" Daniel asked.

"What was happening to my house tonight. I saw the doctor's carriage outside."

"Nothing is happening to your precious house"—Olive really disliked this man—"it's happening to Esther."

"More fires?" He walked quickly into the room, sniffing the air. "I told you, Daniel, I won't have any more fires."

"There have been no fires," Daniel replied. "Esther is ill. She had another—"

"Fit," said Mr. Davison. "Esther had another fit."

"It was not a fit!" Hubbell said loudly.

"Call it what you will," Davison said.

"She was ill and we called the doctor," Olive added. "That's normal."

"Nothing's normal when that girl's around," the judge replied. "I can't have her destroying my house."

"Look at her, for God's sake!" Hubbell grabbed the little man by his arm and shoved him toward the bed. "Does that unconscious girl look like she is harming your house?"

"Mr. Hubbell!" Daniel didn't want any trouble. He knew how to deal with his landlord; this American didn't.

"She's passed out cold because of the things that are happening to her. To *her*, not to your property, this house, this pile of old wood that should be torn down anyway!"

"Mr. Hubbell!" Daniel's voice was loud. "I must insist that

you refrain from actions such as these! You are a guest in my home. Please comport yourself accordingly."

"I'm sure Mr. Hubbell didn't mean—" Olive started to say.

"Oh, yes, I did. I meant every word of it. This is what I meant by no understanding of Esther's real problem. This man doesn't give a damn about *her*. All he cares about is this miserable rental property."

"I assure you that Judge Bliss—" Davison began.

"You can't assure me about anything!" the American shouted over him. "His bank balance is his main concern, and your job in his court is *your* main concern! If this doctor really was on Esther's side, he would throw both of you out of here for taking up valuable oxygen that she needs to breathe!"

"Mr. Hubbell! That's enough!" Daniel's face was red with anger.

Walt paused, then sighed. "I'm sorry. I forgot my place. You have to live with these people in this town, I don't. You have to kowtow to them, I don't. I just hope to God that after I'm gone there is someone in Amherst strong enough to defend this child. She can't battle the medical profession, court clerks, and judges all by herself." He walked toward the door, turned, swept off an imaginary hat, made a deep theatrical bow, and put the hat back on his head. "Learned gentlemen, good-bye and good luck."

Davison broke the silence after Walt had gone. "What an unusual man."

"I've heard about him," the judge said. "None of it good."

"I really must apologize for my houseguest," Daniel said. "He didn't know what he was saying."

"I think he did, Daniel." Olive had a faint smile on her lips. "I think he knew exactly what he was saying."

The bedsprings creaked. Because of Hubbell's exit, they had momentarily forgotten the sleeping girl. The springs groaned. The bed shook. The springs groaned again.

"That looks like . . ." said the judge slowly ". . . like someone else is in there with her!" His eyes were wide and unblinking.

"There is!" Davison pointed. "Look! Under the sheet! Like a body!"

"Like a man's body," the judge added.

"Who could be . . . I don't understand. . . ."

"The lines of a back . . . and the legs . . . and the rear. Look at the rear end!" Judge Bliss was frightened, yet fascinated. "Look at that! Under the sheet!"

The bed creaked again, then again. Then the mattress started rising and falling, rising and falling as the headless form under the sheet pushed down on Esther and then rose up. The girl, awake now, started beating at the form with her fists. She cried in pain. The sheet rose and fell faster.

"Stop him, for God's sake!" Olive screamed.

Daniel and Dr. Carritte both lunged at the form. They grabbed the sheet. It deflated. They pulled the sheet from the bed and threw it against the wall. The movement of the bed ceased immediately. Esther closed her eyes while the tears ran down her face. There was no movement. Whatever it had been had ceased.

"I think you had better leave," the doctor said. "All of you. I need some time alone with my patient."

No one spoke as they went down the stairs. The court clerk and the judge were trying to make sense of what they had just seen. It looked like Esther was getting . . . but there was nobody under the . . . how could a man with no head make a sheet rise and . . .

The first flaming match fell directly in front of Judge Bliss. He reacted as if it were a snake. Daniel stomped it out with his foot.

The second flaming match landing on the judge's coat sleeve. He brushed it off in horror.

The third touched the judge's hand, and there was the odor of singed hair for just a second in the hallway.

The fourth was caught in mid-air by Mr. Davison.

The fifth Daniel grabbed.

The judge sidestepped the sixth, putting it out with his boot.

Then a shower of lighted matches fell on the group. They brushed and scrambled and stomped and managed to get them all.

The judge hurried toward the front door, his eyes searching the darkened hallway for more falling fires. "She's got to go, Daniel Teed. That girl is dangerous to life and property. And she's"—he searched for a word to describe what he just saw—". . . she's *immoral.* I can't have immoral women in my houses. Can't have fires, either. Get her out of here. Tomorrow or Friday by the latest! But I want her *out.*"

Thursday, July 17, 1879

"The Van Amburghs have agreed." Daniel told Olive and Jennie as he came into the kitchen. He was perspiring, for even though it was only a little after 8:00 A.M., the sun had already started heating up the land and the waters of the marshes. He had ridden out to the Van Amburgh farm, found them just as they were having their breakfast, and got them to agree to take Esther in with them. She had spent two months with them this past spring and they had treated her like a daughter. There had been no manifestations there. Esther's ghosts had not followed her to their place. Of course they would be glad to have her again. Esther was a good worker, she could help with the canning. August would soon be here and the tomatoes and beans, beets and peas would need canning. Of course she was welcome, and tell her that her old room is waiting.

Esther didn't get out of bed until almost noon. The sedative Dr. Carritte had given her knocked her out, and she slept soundly. When they heard her stirring, both Olive and Jennie went into her bedroom and closed the door. Jennie didn't go to work that day. Her sister needed her more.

They sat on the edge of the bed and told her what had happened last night. She remembered most of it, had tried to block out part of it, felt ashamed for all of it. She hadn't been aware that Judge Bliss had been there. She was afraid of him. She didn't want important people like the judge to see her lying in bed. She waited for her sisters to tell her about Bob Nickle and what he had done—again—to her body. She waited to hear their impressions of how he lay heavy and stinking and hard against her. Did they know what pain he caused her? Could they know how she ached this morning down between her legs? Did Olive go through such pain every time she and Daniel were together? Someone said that was how babies were made. If so, then poor Olive had had that terrible thing done to her at least twice.

They didn't mention that part. They did, however, tell her of the falling matches and of the landlord's demand. Her eyes grew wide; then she closed them and shook her head. It was becoming too much. It was becoming more than she could bear. "If Bob Nickle wants to kill me, why doesn't he go ahead and do it? Get it over with."

Jennie took her hand. "Now, don't cry."

"I'm not crying. There's no sense in crying. It does nothing. I just feel empty, like an old bottle that's been all poured out and then thrown onto the trash heap."

"Now, don't talk like that." Olive took her other hand. "You have a lot of life left in you and many years ahead. But you understand, darling, we do have to do as the judge said." Esther nodded her head. "If we don't, then the entire family has got to get out. And where would we go? There aren't many houses available in Amherst. We were lucky to get this one."

"I know," the girl replied.

"And we'd have to find a place with at least three bedrooms and a yard for the boys to play in. Fenced in like this one so they wouldn't get run over by the horses and wagons."

"I know," she said.

"And"—Olive hesitated—"it would, in truth, dear, be quite difficult for us to find a place where they would agree to take *you*. I don't mean to sound cruel and don't mean to sound as if we don't want you to stay with us, but people around here are strange. They just wouldn't rent to us if they knew you were moving in, too." Olive sighed. How difficult all this was.

"I know all that," the girl said.

"So Daniel went this morning and talked with the Van Amburghs. They want you to come and live with them. For a while."

"Esther looked at Olive. "How long is 'for a while'?"

Her sister reddened slightly. "Until . . . until whatever it is that is causing all this goes away. Until your ghosts let you go."

Esther's eyes were dry. "That'll be never. They'll never let me go. They'll kill me first."

"Nonsense." Jennie squeezed her hand. "It'll be over soon. You'll see. One day they'll just get tired and they'll go bother someone else and you'll be back with us." She forced a smile. "You'll see."

Esther shook her head. "One day they'll kill me. One day the butcher knife won't stop just at my skin. It'll go deep. They'll cut my throat, and that's how my body will be found. Then I'll join them. Then I'll join the group. Then I'll be a ghost and I'll run with the pack and be just like them. That's what they want. They want me off this side and over onto *their* side." She closed her eyes and lay very still for a while. Then she sighed deeply and looked at her sisters. "Oh, well. What's to be is to be. Let me get up and get washed and dressed. I'll pack my bags myself. Tell Daniel I should be ready in an hour."

They tried to be casual around the table, tried to think of funny things to comment on, light chatter while the girl drank a little coffee and ate a bit of toast. Olive and Jennie fussed at her, asking if she remembered to pack this item and if she wasn't going to take that item. The two small boys played around her feet under the table, unaware that their Aunt Esther was going away for good.

Hubbell didn't come downstairs. He was awake, had been since sunrise, but had stayed in his room. This parting was a family matter. He had upset the head of this family last night, had worn out his welcome with Mr. Teed. It would be best to stay away from this family leave-taking. He'd go out to the farm before he went back to New York, he'd see Esther before he left.

There were embraces and kisses and promises to see one another every chance they got. Two suitcases were carried to the buggy, and Olive had to get both boys down from the seat and firmly tell them they couldn't go with their father and Aunt Esther. When the horse finally pulled away from the picket fence, both Olive's and Jennie's faces were streaming with tears. Esther's was dry. As she had said, "There's no sense in crying."

Olive ran alongside the buggy as it headed toward Havelock Street. She reached up to touch her sister one more time. "You remember, now. Whatever happens, we're here. Remember. This is your home."

"No, Olive," Esther said unsmilingly, "this is not my home. I don't have a home anymore. I'll never be back here."

Friday, August 1, 1879

She looked up from her work, shielded the sunlight from her eyes, and watched the carriage as it came up the long driveway. She stood up, pushing the basket with the patchwork pieces aside. Mrs. Van Amburgh had gone to town, and Mr. Van Amburgh was selling a cow to a neighbor. Then she smiled as she saw him wave.

"Esther!" he called before he had fully stopped the horse.

"Mr. Hubbell! How nice to see you. How good of you to come." She hadn't seen anyone from the house on Princess

Street for two weeks. She had tried not to think about that place, tried to imagine it not being there. She had spent the past fourteen days reminding herself that she was an orphan, no relatives and no future. Now here—suddenly—was the American. He had never really understood her, yet his attitude had changed. He had gone from skeptic to friend, from being a famous actor to just folks.

He jumped down from the seat, wanting to embrace her yet going no farther than shaking her hand. "Olive sent you some clothes and a batch of oatmeal cookies."

"How is she? And the boys? How are the boys?"

"They're fine. Everybody's just fine. They all miss you." He looked around the backyard of the farmhouse. "This is quite a place."

"Oh, yes. It's a large farm. It stretches that way to those tall trees and over that way to the fenceposts. You can breathe here," she said. "It's not like being in town at all."

"Are you happy?" he asked.

She shrugged. "I suppose so. I get lots to eat, and the Van Amburghs gave me a large bedroom all to myself. They even have a player piano in the parlor. You put on a roll of paper that has holes in it and the piano plays all by itself. It's just like"—she stopped, her smile turning to a frown—"like my ghosts," she said finally. "Just like my ghosts."

"Are they here? Did they follow you?" He really wanted to know because he didn't want any of them following him. Especially Mattie.

She shook her head. "I haven't seen them."

"Not in the whole two weeks?"

"No, there's not been one thing out of place nor poundings nor nothing. I think they're gone. At least I hope they're gone."

"I hope so, too."

"I'm going to wait till the end of the year, and if they stay gone till then, I'll go back to Daniel's and Olive's and spend Christmas with them. Then I'll move somewhere and get employment. I've talked about it with the Van Amburghs, and they say I can stay here as long as I like, but I think till Christmas is long enough. I'm nineteen years old. It's time I was on my own."

They walked together across the lush grass of the backyard. Large shade trees blocked out the August sunlight, and over beside the house, zinnias and hollyhocks flowered. "Come on in," she said. "I was thinking to make some lemonade before you came. Would you like some?" He smiled and nodded his head. They went up three stone steps and into a large kitchen, at least four times bigger than the kitchen on Princess Street. He leaned against the wall and watched her as she sliced the lemons, added the sugar, filled the pitcher with water, and chopped a few chunks of ice from the block in the top of the icebox. "Here," she said, handing him a large and chilly glass, "wet your whistle."

"You seem happy here." He sipped the tart liquid.

"I guess so," she said. "It's not like being with my own kin, but they treat me well. I feel more like a relative than a stranger. And the ghosts aren't here."

"They're not at Daniel's, either," he said.

She smiled. "I was afraid to ask you that. I was afraid they had stayed behind. To bother everyone even though I was gone. I'm glad," she said. "Now maybe Olive will get some peace."

"I came to say good-bye." He looked at her over the rim of his glass. "I'm leaving for St. John tonight. There's a new theatrical company being formed, and they've asked me to become part of it. We're going to play other provinces, hopefully all the way to Toronto. I'm looking forward to it."

"That's nice." She turned and chopped a few slivers from the block of ice. She wanted to say, "You, too. You're abandoning me, too." But she didn't. Instead, she turned to him and said, "We all knew you had to leave sooner or later. I'll miss you."

"And I'll miss you." He held out his glass as she dropped the ice into it. "You know, I thought I knew it all when I first came to Amherst. I didn't think there was anything anyone could teach me. I was wrong and I admit it. I learned from you." She made a face and a gesture that meant "get away with you," but his comment pleased her. "I saw things around you that have no explanation. You weren't hoaxing people. There was no way you could."

"There was no reason for me to."

"No. There wasn't. I didn't understand that when I first heard about you. I supposed you were out for fame or money or whatever. I'd been with theatre people and stage magicians for so long that I thought everything was a carnival con. I treated you unfairly," he said. "On the tour, especially. I shouldn't have done that to you. I know that now."

"What did it hurt?" she asked. "It wasn't pleasant at the time, but it's over. Nobody really suffered from it. And I did get to ride on a train and eat in nice restaurants. I never stayed in a hotel before. I gained from it, too. It wasn't all one-sided."

"I also learned about injustice," he continued. "The injustice the people have done to you. Your friends, your neighbors, even ministers of the gospel. They've treated you unfairly."

"They didn't know any better," she replied. "They didn't know what was really happening. All they saw and heard was strange to them. I've had time here to do a lot of thinking, and I guess it's natural to be afraid of something you don't understand. Folks can't deal with things that scare them, and they get scared because they don't understand." She watched his face, then she laughed. "I figured that out all by myself. People think I'm dumb, but I can figure things. If they let me alone and give me some peace, I can figure out almost everything."

"I'll be truthful in the book," he said. "I won't add things that didn't happen or embroider things that did. I promise."

"I appreciate that," she said softly. "I know you'll make it a good book, and maybe people who read it will understand a little more about me and what's been happening to me." Then she laughed again. "You'd better make it a good book, because someday I'll learn to read good and then I'll see for myself exactly what you said about me!"

He laughed. "I promise." The wall clock chimed three quarters. "I've got to get back," he said. "The train leaves in a couple of hours."

They walked back to the waiting horse and buggy. She stretched out her hand; he took it and held it. Suddenly he didn't want to leave, didn't want to abandon this little girl who had suffered so much and had been hurt by so many. "I . . ." he started to say; then he reached out and brought her to him in a long and emotional embrace. They stood there, arms around each other, two people from two different worlds, touching at last for the first—and the last—time.

should [illegible] have come that to you. I know that [illegible]
"[illegible] like it?" [illegible] asked. "I would [illegible] at the [illegible] out of sight. Nobody [illegible] [illegible] I [illegible] get my [illegible] and [illegible] [illegible]. [illegible] and [illegible] [illegible] [illegible] [illegible] [illegible]

[illegible] [illegible] [illegible] [illegible] [illegible] [illegible] [illegible] [illegible] [illegible] [illegible] [illegible] [illegible] [illegible] [illegible] [illegible] [illegible] of [illegible] [illegible]. They've [illegible] you [illegible].

[illegible] didn't know [illegible] better," she replied. "They didn't know what was really happening. All they [illegible] [illegible] [illegible] [illegible] [illegible] [illegible] here to [illegible] [illegible] [illegible] [illegible], and [illegible] [illegible] [illegible] [illegible] of something you don't understand, [illegible] [illegible] with things that scare them and [illegible] [illegible] [illegible] understand." She watched [illegible] [illegible] [illegible] [illegible] [illegible] [illegible] [illegible] [illegible] [illegible]. People [illegible] [illegible] [illegible] I [illegible] [illegible] [illegible] [illegible] [illegible] done and [illegible] [illegible] [illegible] [illegible] [illegible] [illegible] [illegible] [illegible] [illegible].

[illegible] [illegible] [illegible] at the [illegible] [illegible] [illegible] [illegible] [illegible] [illegible] [illegible] [illegible] understand things that [illegible] I [illegible].

"I appreciate that," she said [illegible]. "[illegible] you [illegible] [illegible] [illegible] and maybe people who [illegible] you [illegible] [illegible] me."

He [illegible] [illegible] [illegible]. The [illegible] [illegible] [illegible] [illegible] [illegible] [illegible] [illegible] [illegible] [illegible] [illegible] [illegible] [illegible] [illegible] [illegible] [illegible]

[illegible] walked back to the [illegible] [illegible] and [illegible]. She [illegible] [illegible] [illegible] [illegible] [illegible] [illegible] [illegible] [illegible] [illegible] [illegible] [illegible] [illegible] [illegible] [illegible] [illegible] [illegible] [illegible] this [illegible]. They [illegible] [illegible] [illegible] [illegible] [illegible] [illegible] people [illegible] [illegible] [illegible] [illegible] [illegible] [illegible] [illegible] [illegible] [illegible] [illegible] [illegible]

PART FOUR

Sunday, August 24, 1879

It was one of those wonderful almost-end-of-summer days, and Esther stretched out on the lush green grass under the maple tree. The Van Amburghs had gone to a family reunion. They had left before the sun was up, the buggy loaded with food and children and expectations. Esther had helped Mrs. Van Amburgh make two kinds of potato salad, two kinds of baked beans, and three different fruit pies. Esther had washed, starched, and ironed the little girl's dress and two shirts for the little boy. He almost always got one shirt dirty before dinnertime. They were gone, and Esther had the entire farm all to herself. Acres and acres of it. Space and time and peace and quiet. The Van Ambrughs were wonderful to her—as good as Olive and Daniel had been—and loved her. She did the work they asked her to do, and then when she was finished they let her alone, they allowed her to have her own thoughts. The two children were no problem, and Esther would go into her large bedroom and relax and think.

This freedom tasted good. It was good to be away from the ghosts again, good that they had not followed her to this farm. For some reason, just like the time before, they stayed away. She imagined them off in the woods, peering out between the large trees and shouting, "Curses, foiled again!" just like villains in dime novels. They couldn't reach her. They didn't seem to be trying. That was good. That was *really* good.

She had been there a little over a month. The month had gone quickly, she thought. She really didn't miss the house on Princess Street. Oh, it came to her mind often, but she didn't miss it—didn't pine to be back in it. It had never really been *home;* it had been a shelter. Olive had taken her there after she married Daniel, and Daniel—bless him—had put up with her right from the very start of his marriage. But it had never been *her* home. It was the Teed home, and she was not a Teed. She was Esther Cox—whatever and whoever *that* was. Like every other teenager, she didn't know who she was or what she was, and when the ghosts started doing those awful things to her, it confused her all the more. While other girls of her age were worrying about boyfriends or employment, she was worrying about demons and preachers and doctors and newspapers and fires and hatred and fear and scorn and abuse and Bob McNeal. Bob McNeal. She hadn't thought about him in ages. She shuddered in the warm sunlight and rolled over onto her side, staring at the broad expanse of fields that were high with corn and climbing tomatoes and pole beans.

That's when she saw the rider slow his horse and turn it into the Van Amburgh drive. She sat up, shielded the sun from her eyes, and squinted to get a better look. It was a man. She got to her feet, smoothing her long skirt and pushing back her hair. "Now, what does *he* want?" she said aloud as she watched the horse come closer up the drive.

"Miss Cox?" the man called.

She frowned. "Yes," she called in return.

"Good afternoon," he called again.

"And to you, sir," she said. She stood watching him, her hands on her hips, as he came closer and then stopped his horse.

"Hello." He looked down at her and smiled.

"Hello," she returned.

His smile grew broader. "You don't remember me, do you?"

She looked into his face. It was a handsome face, white skin, square-jawed, needing a shave, and then those blue eyes . . . those blue eyes looked strangely familiar.

He laughed and to save her more embarrassment said: "Adam Porter. We met when you were employed at White's Oyster Saloon. The waiter, Chip, introduced us." He paused. "Now do you recall?"

"Of course!" she said quickly. Those blue eyes, how could she forget them? "Of course I do!"

"I only talked to you for a minute. It wasn't one of your better days."

"None of those days were that good." She smiled and extended her hand. He slid from the saddle, landed easily on his feet, took her hand in his, and held it just a bit longer than she thought he should have. "How nice to see you again," she said, taking her hand back. "What a pleasant surprise."

"Well, I heard you were living out here now, and as I was going by I thought I'd stop by and do the neighborly thing. They don't mind, do they?"

"They?"

"The people you're working for. They aren't going to fuss if I stop and say hello?"

"Oh, no, they're wonderful folks. It's a pleasure to be their hired girl. Besides, they aren't at home today. The whole family went to a reunion over near Springhill." As soon as she said it, she wished she had bitten her tongue instead. Why tell this stranger she was all alone? What a silly thing to have done. Yet . . . how blue his eyes were! "Anyway," she added, "they give me Sunday afternoons off, whether they are here or not."

"Well, I'm glad I'm not causing you no trouble." Again that smile.

"You're not. Please feel welcome." She didn't know what to do with her hands. There were no pockets in this skirt. Did she clench them in front of her? Put them behind her? Fold them around her middle? Put them in her hair? Reach up and let them touch that strong masculine face? "Please," she said, and gestured to the front porch, turning so that he couldn't see how red her face had become at her own thoughts. "We could sit up there for a spell. Out of the sun and all."

He followed her across the lawn and up onto the large wooden porch. An oak-slatted swing, painted green and with a seat and back padding sewn from multicolored cloth, hung on link chains between two large potted palms. The pots had been in the parlor all winter, and Esther had moved them onto the porch for the summer. They thrived on the fresh air and warmth even though Mr. Van Amburgh joked that it made his front porch look like "that fancy house where Arabs keep all their women. You know, a harlem."

Esther sat at the far end of the swing and he, thankfully, sat at the other end. She let him start the rocking motion, watching as his boot-clad heels pushed against the scatter rug on the floor, sending the swing backward. On its return, his heels pushed again, and by the third push the swing was swaying easily in the warm August air.

"Hear from Chip?" he asked.

"No," she said, "I haven't seen him since I quit there before Christmas. I . . . I just never wanted to go back there." She sighed. "Too much happened."

"I know. I heard about some of it. Too bad you had to quit. Everyone there really liked you. Mr. Crowe the bartender, Chip, everyone."

She smiled at him. "That's good to hear. The way I carried on like some looney bird it's a wonder they weren't delighted when I left. I can't talk badly about the people who worked there. What happened to me was awful, but Chip and the others, they were real kind. They all treated me real nice."

"Chip got married."

"Oh?"

"To some girl in Moncton named Angela. He moved over there. Her father has some sort of mercantile business."

"I hope he's happy," she said. "I really do."

"Yep. Old Chip got married. Really did. Just up and *married.*" He glanced at her. "Claims his whole life has come together now that he's married. I guess that marriage is a wonderful thing."

"For some," she said.

"Well, it sure is for Chip. Just changed him around completely. He comes home at nights on time and doesn't carouse with the boys and talks about a family and insurance and going to church and all those things."

"I'm happy for him," she said.

"Yep. He says marriage is something he thinks everybody ought to do at least once."

"That sounds like Chip."

"He says it's not natural for a person to remain alone, to stay single and never get married. Chips says it says that in the Bible, too."

She looked at him. "Chip is quoting the Bible now?"

"Ever since he got married he's been studying religion. Married life is really good for him."

A light began to go on somewhere in the back of Esther's mind. "Mr. Porter, you are a married man, aren't you?"

"No, I'm single."

"But . . . I seem to recall you telling me that day in the saloon that you had two children. And that they were living with your mother."

"That's correct. You have a good memory. I also told you that I was a widower. My wife died of diphtheria. No, Miss Cox, I'm a single person. A very single person."

"It's difficult to be *very* single with two children, sir."

"Well, they're perfect tots," he said. "You'll see when you meet them." She ignored that, didn't bat an eyelash at it. "Of course, as long as I have my two babies to care for, I'll never be *single* single, but I don't have a wife, and so I'm single as far as the law is concerned." He looked directly at her. "And I'm single in my heart. That's where it's important."

Esther's feet touched the floor, stopping the swing. She rose quickly and hurried toward the front door. "Would you like some ice water?" she asked without looking at him. He didn't have time to answer. "I'll be out with it in a minute." She closed the door behind her. As she hurried down the corridor to the kitchen, she noticed how difficult it was to move her feet. They seemed to be attached to someone else's ankles, not hers. Her hands, those hands she knew so well, were shaking. "I swear," she said aloud as she opened the icebox, "if that don't beat all! Coming over here and telling me about his motherless babies! As if I needed *that.* As if I don't have enough commotion in my life but what I'd want to take on some man's ready-made family." Her hands shook as she poured the cold water into the tumblers. "If he had kept that up for another minute, I don't know what I would have done. I might have found myself agreeing to seeing those young ones of his! Imagine! Just because Chip went off and got married is no reason for him to think that he can come over here while I'm alone and ask me to . . . to . . ." She stopped. "He didn't ask me anything, did he?" She paused, trying to recall his exact words. "All he did was tell me about his being single. That's all." She shook her head and smoothed her skirts and put the two water tumblers on a tray. As she headed back toward the front porch, she paused and looked into the hall mirror. "You silly goose," she told her reflection, "he just came for a visit. He just happened to be passing by the farm, that's all. It's just a visit and all he's doing is getting acquainted. That's all." She was almost at the door. "He'd better stay on his end of the swing. The Van Amburghs don't want any hanky-panky on their front porch." He was still there, waiting her return. She handed him the cold tumbler and looked straight into his eyes. "They are blue!" she said aloud.

"What?"

She turned bright red. "The tumblers," she stammered, "they're *new.* Be careful with them." She plopped down on the other end of the swing and sipped her ice water, keeping her head turned away from him most of the time.

He talked about his profession. He was a farmer. He hadn't always lived in Nova Scotia. Once he had gone into Quebec Province and worked as a miner. Iron ore it was, but he didn't like that. He preferred to plant things so the ground could reproduce them, not tear it from the earth with a shovel and dynamite. He owned the farm he lived on. Actually, it had been his father's farm, and his father had inherited it when he married Adam's mother. She was still alive, living on the farm and complaining of several illnesses all at once. The farm was over near Port Philip, some twenty-five miles from Amherst.

"And your . . . wife . . . she was a local girl?" Esther asked.

"No, I met her in Quebec. The two babies were born in Quebec. Then when she died I couldn't work and take care of them by myself, so I came back to the farm. My babies need a mother."

"They have their grandmother," she said cooly.

"That's not the same thing as having a mother."

"But it'll do."

"It'll do until I find the right woman. It'll have to do. I'll take care of things till then. I have to. The farm is going well. We always have enough to eat, and I'm still strong and young."

She stole a glance at the well-muscled legs that were encased in the tan trousers. Then upward to the masculine hands and the forearms and the biceps that showed up to where he had rolled his shirt sleeves. She had to admit, he *was* strong. But how old was he? She didn't want some infant who still clung to Mama, yet she didn't want an old codger, either.

"I'm still young. I've just turned thirty-three. I've got a lot of fight and life left in me yet." He reached out and gently pushed a lock of her hair from her forehead. She waited for the lock to sizzle and burst into flame. "I thought about you ever since I saw you at White's. I asked Chip to introduce us. I had been there a couple of times before, but you didn't notice me. I was there the day the chairs piled up by themselves."

She felt a chill run down her back. "And you still wanted to meet me? After that?"

"Sure. Why not? I thought you were pretty."

"Standing there screaming the way I did that day?"

"It wasn't your fault." The lock had fallen and he pushed it away again. "It wasn't your fault," he repeated.

She stared at him. "You don't think so?" He shook his head. "You don't fault me for those crazy things that happened?" Again he shook his head. "Didn't what happened frighten you?" she asked. "Didn't it make you wonder?"

"Oh, it made me wonder, but it didn't scare me. I don't scare easily. I've been through too much to be scared by things I can't account for. If a thing doesn't touch me personally, I don't pay it no mind. I can't get scared by ghosts or whatever they say you had with you. There are too many problems on *this* side of life to be worried about what some ghost might do. Dead people don't bother me. The ones that are alive trouble me more." He laughed, and she smiled at him. "I've learned to cope with problems as they arise, not run from them in fear. My old man died and left me and my mother to manage the farm by ourselves. Then I went off and got a job deep in the ground where there was no light or air and saw chaps working next to me drop dead from fumes or get crushed by slides. Then my wife died on me. She got a cold on Sunday, was feverish on Monday, couldn't breathe on Tuesday, and was dead on Wednesday. That's how fast it happened. That's how fast my life changed."

"Mine changed fast, too," she said. "One night I'm normal and living calmly with my sister's family and the next night the house is shaking, my body is all swelled up, and my life is threatened. You have adapted to your changes," she said. "I haven't."

"Why haven't you?"

"Because the changes aren't over. When your father died and when you left the mine and when your wife died, those things were over. They'd happened. Taken place. My ghosts aren't finished with me yet. I haven't seen them since I came to this farm, but I sense them. I sense they are out there just waiting for a moment to start in on me again." She reached out and put her hand on his wrist. Fashion said a young girl didn't do such a thing, but she needed to touch him, needed to absorb some of his strength. "I can only adapt to these changes one day at a time. Today is Sunday and I can adapt to what's happening now. Tomorrow is Monday. Twenty-four completely unknown hours. I have no idea what will happen tomorrow. Maybe nothing. Or maybe they'll kill me."

He looked at her for a while before he spoke. "You don't appear upset about it," he said. "You're taking it all very calmly."

"I'm past the stage of emotion about it all," she replied flatly. "I had months of tears and screaming and terror. That's all over. It didn't do any good. I asked people to help me. I *expected* people to help me, yet no one did anything."

"Why?"

"Because there was nothing they could do. Doctors, preachers, family. Even an actor from America; they all tried and failed. So I have to go it alone."

"You have me now," he said.

"No. No, I haven't." She rose quickly from the swing and walked down the steps onto the front lawn. If she stayed beside him another moment, she might do something foolish, like touching those blue eyes with her lips. "No. I haven't you nor anyone. What I have must be faced alone. I will not permit you to become involved, Mr. Porter. I've involved far too many as it is."

"But what I'm offering is—" She moved away before his hand could reach up and brush that fallen lock of hair again.

"I know what you're offering and I appreciate it. I truly do. I'm grateful. But I can't accept. It would be wonderful but it won't work."

"It *will* work," he insisted. "When you get to know me better, you'll see. I didn't come by here today to say all the things I did. I thought I'd stop by, renew our acquaintance, and then little by little get to understand you . . . let you understand me . . . but all of a sudden I'm sitting there and I hear myself practically proposing marriage. . . ." He stared at the ground, looking for a stone or anything that could be kicked with his toe.

"That *was* what you were doing, wasn't it?" She stood in front of him and had the audacity to put her hand under his chin and tilted his face so she could see into those blue eyes one more time. "I thought that was what you were doing. No man ever did that. I thank you for it."

She put her arm through his and walked him to where his horse was waiting. She watched as he got up into the saddle. "I never really proposed, you know," he said. "I never really asked you the question."

"I'll pretend that you did," she said. "It's more romantic that way."

He pulled the reins tightly and the horse turned to go back down the drive. "You know," he said stopping a few feet from where he started, "you sure don't act like you're nineteen years old."

"Mr. Porter," and she smiled, "I'm only nineteen on the *outside*. Everything that's happened to me has given me a century's worth of wisdom on the inside."

"May I call next Sunday?"

"It won't do any good."

"Not even if I'm thirsty?"

She laughed. "If that's the *only* reason you're calling, I'll have a pitcher of lemonade waiting."

Now he laughed and waved, then rode down the drive and out onto the road. She stood there watching until he was out of sight. "Crazy man!" she said with a smile. "What a crazy man. But what a beautiful man." She sighed and walked back into the house. "What a beautiful man!"

Monday, August 25, 1879

Crash!

The milk pitcher jumped from the table and smashed into fragments on the kitchen floor. Then the children's glasses, filled with milk, rose into the air, hovered over the table, and were thrown violently onto the floor with the pitcher. Both children watched in fascination as the oatmeal cereal in their bowls came up and out and across the oilcloth covering, skittering like some startled sea creature looking for a place to hide.

The little girl cried out and grabbed for her hair. Too late. The bows of the red ribbon that Esther had so carefully tied in it yanked themselves apart, then pulled themselves upward and tied a hurtfully tight knot atop the child's skull. Mrs. Van Amburgh ran for her daughter, got only a foot away, and couldn't get closer. She couldn't budge, and her arms gestured frantically in the child's direction. The little boy, who had only just started to walk, was twisted from his chair, thrown onto the floor, and held face down in the puddle of spilled milk.

Esther didn't move; couldn't move. Her back was against the sink, and the terrible fear and disappointment inside her wouldn't let her body function.

Mrs. Van Amburgh became freed, her feet moved across the kitchen floor, and she was beside her daughter, untying the sailor's knot in the hair ribbon. Esther then ran to the little boy, lifted him up, and wiped his face and shirt front. Everything had returned to normal.

Mrs. Van Amburgh looked at Esther. "What was *that*?" The girl didn't reply. "Esther, what was it? What happened? Did you see it?"

She nodded. "Yes, ma'am." She held the little boy closer. "Yes, ma'am, I did. I saw it." She closed her eyes and drew in a deep breath. "And I'm sorry."

Both children were crying now. The feeling of surprise had given way to the feeling of outrage, and now they howled that they should have been treated so indignantly. Amid sounds like shoe-shoe-shoe and murmurings of "you're okay," the mother soothed the children and shoved them gently through the back doorway. "Go on, go on out and play. The fun's over in here. Go on!" She closed the door behind them and turned to Esther. The hired girl was leaning in the doorway, her face in her hands. "Esther," the woman said slowly, "is this what I think it is?"

She nodded, not taking her hands from her face. "I'm sorry," she said in a dull voice. "I'm real sorry."

The woman gently pried the hands away. "It's not your fault. You don't have to blame yourself."

"They're back," she said dully. "They've come back."

"It appears so." The woman looked around her kitchen at the dirty table and the milk-spattered floor. "They can do a lot in a little, can't they? Just look at the mess!" She straightened the skirt of her apron. "Well, it's got to be cleaned up." She put her hand on Esther's shoulder. "Come on, give me a hand with it, will you? Or do they"—and she smiled—"come back and clean up their own messes?" Esther shook her head no. "That's what I was afraid of. Like a bunch of kids leaving their toys all over the yard."

Esther got out the mop and broom and dustpan and worked on the floor while Mrs. Van Amburgh took care of the smeared milk and oatmeal on the table. As Esther swept up the broken glass, Mrs. Van Amburgh said, "They did me a favor, you know." Esther looked at her and received another smile. "My sister-in-law gave me that pitcher and I've always hated it. Now I can get another one, one more to *my* liking!" Then it was Esther's turn to smile.

Ruth Van Amburgh refused to listen to any of Esther's apologies or entreaties to move out and go somewhere else. It wasn't her fault, the woman kept telling her, so she shouldn't take it so personally. She had been in the kitchen when it happened, and she had seen that Esther was on the other side of the room during the incidents, and unless Esther was the greatest magician alive, there was no way she could have done those things. "And if you are that good a magician, then you should be on the stage . . . and if you go, take me with you."

Esther went to her room and rested afterward, but it was difficult even to close her eyes. Why had they come back? They had been away for over a month. They had given her a false sense of security. Now they had come back and were taking it out on the little ones of the house. Why? Why didn't they take it out on her? Why didn't they do what they wanted to do and have it over with once and for all? Why prolong this damnable agony? How much more of these tortures did they think she could take before she did something rash? Before she either went crazy or else tried to kill herself? Is that what they wanted? Did they want her to kill herself? Weren't they strong enough to do the job by themselves?

She jumped from the bed and stood in the middle of the room. "I can't take any more!" she shouted into the air. "You want me? Come get me now!" She closed her eyes and clenched her fists and waited to be struck dead. Nothing happened. "All right," she said in a calmer voice, "if that's the way it's going to be, then I'll have to play your game. It's unfair, you know, this game of yours. You know the rules and I don't. You also know how it will come out. I don't. That's the real unfair part of all this, the fact that I never know when you're going to *end* your game."

Tuesday, August 26, 1879

John Van Amburgh had not been told by his wife that Esther's ghosts were in the house with them. Ruth didn't tell him a lot of things; she thought it was better that way. He had high blood pressure brought about by years of traveling as a merchant sailor, getting in and out of scrapes and drinking. He was over fifty, tall and lean and bearded. Ruth was under thirty, small and blond. When their first child had been born, she insisted he rent a house and put down some roots.. He wanted to be beside the sea; she wanted forests and solid earth. Amherst, flat and dusty but with ocean and river waters just hours away, was an ideal compromise. The old sailor had heard about Esther's ghosts, but they didn't worry him. He had been through a helluva lot in his lifetime, and ghosts were the least of his concerns.

But he was upset when the coffee cup broke off from its handle and spilled the hot liquid all over his lap. "Damn!" he shouted, pushing back his chair and jumping up. "Damn!" He waved the handle, still clutched in his fingers, at his wife and Esther. "Just look at that! Cheap junk! That's what they sell nowadays! Cheap junk!" His wife threw him a towel and he stormed outside to dry off.

Esther went for the mop automatically.

Wednesday, August 27, 1879

"Mrs. Van Amburgh, why did you do that?" John stormed into the kitchen, still pointing in the direction of the parlor, where he had been sitting and reading the *Amherst Gazette*.

"Why did I do what, sir?" Ruth looked at her husband as if he had gone crazy.

"My dear mother's portrait. Why did you do that to it?"

"I'm sure, sir, I don't have the foggiest notion what you are referring to. I've done nothing to your mother's portrait. Although," she added, "it's not that I haven't considered a few things."

"Very droll, my dear, very droll, but this is serious. Why you did this I'll never know, unless . . ." and he looked at Esther, who was holding a dish towel exactly as she had been when he came into the kitchen. She moved the towel, but it wasn't touching the wet plate. ". . . it wouldn't have been Esther, she's no reason to do that to my mother's portrait."

They followed him out of the kitchen, down the hallway, and into the parlor. He planted one foot dramatically on the rug and pointed rigidly with his arm. "There. There it is! Do not deny it, Mrs. Van Amburgh!"

Both women looked. Esther gasped and turned away. Ruth Van Amburgh gasped and then laughed, then swiftly reconsidered the matter and forced a mock frown. "Dastardly, sir!" she said, trying to control her voice. "Whoever used that white paint to erase her dress and make her appear as if she were without clothes has a villainous soul!" She giggled and stepped closer to the painting. There was old Mother Van Amburgh, hair in a bun, glasses on her nose, and scowling at the world—as always—but naked from the neck down.

Crudely drawn shoulders, enormous exposed drooping breasts. "Maybe it will come off with water," she suggested.

"By thunder, it had better come off with water, or I'll have the head of the blackguard who did this! Imagine, in my own house! We must keep watch on door and window from now on. Someone crept in and did this and crept out."

"We'll find the creeper," his wife replied. "Come, Esther, help me take this off the wall and into the kitchen."

"A man isn't safe in his own home!" her husband continued to bluster. "And neither is his mother!"

"Absolutely, my dear. You're absolutely right." They carried the large oil painting to the kitchen, and Esther brought a pan of fresh water and a cloth while Ruth wiped the slapdash paint job away. "Too bad," she said to Esther, "it comes off. I was hoping it wouldn't. I thought I'd be able to consign this monstrosity to the junk pile along with that broken milk pitcher."

"I'm sorry, Mrs. Van Ambrugh," Esther said with a sigh, "I really am."

The woman brushed her off with a light gesture. "Nothing to be sorry for, actually. The picture's all right. You know, Esther, I kind of like your ghosts. They have a sense of humor."

"Not all of them," she said. "Mattie probably did this. Mattie is always doing crazy things. You remember me telling you about that actor, Mr. Hubbell, from America?" Ruth nodded yes, "Well, one night, as I found out later by overhearing Daniel telling Olive, one night Mattie came into his bedroom and got into the bed with him and—"

"Really?" Ruth stopped wiping the portrait and listened. The coffee was still warm and she poured two cups, they sat at the table, and Esther told her every detail she could recall. When Van Amburgh came in he found them head to head, whispering and laughing. In frustration, he hung the picture back on the wall all by himself.

Saturday, August 30, 1879

There was no energy. No energy anywhere in her body. She had felt it leaving yesterday and now, this morning, there was nothing there even to let her slide her body out of bed.

Her energy began to drain as the bangings grew louder. They started just after the supper dishes had been cleared. They were faint at first, like someone rapping lightly on the back porch door. Then as the evening grew darker, the knocks grew louder and finally the entire house seemed to shake with them. The Van Amburghs had been alarmed, then curious, and then accepting. Unlike Daniel and Olive, this couple actually seemed to enjoy the sounds. They would try to listen to the exact spot where the rapping came from and then put their own hands (or press their ears against the wall) to feel the vibrations. They both knew the poundings meant nothing. The sounds had never done any damage to the house on Princess Street. The matches and the fires, yes, but the poundings were window dressing and both the Van Amburghs were fascinated.

Unfortunately just as the poundings were the loudest, Clerk of Court Arthur Davison pounded on the front door, but nobody heard him. He had been driving past in his buggy (his farm was the next one down) and had heard the sounds way out on the road. When no one answered his knockings, he came in, uninvited, and listened for himself. Mr. Van Amburgh was not at all happy to see him and told him so. Not only had he barged into his house, said the old sailor, he knew he was not welcome. This past spring one of the Van Amburgh milk cows had strayed into the Davison herd and given birth. Davison claimed the calf for his own and insisted the Van Amburgh cow remain there until the calf was weaned. Van Amburgh fumed but Davidson quoted some archaic law about birth rights and property boundaries, and Van Amburgh gave in. Last evening, he claimed his right as a county official to see what was causing the disturbance. He would have been bodily thrown out of the house had he not quoted another ancient law about elected officials and keeping the peace. Once he had gone, the manifestations ceased.

Esther shuddered as she remembered seeing the man standing there with his arms crossed and listening to the rappings with a smile on his face. She hadn't said a word to him, just run into the kitchen, then into the pantry, and shut the door.

Now this morning, no pep. No desire to do anything but lie there. When Ruth called her, she could barely muster an answer. The woman was going into town shopping—it was Saturday, she reminded the girl—and she had expected her to go with her. When she saw how weak Esther was, she brought her a cup of tea and told her not to worry about it. She'd do the

Saturday marketing by herself. She'd take the children and give Esther a morning of peace.

Esther fell asleep after that and awakened only when she heard voices in the kitchen. She glanced at the clock on the bedside table to see if it was time to prepare lunch. With a start, she saw that it was almost 5:00 P.M., time to get *supper* ready. She managed to force herself out of the bed and out of her nightdress and into her clothes. She splashed some water on her face and brushed her hair a couple of times so the strands wouldn't be sticking in all directions. She was sure Mrs. Van Amburgh would be furious at her, spending the entire day in bed! She would make it up to her, she promised herself aloud.

Both the old sailor and his wife were in the kitchen when she hurried in. "I was just going to go up and see if you were awake," Ruth said.

"I am awake, and I'm sorry. I didn't mean to spend the entire day in bed. I don't know what came over me. I was so weak but I'm better now, I'm much—"

"You look terrible," said the old man. "I've seen healthier faces at the county morgue! Sit down there, right there"—he pulled a chair from the kitchen table—"and I'll fix you some supper. Can you eat? You can? Oh, you can't. Well, it doesn't matter. I'll fix you something anyway. How about an omelette? Cheese and stuff in it? Used to make them all the time for myself before I got married. Now I never get 'em. Wife can't cook 'em to suit me. You want one?" Esther nodded, not daring to refuse. "Good. I make 'em great. You haven't had a bite all day. Need something substantial in your innards." He took several eggs from a crock on the sideboard and broke them into a bowl. "Used to feed these to my crew when they got sick. They never forgot it."

"Because they were dead by nightfall," his wife said.

"They were not! Used to thrive on 'em. Told me I was the greatest cook they'd ever seen."

"They were trying to get you to open a restaurant and stay on land." Ruth handed him a cup of cheese she had just grated.

"No such thing! I was a good sailor. My men all loved me! I remember one time when I mixed up some of these omelettes, we had just seen the shoreline of the Cape, and as we headed straight for it, one of the dogs on board came into the—"

Scratch. Scratch. The sound came from the window over the sink. Their eyes turned toward it. A nail no bigger than a shoemaker's nail was jerking stiffly in the air, its point digging into the window glass and leaving a white line where it scratched.

"What the Hell . . . ?" Van Amburgh said slowly.

No one moved, especially Esther, as the nail slowly formed four capital letters. Then it fell lifelessly into the sink.

"A. D. A. M.," Ruth read slowly. "What's that?"

"Could be 'Adam,'" her husband said. "A man's name. Adam."

Esther took a deep breath. It was the only way she could keep herself from crying out.

"That's what it is," Ruth said. "It's a man's name. Adam. I don't know any Adam." She looked at her husband. "Do you?"

"I do," Esther said in a small voice. "I'm afraid I do."

Then there was a crash. The entire window, where the name 'Adam' had been inscribed, smashed into slivers and exploded outwardly onto the lawn.

Sunday, August 31, 1879

"And that's when they smashed it," Mr. Van Amburgh told him. "Just as soon as we had figured out that the name was *your* name, they smashed the glass to smithereens. What daya think of that?"

"It sounds as if they don't like me, that's what I make of it." Adam Porter shifted his weight on the parlor chair. "Sounds as if they're jealous that I've come into Esther's life."

"You haven't come into my life," the girl said loudly. "You came for a visit and they didn't like it. They don't like it when I have friends."

"No," said the old sailor, "there's more to it than that. Mrs. Van Amburgh and I are your *friends*. If your ghosties had only been after friends, they would have made mincemeat out of us a long time ago. No, it's more than that. They see young Mr. Porter here as a threat."

"A threat to what?" she asked.

"To them. A threat to them because he is young and strong and on your side. They don't want anybody like him on your side. They don't know what to make of him and so they aren't going to tolerate him. Not for a minute."

"But what about Mr. Hubbell, the American actor? They

did even worse things when he was around. And he wasn't on my side, as you call it. Not in the beginning, anyway."

"If I recall," put in Ruth Van Amburgh, "in the beginning they didn't do anything that the actor wanted. They refused to cooperate when you went on that stage thing with him. It was their way of getting at him. He wanted to see them in action, and so they didn't do a thing."

"But later?"

"But later their egos got the best of them," she continued. "He was more interested in them than he was in you. He didn't stay in Amherst because of you, Esther, he stayed because of *them.* He wasn't interested in you in the same way that Mr. Porter is . . ." She flustered. "I mean . . ."

"No, you're right," said Adam. "I *am* interested in Esther, not in her damnable ghosts."

"And your ghosts," the woman continued, ignoring Esther's blushing, "were delighted to show him everything they could do. Especially that Mattie. She obviously enjoyed having the American around." Esther's blush deepened considerably. "Then that awful Bob Nickle must have got tired of it all and started in with his fires and threats of destruction. Hubbell was leaving anyway, and they had shown him their bag of tricks."

"What about when Mattie tried to stab me right on the stairs? Olive and Mr. Hubbell were helping me up to my bedroom."

John Van Amburgh answered that one. "Hell hath no fury like a woman scorned! She wanted the actor for herself and didn't want you all fluttery in his arms."

Esther's voice rose. "I never intended anything with Mr. Hubbell! And Mattie knew it."

Van Amburgh shrugged his shoulders. "Try to convince another woman you don't have designs on her man. Hell hath . . ."

"That's a relief, anyway," Adam said with a smile. "I did kind of wonder how you felt about that actor."

"Now, that's the most ridiculous thing I ever heard!" Esther got up from her chair and arranged a doily that was already perfectly in place. "Me and Mr. Hubbell! Indeed!

"I was just wondering," the young man replied.

"Only natural," Van Amburgh said. "A small house, a pretty girl, and a handsome young man—"

"Mr. Van Amburgh!" his wife said quickly. "We are discussing an innocent girl in Nova Scotia, not one of your crew members loose in a Turkish seraglio!"

"What's that?" Esther asked.

"It's a kind of church," the old sailor replied. "Where you pray a lot. You pray that everything works out." He winked at his wife, who made a face and turned her head away. "Anyway, that's not the problem here. The problem is that your ghosties don't like Adam, and you do. So what are you going to do about it?"

"Who said I liked him?" She paused. "I'm sorry, Adam, of course I *like* you. As a friend. I like you just as a friend, and that should not be reason enough for Bob Nickle and his band over there to make such a fuss about it."

"He is your friend and nothing more. Correct?" Van Amburgh looked at her.

"Correct."

"Say it louder, so your ghosties can hear."

"He is my friend and nothing more!"

"That's good and loud. I'm sure they heard that. Now say, 'will always remain a friend.'"

"Will always remain a friend." She was almost shouting.

"And will never be a lover or a husband," he concluded.

"And will never be a . . . a . . ." Her voice dropped. "Will never be a . . ." she looked at Adam sitting there watching her every move, ". . . a lover . . ." her voice lowered almost to a whisper, ". . . or a husband." The last was almost inaudible. Adam reached toward her and she took his hand.

"That's better," said the old sailor. "Now you two just stay that way while Mrs. V. A. and I go into the dining room and see if we can come back with a couple of glasses of port wine. I think we should celebrate."

"Celebrate what?" Esther asked softly.

"Celebrate you. Celebrate your finding a . . . a *friend*." He laughed and grabbed his wife by the arm. "Let's find that bottle I brought back from England unless, of course, you've tippled it all away, woman." She slapped him lightly on the arm and smiled.

Adam watched them go. "Very nice people," he said, and she nodded her head. "I don't want to bring you any problems, Esther. I truly don't. And I don't want to rush you into anything that you'll regret later. I just stopped by last week to get reacquainted and for the same reason this week. Mr. Van Amburgh and your ghosts are rushing things."

"They are. I'm not prepared for any of this. It's all taken place so suddenly. There are all those other things that must be resolved before I can resolve this with you. I do like you, Adam." She looked up at him and he saw a faint smile. "I really do, but I can't give you an answer—"

"I haven't asked the question—"

"I can't give you an answer until I know I'm free of them. And that will take time. Time and a miracle."

"Let me do something to help you."

She shook her head. "No. There is nothing you can do. There is nothing anyone on this side can do. The decision to let me alone must come from them. Over there on the other side. They want me. I don't know why, but they do. They've hurt me and hurt everyone who comes around me. I can't marry you until—"

"I haven't asked you—yet."

"I can't marry you until I am positive they have gone. I can't move in with you and your children and bring my spirits with me. It wouldn't be fair."

"Even if I agreed and said I didn't care?"

"You can say that now," she said, pulling away from him, "you can say all you want now, but you haven't seen them destroy furniture and set fires to walls. You haven't seen what my skin looks like after they spent the night scratching me and sticking me with pins." She walked farther away and then turned back to face him. "You haven't seen how horrible I look when they blow me up like an India rubber doll and haven't heard how I scream and cry. And if you were my husband, lying next to me in bed, I don't think you could take some of the other things they do to me. Things no real husband would ever stand for!" She had started to cry and she became angry with herself, because she had been determined never to shed another tear. "If you loved me, you couldn't bear what they do to me. It's not fair. It's not fair to either one of us. But it's there. That's the fact, the cold fact. It's there and it wants to destroy me. 'Esther Cox, you are mine to kill!'" she quoted. "I didn't tell you about that, did I? I didn't tell you about the death threats along with the pain and the blood and the shame."

"What's there to be ashamed of?"

"The shame comes from walking down the street in

Amherst. Knowing that everyone you meet thinks you are some sort of monster, some doomed mongrel with an unknown disease that just might infect everyone in contact. The shame that I can't go to church. That I can't get a position of decent employment. That I can't even become a barmaid but have to hide myself out on a farm as someone's hired hand. The shame that I'm talked about, not just in saloons but in homes and schools. Oh, yes, they talk about crazy Esther! Just listen sometime. Hear them gossip about how I am possessed by the Devil or how I made their milk cow run dry or their chickens stop laying or how I tried to burn Olive and Daniel out of house and home. Some say I should be arrested. Others say I should be locked away in a looney bin, and others say that I should be burnt as a witch or have a stake plunged into my heart. And this from friends and good people. Good people who go to church on Sunday and wish me dead on Monday. Good Christian people who don't understand what's happening to me . . . who don't *want* to understand . . . good Christians all, who rather than believe the facts, want me dead. As long as I remain alive, these good people have to deal with me, have to wonder if what is happening to me is true. Are there such things as ghosts? Can the dead come back to haunt the living? Does a man's personality remain even though his body is dead? People don't want to think about these things. My staying alive forces them to think, and they resent it. It would all be easier if I was dead. Dead, I'm like a book that's been read. Like last week's newspaper. Like yesterday's potato peelings. Dead, I'm not a bother either physically or mentally."

"You've given this a lot of thought," he said.

"I've had to think about it. It's my life. It's my very existence that I'm talking about. I've had to think on it. No one else could. The thoughts have to come from me, have to be mine."

He reached out for her and held her. For the first time, he held her. "Well, where does that put us?"

She didn't pull away. "There is no *us*. Until all this is over, there is just me and there is just you. I deeply, truly and deeply, appreciate what you are offering me. You don't even know me, and you are offering me a brand-new life. Adam, I *do* appreciate it, but it cannot be until they either leave me . . . or kill me. Neither of *us* can make that decision. It can only come from *them.*"

"But I can see you until they make that decision, can't I?"

She shook her head. "No. It's best that you don't. They tormented this household all last week because you came to visit me. God knows what they will do this week. As much as I would like to see you again, I can't. I don't dare inflict them on the Van Amburghs. These are good people. They don't deserve to suffer."

"So I can't call next Sunday?" She shook her head no. "The Sunday after that? In a month, maybe?"

"I don't know. I can't tell you. A month is an eternity for me, and as for next Sunday"—she laughed, but it was a bitter laugh—"by then I could very well be dead."

Monday, September 1, 1879

They waited all day for something to happen. The Van Amburghs and Esther were out of bed and having coffee before the sun was fully up. Whatever it was that "they" were going to do, everyone wanted to be there to see it and to take care of it quickly, if possible. They had worked out a plan should there be falling matches or a fire. Those were the only tricks that worried them. The Van Amburghs didn't own the farm they were living on, but they did own the furnishings. Ruth had no intention of having her things destroyed.

The morning passed. There were no bangings, no sliding furniture, no names etched in windows.

The afternoon passed. Flower pots remained where they had been set. Knives remained in drawers. Dishes put on the table in readiness for supper sat unmoved.

Esther fed the two young children. Nothing had happened to them. No scratches, no bruises, no sudden ripping of clothes. They went to bed and fell asleep.

The chicken pie, John Van Amburgh's favorite, was almost ready. It sat on top the stove cooling off after having its crust baked for almost an hour in the oven. Esther had pared the potatoes for it, scraped the carrots, and peeled down the onions. Ruth Van Amburgh had cleaned the chicken and spiced the broth. The side dishes of pickled beets and steamed Swiss chard and sliced garden tomatoes in homemade mayonnaise were already on the table. John sat at his place at the head of the table, waiting for the women to dish up the hot meat pie and sit themselves down.

Ruth arranged her napkin on her lap. "Before we begin," she looked at her husband, "I think we should say grace. It couldn't hurt."

He scowled, took another look at the chicken pie, and closed his eyes. Esther bowed her head. "Father," he began, "we ask you to look down upon this table and bless the food that you see here. Bless the people you see around this table. Especially Miss Cox. Bless her, Father, because she has been going through some mighty rough seas lately and she needs your calming hand on her bow. Amen."

He opened his eyes just in time to see the chicken pie, the entire pan of it, coming at him. He pulled to one side as the pie continued past him, past the stove, past the pantry door, and slammed into the back wall. Ruth's scream was drowned out by the clatter of the tin pan and the gurgle of the steaming ingredients as they ran down the wall surface and onto the floor.

Tuesday, September 2, 1879

"What in the god-damned Hell!" John Van Amburgh jumped up from his favorite chair and ran from the parlor for the front door. Esther and Ruth watched him in amazement. When he came back, he was mopping his mouth with his handkerchief and sputtering. "God damn the god-damned Hell!"

"Mr. Van Amburgh, control yourself," said his wife. "Whatever is the matter?"

"The god-damned Hell in my chewing tobacco!" he said. "Put a chaw in my mouth and it tastes like somebody pissed in the jar!"

"Mr. Van Amburgh! Control your language. There are ladies present." His wife was embarrassed for Esther.

"Well, there was a pisser present, and he pissed right in my tobacco jar! God-damned Hell!"

"Couldn't be," she said soothingly, "must be your imagination."

"It was piss and it was in my chewing tobacco. God, woman, I know what piss tastes like!"

"You do?" she said, her eyes opening wider. "Why on earth would you know anything like that?" She turned to

Esther, who was trying hard not to smile. "I, myself, have no idea what urine tastes like."

He grabbed the jar. "I'm going to dump this in the trash. And, like yourself, madam, I don't know what urine tastes like, but I sure as Hell know what piss tastes like, and one of her ghosts pissed in my jar!"

Both women had to stop giggling, wipe the tears from their eyes, and settle calmly on their chairs before he came storming back into the room.

Thursday, September 4, 1879

The pains had started in the middle of the night and Esther, all alone in the room at the end of the upstairs corridor, didn't have the strength to get out of bed and call Mrs. Van Amburgh for help. So Esther lay there until long after sunup, when they found her, unable to talk and breathing with great difficulty.

John Van Amburgh went for Dr. Carritte, and he came only after he had finished with his list of patients for the day. He wasn't in much of a hurry to see Esther. From what the old sailor had told him, he knew it was something he couldn't remedy. It was another of "their" inflicted illnesses, and he was powerless against "them." And "they" knew it.

He sat on the edge of the bed and listened with his stethoscope. He took her pulse, then ran his hand, tapping and probing, over her chest and stomach. "Esther, can you hear me?"

She nodded.

"It's nothing serious," he said assuringly, "it's the same old thing you had on Princess Street. We can't do a thing. You know that, don't you?" She nodded again. "What I'll do is make you a sedative and leave it with Mrs. Van Amburgh. She can give it to you whenever you feel the need for it." He turned to the Van Amburghs, who were standing at the foot of the bed. "Before, when she's had one of these, we've had to let it run its course. Whatever might happen, don't get alarmed. It won't harm her, no matter how bad it may appear. You have, I'm sure, been apprised of her previous attacks?" They nodded yes. "Then get prepared, but don't panic. I wish there were something medical science could do for her. I wish there were something *I* could do for her, but there isn't." He got off the bed, put his stethoscope in his bag, and snapped it shut. As he walked to the door, he said to the couple: "You are very brave to have invited her here. I warned the Teeds what could happen, and now I have to warn you. She is dangerous. Oh, no"—he put his hand up as he saw Ruth start to protest—"not deliberately dangerous, poor child. The things are out of her control. If she could control it, there would be no manifestations, no fires, nothing breaking against walls. But she can't control it."

"What is this god-damned 'it'?" John Van Amburgh demanded to know.

"She says it's ghosts," the doctor replied.

"And what do you say it is?" the sailor insisted.

"I really don't know. At one time I believed it was imagination. Then I thought it could be hypnotism. Then, for a while, I believed in her story of spirits and demons and that ilk. I even devised a method of communicating with them. But that was *then*. I don't know *now*. I've had a chance to do a great deal of reading. What she has sounds like hysteria, some form of mental aberration where her imagination takes over—somehow—and creates tangible results."

"Her imagination?" John looked at his wife. "It sure as hell wasn't her imagination that threw my supper across the kitchen the other night."

"It could have been," the doctor replied. "She could have so strongly wished for something to happen that she created the energy to make the food move."

"She created *what*?"

"The energy. In her troubled mind, she wanted some kind of diversion. She wanted some kind of thing to happen. Something to make you both believe that her ghosts were really there. That she was really under attack. In other words, 'Oh, poor Esther. The terrible things are happening to her again.' So she created the force that lifted your dinner and carried it across the room."

"Nonsense." John Van Amburgh never did have much respect for medical men. "Pure nonsense. Nobody can create such energies from their minds. I never seen it."

"You did this week," the doctor said. "You saw it on your window glass and you saw it at your supper table. The mind, sir, is a powerful thing. We don't yet understand everything it is capable of."

"So you think," Ruth put in, "that she creates all this around her for effect, to get attention."

"That's what I'm saying. To get attention. But," he added quickly, "she doesn't *know* she's doing it. She doesn't *deliberately* make things happen. It all takes place somewhere deep inside her, somewhere she is not conscious of. That's why she is as surprised as the next person when these things occur."

"So she's not doing it out of spite," Ruth said.

"That's correct. She's doing it without knowing she's doing it. It's unconscious. It's not with thought."

"But you just said she was doing it to get attention," the woman insisted.

"That I did, but it's a part deep inside her that's looking for the attention, not the girl you see on the surface." He started down the stairs. "I'm pretty sure of it. Of course, there's not an expert within five hundred miles of here I could call in to agree with me, but that's pretty much what I believe. There are no ghosts. She is not possessed by evil spirits. It all stems from her own twisted inner imagination."

It was at that moment the two pillows that had been under Esther's head came sailing down the staircase and hit the doctor squarely in the face.

Friday, September 5, 1879

"I trust we are not intruding on your work schedule. But Mr. Davison and I both found this time agreeable for a visit." Reverend Temple had his hat in one hand and his Bible in the other. Arthur Davison stood beside him, waiting for John Van Amburgh to invite them inside. "Actually, we came to see poor Esther," the preacher continued.

"Dr. Carritte said she was ill," Davison said rather loudly. "I came to see for myself. And in case you won't let me in, sir, I have come in the capacity of an official of the county courts."

John opened the front door wider and the two men came into the hallway. "She's upstairs," he said. "My wife's there with her. She is sleeping, the last I knew." Both men headed for the stairway. "I said she is sleeping! You two can wait down here till I go up and check." He thumped up the carpeted stairs; the minister and the court clerk waited below. They could hear the sound of his voice as he told his wife about the visitors. They couldn't hear everything he said, but one phrase—"god-damned busybodies"—rang clearly down the stairwell.

In a few minutes, Ruth appeared at the top of the stairs. "You may come up now," was all she said.

They found Esther lying in bed. Ruth had quickly brushed her hair and pulled the summerweight coverlet up around her chin. Esther, who had been dozing off, was fully awake now. Ruth had warned her who her visitors were, and she kept a smile on her face even though she wished both men had never stopped by.

"We heard from Dr. Carritte," said the minister, "that you were ill. That you had another of your spells. Again. That's why I came to see how you were, along with Mr. Davison here, to see how you really were." He paused. "Oh, yes, Mrs. Temple sends her love."

Esther returned his smile. "I'm just weak, that's all," she said. "The doctor didn't inform you quite correctly. I didn't have one of my *spells*. I'm just not feeling well. I'll be up and around in a day or two."

"I heard there was a window broken," said Davison.

"None of your concern," Van Amburgh spoke quickly. "It was my window, it wasn't yours."

"But it broke, didn't it?"

"It did. Have you come to measure for a new one?" John asked. "When did you get into the window business?"

"The window broke," Davison ignored John, "and there was nobody there to break it. Just like what used to happen on Princess Street. Windows breaking and nobody around."

"I asked you what business it was of yours," Van Amburgh said loudly.

"Things that disrupt the continuity of this county are my business," Davison said. "Mine and the courts. A community cannot survive without law and order."

"A community of fools can."

"There are no fools in this community, sir!"

"Ruth, go and fetch him the hand mirror."

Davison took a step toward the old sailor, who took a step toward him. Then the clerk backed away two steps. "I didn't come here to argue with you, sir, nor to be insulted. I came here in the name of the county to see what this girl is up to now. From what the medical profession tells me—"

"Medical profession!" Van Amburgh turned and spat a load of tobacco juice out an open window.

"—what the medical profession tells me, we have a dangerous person here in the form of Miss Esther Cox. She is dangerous to the people of the area because her thoughts can trigger disasters. The way I heard it, anything she can imagine, she can conceive."

"Esther," John Van Amburgh smiled at her, "if that be the case, then imagine these two lunkheads out of here."

"Sir! You may be taking this lightly, but this girl is a meance to society, to decent, God-fearing people! She can break things, she can move things, she can produce sounds."

"She can make hymnbooks fly," the preacher said, and Van Amburgh laughed at the mental picture.

"She can deliberately, and I emphasize the word *deliberately,*" said Davison, "create havoc and instill fear. She can produce matches from nowhere and start fires that can burn down houses."

"You make her sound like a one-man vaudeville show. Hell, I'd pay a dime to see her do all that!" Van Amburgh had started to enjoy his visitors.

"You may *have* to pay if you want to see her, sir." Davison took a paper from his coat pocket and handed it to the old sailor.

"What's this?"

"Read it. You can read, can't you?"

Van Amburgh shot him a glance and scanned the document. "It says that Esther has been declared a public nuisance and that you have been empowered by the county to take Esther away with you. That you have become her legal guardian until the court sees fit to put her someplace else." He looked at Davison. "You son-of-a-bitch! Who do you think you are?"

"I am a representative of the county and with the powers invested in me by the public, I have decided to take charge of this girl, who has become a public nuisance."

"Public nuisance, my ass! If anybody is a public nuisance, you are!"

"Mr. Van Amburgh, please!" Ruth put her hand on her husband's shoulder. "Is the paper legal?" The minister nodded. "We can't fight this," she said to John. "As much as we want to, we can't. You know that. Esther's not ours. We love her like a daughter," she said to the minister, "but she's not ours."

"I'm not anybody's," Esther said. They turned to her in surprise, as if they had all forgotten she was there. "I'm not going anywhere. I'm going to stay right here! I'm tired of running!"

"You'll go and you'll go tomorrow," said the court clerk. "That gives all day today to get your things ready."

"Go where?" Ruth asked.

"I don't know yet," said Davison. "It'll be someplace where she can be watched."

Tears came to Ruth's eyes. "You're not going to put her in jail, are you?"

He shook his head. "Nothing like that. But I will decide where the best place will be. The hospitals won't have her. Dr. Carritte refuses to sign a paper saying she's ill."

"She doesn't belong in a hospital," Ruth said. "She belongs where people love her."

"I'm afraid those kind of places are few and far between around here," Davison replied.

"I will continue to give her spiritual guidance," the minister added.

"Oh, wonderful! said John Amburgh. "She needs a wagonload of that!"

"Doesn't anybody care what *I* want?" Esther said loudly.

"No, my dear, they don't." Van Amburgh came closer to her bed. "You're a public nuisance now. How about that? A certified public nuisance. That means you don't have any rights. People can throw stones at you. They can chase you and tie tin cans to your tail. You don't matter. You've become a 'thing.' Isn't that wonderful? What Esther Cox wants—what you want——doesn't matter at all!"

Monday, September 8, 1879

Judge James Z. Bliss
County Court House
Amherst, Nova Scotia

Sir:

Esther Cox, female, white, nineteen years of age; was removed from the premises of Mr. John Van Amburgh on Saturday, September 6, this year as per legal writ and decree. The female in question went with the below signed peaceably and without incident. Being as it is the court's wishes not to have the above named female incarcerated in a public facility I, the undersigned, have assumed the civic duty of keeping surveillance upon her at my own place of residence. Both Mrs. Davison and myself undertake my legal guardianship of the named female willingly. We feel the interests of the community are best served having her confined to my residence and under the watchful eye of a member of my family at all times. While she resides at my residence she will not be a financial burden to the taxpaying public. She will, however, be expected to reimburse my family for her room, board and care by performing such domestic tasks as deemed necessary, i.e. washing, cleaning, cooking, gardening, child care, lawn care, etc. This surveillance is to continue until further instruction from the courts.

I remain your most obedient servant:

Arthur Davison, Esq.
Clerk of Court

Sunday, October 5, 1879

Dearest Martha:

I have a few moments today (Ezra and the boys have gone to some livestock exhibition) to drop you a few lines. I sincerely hope your father's health improves so that you can come quickly back to all your friends here in Amherst. The church bazaar is just six weeks away, you surely must recall, and the committee has yet to receive the parlor set you promised to crochet them. (Sara Finch has decided *not* (!!) to help out on the pie and cookie table this year! Does that surprise you (???), it doesn't *me*!) Yesterday I spent the most enjoyable afternoon and thought of you while doing so. A group from the Bible study went out to the Davisons' for our lesson and tea. (First time in ages I've been inside that house and I don't know where she gets the wherewithal to furnish it the way she does!) Anyway, the *Cox girl* was there! Working there! Can you imagine it? You know the one I mean, the one who tried to burn down that ugly little house on Princess Street. (I agree with you, that *entire* section should be burnt down and then rebuilt!) I had wondered what became of the Cox girl as there had been nothing about her in the papers and I never saw her on the street anymore. Well, it seems that Mr. Davison was made legal guardian (!!) by the court (how did *that* happen—ha ha) and has taken her in to stay with them as a kind of protection. Well, I wouldn't want that crazy firebug living with me, but they don't seem to mind. Mrs. Davison has to keep an eye on her and did tell us that the girl is not the *best* shirt ironer in town but that she does know how to handle a mop and broom and take care of little children. (You know that Davison brood!) Esther served us and everything, just as if she was a colored maid. She is prettier than I recall but then I never really knew her that well. Eating a lot and working it off at the Davison's must keep her looking so good. (Of course she's only 19!!) She didn't smile a lot, but the folks there yesterday were not *her* kind of people. I understand that Olive Teed and Jennie Cox do visit from time to time but they have to stay on the porch and always be with someone from the Davison family. It's like being in jail but not quite. I heard rumors about some young man wanting to visit her but Mr. Davison put his foot down on that! As I should well imagine! (Can you believe *any* young man would be interested in *her*? After all that's happened??) Well, after the lesson and the tea they made Esther do tricks. She obviously didn't want to, and spent most of the time with a hang-dog face but she did do them. She correctly gave the date on a silver dollar that Grace Smithwaite had in her purse and described the contents of a letter that Agnes Froman had in her purse. Even down to the name of the cousin who had written it! You know that gold ring with the red stones that I have? Well, I handed it to her and she told me who gave it to me, when I got it and the fact that it had belonged to Ezra's grandmother who had worn it over here from Scotland!! I still can't imagine *why* the Davisons keep her there, tho. It can only be because they get a lot of work out of her! She's almost like a common criminal. I think I'd rather have Ezra's mother (God forbid!!) back here again than have a crazy woman like that running around my house!!

(They do lock up the kitchen knives before going to bed, I'm told.) There have been none of those awful knockings that she is so famous for. We did hear that one evening, last week, when she was laying things on the table for tea, a dinner fork rose out of the silverware drawer and struck Mr. Davison on the back of his head. He swears there was no way she herself could have done it. It must have been one of her ghosts! Can you imagine living with a girl like that?? Anyway, when you return maybe we can go out there and she can do some of her tricks for you. Bring something that belongs to your father and let's see if she can guess where it came from!! I pulled up all my zinnias and pruned back my roses last week. Everyone says it's going to be a very cold winter!! Don't forget that crochet set for the bazaar!! Your friend,

Sabrina

Wednesday, October 29, 1879

A snow had fallen during the night, a thick, wet layer about four inches deep that covered everything in sight. Before Esther could prepare breakfast, she was sent to dig a path from the house out to the road so the Davison children would have a clean place to walk to get the shcool wagon. The wagon, enclosed with a portable leather and isinglass top when there was bad weather, had converted from wheels to sleigh runners. The horses were special ones, trained to step high over the snow rather than plow through it.

Once the children were out of the way, she had to dig another path to the chicken coop, the pigpen, and the barn. Farm animals needed caring for all year round, and snow or no snow, eggs had to be gathered, hens fed, cows milked, and fresh hay put in their feed troughs and stalls.

After that, the usual indoor chores were taken care of—bannisters oiled, floors scrubbed, windows cleaned, chamber pots emptied, the woodbox stocked, lamp wicks trimmed, beds made, linens boiled, coal stoked, and ashes scattered. In between all this, food had to be procured, cleaned, cooked, served, rid up, and put away. The next day, it started all over again.

Mrs. Davison did her share of the housework, as she had

always done. But it became easier as the weeks wore on to delegate more to Esther. The girl was a hard worker—the best house help they had ever had—and Mrs. Davison found herself acting like a supervisor instead of a helper.

She wasn't sure she liked the girl. Esther did what she was told but never seemed to enjoy doing it. The family wondered if Esther knew how to smile on weekdays because the only time they ever saw her smile was on Sundays, when one or both of her sisters would come calling. Since the cold weather and the snow, it was more difficult for her to visit with them on the front porch. Mr. Davison decreed that the girl was not permitted visitors inside the house. After all, clerk of court or not, a man's home *was* his castle.

This particular evening, Davison got home later than usual. The snow had slowed his horse, and the buggy was pulled carefully from the municipal barn in town to his own barn in the country. Esther was in the barn when he drove in. She was milking his one cow and was almost finished. Davison nodded to her as he passed and took the horse into the rear of the barn. He undid the harness, backed the horse into the stall, and reached for the currycomb that hung near the stall gate. It wasn't there.

"Esther. Where's the horse comb?" he called. "It ain't here."

"I don't know," she called her reply. "It should be there."

"I know it should be, but it ain't. Have you let the children play with it?"

"I haven't seen it," she said loudly. "The children didn't come out here tonight. Mrs. Davison kept them in the house."

He searched the floor and kicked at a few wisps of hay. "Well, I don't know what you did with it, but it ain't here." He walked past her seated figure, bent over by woolen clothes and fatigue. "It's too cold for me to stay out here and look for the darned thing," he said. "When you're done with the milking, find it for me."

"Yes, sir," she said softly, "just as soon as I finish this."

He walked to the door and stopped to examine one of the hinges. He heard a noise and turned quickly. It was Esther, walking toward him with a heavy pail of steaming milk that she carried in both hands. He started to say something about looking for the comb when he saw it.

It was sneaking behind her, all by itself, like a snake trying not to be seen. This comb, this oval hunk of wood with metal teeth, was following, slithering, after her.

"There!" he called out. "Behind you! There's the comb!"

She turned, saw it, and jumped to one side. The comb paused, stirred up dusty motes on the floorboards, and came forward. It crossed in front of her, passed her open-mouth stare, and headed for Davison.

He stood there, frozen at the sight, then turned for the door. The comb raised itself from the floor and sailed out into the open air, circling the clerk of court and forcing him back inside. He stumbled as he tried to escape, and felt himself come up against one of the empty animal stalls. The comb hovered in the air, its metal teeth catching the rays of the setting winter sun. Then it charged straight for the man's face. He shouted. Esther screamed, dropping the pail and spilling the milk across the rough-hewn floor. Davison twisted to one side, the comb caught itself on the brim of his woolen hat and veered sideways, then fell lifeless to the floor. Davison stared at the comb and then at the sobbing girl and then back at the comb. That night as he relived the incident with his wife for what seemed to her the hundredth time, he said: "I don't understand it. It wasn't her. The comb was behind her and then in front of her. She didn't throw it. Her hands were full. It just came alive. The god-damned thing just came alive!"

Sunday, November 2, 1879

"I suppose it can't do no harm," Davison told his wife. "As long as Van Amburgh understands his responsibility and has her back here before nightfall, it should be all right."

"She has been wanting to see them again," his wife said. "They were awfully good to her while she was there."

"Well, I don't especially like that old sea snake," Davison said, "his mouth's always full of opinions that nobody wants to hear, but Esther likes him, that's sure. She's been here almost two months now. I guess a day with those folks won't do any harm."

"And it is her day off," his wife reminded him.

Esther was actually humming when Mrs. Davison knocked on her bedroom door. She had put on her best brown dress, added a garnet brooch that Jennie had given her, and had put a red ribbon in her hair. "My, you look real nice," the woman exclaimed. Esther blushed and murmured her thanks. "What's in the package?" she asked.

"I'm taking some things over to have Ruth Van Amburgh alter for me," she replied. "She has one of those new machines that sew, and these clothes don't fit me anymore. I've lost weight since I got them." She smiled. "I'm glad she'll be taking them in instead of letting them out!" She unfolded the brown wrapping paper that was around the package on the bed and showed the contents to Mrs. Davison. "This green blouse fit fine a year ago. Now it's like a sack. And this blouse could have the collar lowered a bit. It's too high and now that I've lost weight, it's kind of floppy." She took out a brown skirt and placed it against her hips. "She has to take in the seams on this one, and this one here with the blue threads in it."

Mrs. Davison helped her put the clothes back in the paper and watched as she rewrapped it. As Esther tied the cord around it, Mrs. Davison put her finger on the string to help make the knot. "I don't know where Ruth Van Amburgh gets the time for extra sewing," she said, "with two children and a husband and all."

"Well, Mr. Van Amburgh doesn't go to work like Mr. Davison does. He tends the farm and has time to help in the kitchen and with the house chores," the girl said. "The two do things together."

"The only time Mr. Davison helps me with the household chores," said his wife, "is when he lifts his feet so I can sweep under them." She laughed. "Men aren't supposed to be in the house all day. That's why God invented doors, so men would get out and leave their womenfolk alone for a while."

They heard the honk of the brass horn. Mrs. Davison jumped. Esther smiled. "There he is. He must have taken the squeeze horn off the buggy and put it on the sleigh. He is a caution!"

"Both Mr. Davison and I agree with you on that one!" Mrs. Davison carried the package of Esther's clothing downstairs while the girl struggled into her heavy coat, muffler, and mittens. She put the parcel in Esther's hands as she held open the door. "You have a nice afternoon," she said. "Just make sure you're back in time."

Esther almost ran across the porch and down the steps to get to the sleigh. John Van Amburgh tipped his hat to Mrs. Davison, who was in the doorway.

Mr. Davison appeared behind his wife and shouted: "She must be returned by nightfall!"

"*¡Plátanos!*" Van Amburgh said loudly, touched his hat, and turned the horse around the drive.

Esther grinned at him as they reached the road. "What did you reply to Mr. Davison?"

"Bananas!" he said, laughing. "That's South American for bananas!"

Monday, November 3, 1879

"I have been waiting for you to come home," Mrs. Davison said to her husband even before he could take off his boots and heavy winter coat. "I have something to discuss with you. It's"—she paused—"it's not very pleasant."

"What is it?" he stared at her. There was a nervousness about her that wasn't natural.

"Finish getting out of your woolens and come upstairs. I'd rather discuss this in the bedroom."

"Where's Esther?" he asked.

"In the parlor with the boys. She's helping them with their schoolwork." She left the kitchen quickly. "Please come up right away."

He joined her in the upstairs bedroom. "Close the door," she said. "I don't want the children to hear." He did as she asked, then stood looking at her. "On the dresser," she said. "Do you see anything unusual?"

He looked, letting his eyes crisscross the dressertop several times. "No," he replied slowly, "I don't."

"Nothing different?" she insisted. "Nothing out of place?"

He looked again. "No," he shook his head, "except the hand mirror isn't beside the comb and the brush, but that's all."

"You didn't take the mirror, did you?"

"What would I want with your mother's silver hand mirror?"

She sighed. "It's gone." She sat down wearily on the edge of the bed. "I noticed it this morning, after breakfast. I asked Esther if she had seen it, and she said she hadn't. I was in hopes you had put it away someplace, but if you say you didn't—"

"Of course I didn't! I haven't seen it." He walked over to

the dresser and picked up the brush as if possibly the matching mirror could be hiding under it. "Was it there last night?"

"I don't recall. I wish I could, but I can't. I don't use it every day, you know. I use the set in the washroom cabinet. That set's mostly for show." She got up and walked to the closet, opening the door. "And up here"—she pointed to the shelf—"up here I had some tweed cloth for a new dress. Remember, I bought it this summer from that Scotsman who came peddling through here?" He nodded, remembering the material. He had hinted that it would make a nicer man's jacket than a woman's dress. "Well, it's gone. It's not here, either."

"Are you sure?"

"Mr. Davison, I'm looking at the empty spot it left on the shelf. It's not here."

"Did you ask Esther about it, too?"

She shook her head. "No. I didn't mention it to anyone. I thought it best to wait till you got home."

"You think she took it?"

"I'd rather not think that, but I can't imagine who else would have taken it. Certainly not the children."

"Of course not."

"I don't like to think of the ingratitude," she said. "After all we've done for her and then she steals from us."

"Well"—he exhaled slowly as he walked over to the door and opened it—"we'd better get to the bottom of this. Esther!" he called loudly. "Esther! Can you come up here?" He turned to his wife. "What else is missing?"

She shook her head. "I don't know. I haven't noticed anything else, but then I've not gone around inspecting."

"Esther!" he shouted again. "Will you come upstairs? Now!"

They could hear her feet on the wooden staircase, and when she came into the bedroom one of the children was right behind her. "Yes, sir?" she said. She glanced at Mrs. Davison, who had her back to them as she looked out the window.

"Esther," Mr. Davison began, "that silver hair set there on the dresser. Do you see it?" She nodded yes. "It's not complete. The mirror is missing." He watched the expression on her face. "It was there yesterday. It's not there today." There was something in her eyes; he wondered if it was fear or defiance. "Did you see the mirror? Did you *take* the mirror?"

"Take? Why should I do that? Of course I didn't! I told Mrs. Davison I didn't."

"Then where is it?"

"I . . . I don't know," she replied falteringly. "It's always been there when I've dusted the room . . ."

"Well, where is it now?" he insisted.

"I don't have any idea," she said. "Maybe one of the children has been playing—"

"Nonsense!" Mrs. Davison turned and glared at her. "The children know they're not allowed to play with things in this room. Don't put the blame on them."

Esther colored. "I'm not putting the blame on them, it's just that they might have been playing with the mirror and left it someplace." She turned to the boy beside her. "Do you know where your mother's mirror is?" He shook his head. "Have you or your sisters been in here?" Again he shook his head.

"They wouldn't have been playing with bolts of cloth!" Mr. Davison spoke sharply. "There's good tweed cloth missing as well. Mrs. Davison bought it and put it in the closet and now it's gone, too!"

The full implication of what he was saying suddenly reached her. She felt her pulse race. "And you think I stole the cloth?" He nodded. "And the mirror, too?"

"I think you did," he said, "and I think it was very foolish of you. Especially in the light of who you are and *why* you are living in this household. It was a very foolish thing to do.."

"I looked in her room," Mrs. Davison said. "While I put her to work peeling potatoes this afternoon, I searched her room. The items aren't there."

The thought of Mrs. Davison going through—touching—all her things made Esther's stomach twitch. "I wish you would have asked me," she said softly. "I would have told you that I didn't have them."

"Where are they?" Davison insisted. "What did you do with them?"

"I don't have them!" she replied, almost ready to cry.

"If they're not in your room, they must be somewhere. Did you hide them in the barn?"

"I haven't hidden them anywhere! Why don't you believe me?"

"Why should we believe *anything* you say?" he shouted.

"You're just a cut above a common criminal! You're here because you are a threat to the community! You have been placed under surveillance by the court. Have you forgotten that?" She shook her head no. "And have you also forgotten that you could be in jail right now? Have you? The only reason you are not behind bars at this moment is because Mrs. Davison and I took pity on you and brought you into our home!"

"I didn't ask for your pity," she answered quickly. "And I didn't ask to come here. Jail would be better than here."

Mrs. Davison gasped and put her hand to her heart. "Ungrateful! After all we have done! Taking you into the bosom of our family!"

"I never asked to come here," she replied. "I was happy at the Van Amburghs'. You people brought me here. Against my will. With a legal paper."

"The Van Amburghs! Of course!" Mr. Davison snapped his fingers. "Of course! That's where your things are, my dear. She took them to the Van Amburghs yesterday. That's what was in that package she had under her arm."

"No!" Esther shouted.

His wife shook her head. "It couldn't have been. I watched her pack it. I helped her, as a matter of fact."

"But this girl is an expert," Davison explained. "She's a perfect con artist. She switched packages on you and you never knew it. She's clever, she is. She must have learned a lot of stage tricks from that American actor fellow who was living with her. Don't you recall that story on him in the *Gazette*? Where he said he knew all about magicians and their tricks?"

"No!" Esther shouted.

"And she learned a couple. You only *thought* it was the same package. She switched it on you and you helped her steal your own property!" Mrs. Davison looked confused, and Esther leaned back against the bedroom wall. "See? You catch these people in the act, you prove you're wise to them, and they don't have an argument. They don't have a leg to stand on."

"Mr. Davison, sir," tears were running down Esther's face now, "please believe me. I did not steal anything from your home. I appreciate being here. You and your wife have been good to me. Why would I ruin it all by stealing?"

"I don't know why you would. But you have. You've ruined it—all of it—and you'll have to pay. Pay as you should have done in the beginning." He grabbed her by an arm and yanked her around. "I'm going to put you in your room and you're going to stay there. I'm going to lock the door to make sure that you do."

She tried to pull away, as his grip was hurting her. "Why don't you ask the Van Amburghs?" she cried. "They'll tell you the truth."

"I intend to do just that," he said. "As soon as I get you under lock and key, I'm going over there and see what was in that package for myself. And if"—he jerked her around so she was facing him—"if my wife's things are in there, you'll go straight to jail."

"We won't be able to keep you here," Mrs. Davison said. "Not if you're a thief."

"I don't want to stay here anyway," Esther said. She and Davison reached her bedroom and he shoved her inside and quickly pulled the door shut. "I don't want to stay here!" she shouted through the locked door. "I want to go away! I want to go home."

"Home?" Mr. Davison shouted back. "What's *home*? After all you've done, you don't *have* a home!"

* * *

John Van Amburgh stood in the doorway with his arms folded and his feet firmly planted. "You want to do what?"

"See that package that Esther brought over here yesterday," Davison said. "I want to see what's in it."

"Whatever's in there belongs to Esther," said the old sailor, "and you can't meddle with it."

"Whatever's in there could be my property, sir! It could be things that she stole from my home and hid over here." Davison wished Van Amburgh would let him in. The wind was like an icy dagger as it blew across the porch onto him.

Van Amburgh raised the hand lamp a little higher to get a better view of this unwanted man at his front door. "Esther is not a thief," he said matter-of-factly. "If things are missing from your house, look for someone else to blame. Not that girl."

"She's the only one who could have done it," Davison said above the wind.

"Your Aunt Fanny could have done it," Van Amburgh said. "The damned things are probably misplaced. Go back and look in your own home. Don't bother us with your nonsense."

Ruth Van Amburgh came to the door. "What is it?" She

saw Mr. Davison and pulled slightly away. 'What is it he wants?" she asked her husband.

"This idiot claims that Esther stole some valuables and brought them over here yesterday."

"That's preposterous," Ruth said. "Esther came over here with some clothes that she needs to have altered."

"Is that what was in the package?" Davison asked. "Her clothes and nothing more?"

"I don't know," Ruth replied. "I didn't bother to open it. She told me what was in it, and I put it in my sewing room. It's still there, still tied with string."

Davison's teeth were chattering from the cold. "Will you get it? Get it and let me see what's in it?"

"Of course," she said. "Mr. Van Amburgh, have Mr. Davison come in out of the wind while I get the package."

"No, you won't," John replied. "That package doesn't belong to us. It's Esther's property. If she wants to come for it, then let her. He ain't getting a look-see into it."

"Esther is not about to come here," Davison said. "I've locked her in her room. That's where she'll stay until this gets cleared up."

"Well, you miserable skunk! That child doesn't need to be locked anywhere! Now you get off my property and don't come back!"

"John Van Amburgh, you are a troublemaker!" Davison shouted.

"Pot calling the kettle black."

"A troublemaker! I am an elected official and I have the authority to look inside that parcel if I choose. I don't need a search warrant."

"Oh, you don't? Well, let me tell you, if you set one foot inside my house without my saying you can come in, you won't need a warrant. You'll need a shroud! And a box to lay yourself in!"

"I'm clerk of courts!"

"And I'm a champion rifle shot!"

"John, just let me get the package," Ruth begged. "It'll settle it once and for all. This arguing is all so silly."

"You're not getting him that parcel," her husband insisted. "That's Esther's property, not Mr. Demented Davison's. He's always spouting legal talk at people, so now if he wants to open that parcel, let him do it in a legal way. He's not marching in here just because he wants to. He has to make it official." He slammed the door, returning the figure on his front porch to the icy blackness of the November night.

"You'll get yours," Davison muttered as he found his way back to his horse and sleigh. "Oh, yes, you old pirate, you and the girl will get what you both deserve."

Tuesday, November 4, 1879

The pounding on the door came just a little after 10:00 A.M.

"Who in the Hell is that?" Van Amburgh put the soldering iron back on the stovetop. Ruth had been after him for months to mend a hole in one of her favorite cooking pots, and this morning he had finally decided to do it. "Wouldn't you know, I'd just get started and the door would have to be attended to." He spoke to himself as he trudged down the hallway. "Oh, no!" he groaned, staring at Mr. Davison. "Not you again."

Davison whipped a folded paper from his overcoat pocket. "My warrant, sir."

"Warrant to what?"

"To search your premises and find that parcel that Esther Cox removed from my home."

Van Amburgh opened the blue cover and read the handwritten page inside. "This looks legal enough," he said.

"It is, sir." A tall, thin man came up onto the porch. "I'm Constable Canbam. I've come to accompany Mr. Davison and see that there's no trouble."

"I know who you are, sir, and there won't be any trouble. There would have been had this idiot come without you or without this piece of paper. Does it make you feel braver, sir, to have help beside you?"

"Stand aside, Mr. Van Amburgh. I'm going to search your house." Davison tried to push the old sailor out of the doorway but he didn't budge.

"No, you're not! You can come into the house but you aren't going to *search* it. I don't give a damn what that legal paper says. You came just to see Esther's parcel, and by God, that's all you're going to see."

"Mr. Van Amburgh," said the constable, "may I remind you that we are officers of the law and there are strict penalties for not complying with us?"

"You don't have to remind me of anything, sir. Let me

remind you that this devil you've got with you is a nosy fool who is not going to get his way with me regardless of how many papers he may bring." He stepped back and motioned curtly with his hand. "Come on in. I'll call my wife."

The two men stomped the snow from their boots and came into the hallway. Davison glanced nervously around him, as if expecting a crew of pirates to come out swinging.

Ruth came into the hallway. "What is it?" She saw Davison. "Oh. You're back."

"Yes, ma'am. And with a search warrant. I demand to see that package Esther brought over here."

She looked at her husband and then at the metal star on the constable's coat. "I'll get it for you," she said haltingly.

"No, ma'am," the constable said quickly. "I don't want you to touch it. Just take us to where it is."

"It's in my sewing room. Upstairs. Really, it would be easier if I got it for—"

"No, thank you," the policeman said. "We'll go ourselves." They walked to the staircase and started up the steps. John and Ruth were right behind them. "Which is the sewing room?" the constable asked. Ruth pointed to the door at the end of the hall.

"That's it," Davison said loudly. "That's the package she carried over here."

"Is it?" Canbam asked Ruth. She nodded. "It's tied up," he said.

"That's the way Esther gave it to me," Ruth said. "I haven't had time to get to it yet, that's why it's still tied."

"Open it!" Davison commanded.

The constable took out his pocketknife and sliced the string. It parted easily. Then he unwrapped the brown paper covering.

The silver hand mirror was right on top.

"I *knew* it!" Davison shouted. "I knew she stole it!"

The policeman set the mirror to one side. Underneath were three lengths of cotton material. He set them aside. Under that was a cut of tweed material.

"That's my wife's!" Davison was still shouting. "That's the material she bought from a peddler to make a winter dress! I knew it! I knew that girl was a thief!"

The next item was a child's blue cotton skirt. There was also a tan skirt, the same size. Davison muttered that he recognized those objects as well. Then a pair of boy's cotton trousers was unfolded. Davison was positive they were his son's. Then a white linen sheet. There were four pillowcases, and from one of them the constable dumped an assortment of silver knives, forks, and spoons.

Davison picked one up and waved it under Van Amburgh's nose. "Look! It's monogrammed with a 'D.' That's 'D' for Davison. These are all *my* things. I knew it! I just knew it!"

Ruth had taken hold of her husband's hand, hoping to gather strength from it. "I can't believe . . ." she stammered.

"This is some trick of yours," Van Amburgh said to Davison. "You'd do anything to get that girl in trouble. I don't believe Esther stole these things. You must have planted them on her!"

"I? What would I want to do that for? No, sir, don't try to get out of this by blaming me. You and Esther are in this together. She stole these things and brought them to you. Oh, yes, you and that girl! I should have known! I'm not surprised."

The constable put his hand on Van Amburgh's shoulder. "You'll have to come with us," he said. "I'm putting you under arrest."

"What?" Van Amburgh thundered.

"As her accomplice," the officer stated flatly. "These items are stolen and were found in your possession. You'll have to come with me."

"I never heard anything so asinine in my life!" John shouted.

Ruth was almost in tears. "My husband didn't have anything to do with this."

"Ma'am, that's for the judge to decide. Not me. I have to take him in. Get your coat, sir."

"I'm not getting my coat! I'm not going anywhere with either of you!"

The constable opened his jacket and patted his revolver. "Get your coat," he said. "Don't make me use this."

It had started snowing again and the constable's sleigh was starting to cover over. Even his docile horse had the white stuff piling up on her back. They motioned Van Amburgh to sit in front while Davison took a rear seat. The snow was blowing so that it was impossible to see even ten feet ahead.

Yet, somehow, Davison saw the smoke.

"My God!" he shouted and grabbed the policeman's shoulder. "Look over there! From my place! Oh, my God!"

Now the other two could see the black cloud struggling up through the humid wet flakes. "Whatever it is is burning badly," Van Amburgh said..

"It's on my property!" Davison yelled. "Something's ablaze on my property!"

The constable slapped the reins against the horse's rump, and the animal broke into a fast trot. Davison almost fell out of the sleigh trying to get a better look at what was going on. "It looks like my barn!" he cried. "God damn, it looks like my barn!"

The reins were slapped again, but the horse ignored it. This was as fast as she was going to go, no matter how hard they stung her rump.

In a matter of minutes (it seemed like hours to Davison) the sleigh pulled into his drive and went quickly up to the house, then behind the house. Now they could all see it quite clearly. It was the barn and the roof, or what was left of it, blazing fiercely.

Mrs. Davison, bundled in an old sweater, came running to her husband. "It's awful!" she screamed. "The whole thing's gonna go!"

He put his arm around her and the two stood and watched the flames licking ravenously at the exposed roof beams. "Where are the children?" he asked.

"In the house. They're safe." She was crying. Not making any noise, just tears running from her eyes. "There's not much wind," she said. "Thank God for that."

"Amen," he replied, remembering a few years ago when the Stillwell barn had burnt and the wind had carried flaming chunks of hay onto all the outer buildings and finally to the house itself. What had been a prosperous farm had been reduced, in an hour, to rubble and char.

Amherst had a volunteer fire department, but there was no use calling them. Not for this. It would be at least twenty minutes before they could get there, and by that time most of the building would be gone. The fire was in the hayloft. The water from their pump would never reach it. There was nothing to do but stand and watch. Stand and watch the barn collapse into itself.

Suddenly Davison remembered: "Where's the horse and cow?"

"Esther got them out. She has them over behind the chicken coop."

"Esther?" he was shouting again. "What is she doing out? She was to remain locked up!"

"Well, she had to have some breakfast," his wife replied. "And clean her room. I just opened the door for a little while. That's all."

"That's *all*? You gave her just enough time for her to set fire to the barn! That's all!"

She pulled away from him. "She didn't set this fire. She was in the house. With me."

Davison stepped back as the main roof beam fell into the flames, taking most of the cross-section structure with it. Sparks flew bright red against the snow-white flakes. "You let her out!" he screamed. He ran to the policeman. "She let her out! My wife let the girl out! She burnt down my barn! My wife . . . that stupid woman . . . let her out!" He cradled his head in his hands. "Oh, my God! That Devil is trying to destroy me. Destroy me!"

Van Amburgh, standing nearby, said, "Now, you don't know that to be true. Esther wouldn't do a thing like that. She's not that kind of girl."

"What kind is she? Don't tell me about your sweet Esther!" he screamed just inches from Van Amburgh's face. "She's in league with Satan! She's a thief! She's a liar! She didn't burn down my barn, huh? Just like she didn't steal my things!"

"You don't have any proof—" Van Amburgh started to say.

"I don't need any proof! My wife let her out of her room and then my barn caught fire! What more *proof* do I need?" He turned swiftly to the policeman. "I want you to get her. Now! I want her arrested and I want her off my property! Now! God damn it, man, do it now, before she sets fire to my house and family!" He pushed the officer in the direction of the chicken coop. "Get her!" He shouted above the roar of the flames, his face streaming with tears of anger and frustration. "If you don't get her, I will. I've got a rifle in the house and I'll use it on her! I swear to God if you don't get her, I will!"

* * *

They sat apart from each other, Van Amburgh near the left wall and Esther near the right. The courtroom wasn't that big (plans for a new courthouse were on the drawing board at that moment), but Constable Canbam and Clerk Davison thought it best to keep the culprits separated.

Esther was still in shock. She had barely time to get over

her surprise and fear at the barn catching fire when she was roughly shoved into the constable's sleigh and driven into town. She had sat in the back with Davison, and once, when Van Amburgh tried to say something to her, he was rudely told by Davison to shut up. She had walked past the courthouse a million times but had never been inside it. She had often wondered what was behind the tall wooden columns that decorated the front of the white-painted building. Now she was inside, forced to sit and wait for a judge to hear her plea. They had made her sign a paper—they said Mr. Van Amburgh had signed one in another room—and then brought her to this larger place. She was not tied nor had she been threatened, but Constable Canbam made it more than obvious that he was wearing a gun and she understood his silver star gave him authority to use it. She glanced at the old sailor. He was staring at the floor. She wanted to talk to him, to tell him she didn't know how those things got into her parcel and to tell him she didn't start the fire in the barn. They wouldn't let her say anything to him. She wanted to put her arm around him and reassure him it would be all right. Suddenly, to her, he seemed so old.

The side door opened and she drew in a quick breath. It was Judge Bliss. "Oh, no!" she said aloud, and the man glared at her as he took a seat behind the raised table.

Constable Canbam read from a paper. He read flatly and without emphasis that one Esther Cox had been apprehended for the crime of stealing and for the crime of barn burning. One John Van Amburgh had also been apprehended. His crime: aiding and abetting the thievery of the said Miss Cox.

"I don't suppose you have anything to say in your behalf?" Judge Bliss made notations on a pad in front of him, not looking at the defendants.

"Just that Esther is not guilty, sir," Van Amburgh said. "And neither am I."

"Not guilty of what? Which crime?" the judge looked at him now.

"The thievery charge. She didn't steal anything from Davison."

"You were there?"

"Yes."

"When the objects were removed from the Davison residence?"

"No, I was there when she brought a parcel to my home. It had some of her clothes in it. Clothes she wanted my wife to alter for her. We have one of those new machines that sew, and my wife offered to fix the clothes for her."

"And when she opened the parcel in your home, it contained those items of her personal wearing apparel?"

"We never opened the package, Your Honor. We just left it. Esther said it had her clothes in it." He looked at the girl and then back to the judge. "We had no reason to open it, at the time."

"So you didn't know what was in the package? When she brought it into your house?"

"No, but Esther said—"

"I didn't ask you what she said. I asked you if you knew, really knew, what was in that package." Judge Bliss glared at him.

"No," the man said slowly, "not really."

"Then you cannot swear, sir, that the girl is not guilty as charged, can you? You really never knew what was in the parcel. You took her word for it." The judge still didn't look at Esther. "Why didn't you open the parcel? Didn't you want your wife to see what was in it?"

"My wife? What does that have to do with . . . See here, sir, I don't know what you're getting at."

"What am I getting at is very simple. You had Esther bring over a parcel of Mr. Davison's valuables and you didn't want it opened in front of your wife because you were going to sell them for the girl."

"What?" Van Amburgh started to stand up, but the policeman pushed him down. "What kind of nonsense are you spouting?"

"It's called plausible supposition," the judge replied.

"It's more like plausible bull-shit! I never intended to do anything like that!"

"Then Esther"—he turned toward her; she wanted to look away, but she held her gaze firm—"you planned to take the money from the sale of the items and leave the area." The girl was so shocked she couldn't find words to answer this charge. "You don't have any money. Silverware and dress material can easily be converted into cash. You were hoping the Davisons wouldn't discover the items missing until Van Amburgh could get them sold."

"Where in the Hell," the old sailor shouted, "did you get that cockamamie idea?"

"From me," Davison spoke up. "Esther wanted to escape but needed money. She brought my valuables to you on Sunday so you could sell them on Monday. She was probably planning on slipping away last night. But I locked her in her room. I foiled her plans. And yours."

"When did you figure that out?" Van Amburgh asked.

"On the way to the courthouse," Davison said proudly. "It's the only thing that makes sense. Then"—he turned back to the judge—"when she saw that her plans had gone awry, she convinced my wife to unlock the door so she could slip away and set fire to my hayloft. Revenge. That's what she wanted, she wanted revenge."

"That's not true!" Esther found her voice. "None of that is true! I don't know how your things got in my parcel. When I wrapped it, it had *my* things in it. Your wife was right there. She helped me with it. Ask her. Ask Mrs. Davison!"

"Your Honor," Davison said with a smile, "need I remind you of what we have already discussed? That this girl spent several weeks with an actor, a theatrical person, who was well versed in the art of stage magic and deception? She's fooled a lot of people around here. I was too much for her." He sat back, content in his own cleverness.

"And that's why you set the fire," the judge stated flatly.

"I didn't! I wasn't anywhere near the barn this morning! The first time I knew it was afire was when Mrs. Davison told me to run and save the animals. I hadn't been out of the house all morning!"

Judge Bliss tried to suppress a grin. "It wasn't necessary for you to be *out* there, my dear. I personally have seen what you can do with fire. Matches and fire. I've been in my house on Princess Street when lighted matches have fallen everywhere. Fallen because you have commanded them to fall! You're a rare little bird, Miss Cox. You don't need to be in a room for something disastrous to happen in it. I've *seen* it. I've heard stories of others who have seen you at work. I've read newspaper accounts of what you can do. Oh, yes, you've made the papers. For a young girl, you're quite a celebrity. You've long been known as a troublemaker and as an incendiary. You light fires. Just by wishing them. You want something to burn and—poof—up in smoke it goes. Don't sit there with those big innocent eyes and claim you didn't light that fire. I know better. And so does the whole town of Amherst."

"You're wrong," said Van Amburgh, "dead wrong."

"Dear sir," the judge said evenly, "the people of this county chose me—yes, and pay me—because I am usually right. Nine times out of ten, I am right. That's why I am entrusted with the power of the people. And I'm right in this case. Miss Cox set fire—one way or another—to the barn. She also removed those articles from Mr. Davison's home to yours. You took them and planned to sell them. I'm right about that. I'm also right in directing you both to spend tonight in jail. You'll have until tomorrow to think about your crimes and tell the truth. And depending on how I view your particular brand of 'truth,' I'll make my decision." He rose from his chair. "Frankly," he said, "it doesn't look good for either of you."

Wednesday, November 5, 1879

The room that Esther awoke in had no windows, just a hole in the ceiling that was covered with clear glass. They had taken her directly to this room after Judge Bliss dismissed them. She didn't know where Van Amburgh was. She called out to him several times in the afternoon and evening but he didn't answer. The policeman who brought her dinner (which sat untouched on the floor) refused to give her any information. She knew the man, had gone to school with his younger sister but he only said "hello" and "you better eat something." She didn't feel rested and didn't recall sleeping. The single bed with the stinking mattress was the only piece of furniture in the room. She wondered how many drunks had thrown up on that mattress and wished she had her bottle of perfume to douse the thing. There was a chamber pot under the bed. She had to use it once, and she was thankful it was clean. It had no lid, however, and the stench of her own waste materials mingled with the stenches that were already there.

She had slept, of course, in the clothes she had on when she was arrested. They were warm clothes, because the Davison house was always chilly and as she went out to the chicken coop and the barn all the time she wore heavy clothes in readiness. When she thought of the barn, she stopped and closed her eyes. She could see it, against the snowstorm, ragged with flame. There had only been a little smoke when she saved the animals; she wondered if she would have gone in for them had the ground floor been on fire rather than the loft.

"But I didn't do it!" she said aloud. She had said it over and over in this cell, but there was no one to hear her.

The door opened. There was no knocking first. The young policeman came in with a basin and a pitcher of warm water. "You're supposed to get ready," he said. "The judge is gonna see you in about half an hour." He had a towel draped over his shoulder. "Here, use this. It's clean. We usually don't have girls in here, so Sadie sent this with me this morning. She said you went to school with her." He reached in his pocket and took out a comb. "No mirror," he said. "Sorry." She smiled at him. He picked up the tray of uneaten food and went out without another word. She heard his key turn the lock.

When he came back for her, she felt much better. She had been able to wash herself with the water and to smooth her hair with the comb. Her dress was still wrinkled from sleeping in it, but she knew there was nothing she could do about that. "I'm not in a fashion show!" she said as she brushed at the creases in her skirt.

As she was led into the courtroom again, she heard her name called. It was Olive and Jennie. Sobbing aloud, they ran to her, grabbed her, and hugged her tightly. They both said things that sounded like "so sorry" and "how did this happen?" and "get you out" and "you're innocent" and "poor baby," but the words didn't register on her. All she knew was that she was holding her sisters again—even if it was in a public courtroom.

They brought in Mr. Van Amburgh. She saw immediately that they hadn't given him fresh water or a comb. His hands were tied and he had a raw bruise on the side of his face. He held his head high, though, and winked at Esther as they pointed him into a seat.

Judge Bliss came into the room and took his place behind the large table. He looked around. "Mrs. Teed," he acknowledged. "Miss Cox," Jennie nodded. "Are we ready to take care of this matter?" The constable nodded. Davison, sitting alone and with his arms folded across his chest, also nodded. "Good. Mr. John Van Amburgh, have you anything to add to what was said yesterday?"

"Just that I'm not guilty of any wrongdoing. And neither is Esther. Everyone in this courthouse has jumped to all the wrong conclusions."

"And why are your hands tied?" the judge asked.

"Because I tried to hit a cop," he said easily. "I would have, too, if I'd had more room to swing."

"But you didn't hit him?"

"No. He hit me. See where it's getting black? That's where he hit me."

"Are you sorry you tried to attack an officer of the law?"

"Well . . . let me think about it."

"Mr. Van Amburgh," said Judge Bliss, "I suggest you think quickly because I have decided that even though you wished to help Miss Cox, outside events prevented you from doing so. The valuables were returned intact. You may have wanted to be an accomplice, but my clerk of court and my constable prevented you. I can only reprimand you, I can't *jail* you, for *wanting* to do something. But," he cleared his throat, "I *can* jail you for willfully attacking a policeman. That is most definitely an offense. However, should you repent publicly of your desire to attack the officer, then I have no recourse but to release you into the protective custody of your wife."

"In other words," said the old sailor, "if I say I'm sorry, I can go home."

"That's correct."

He looked at the judge and then at Esther. He smiled at her and shrugged. She understood. "Then I'm sorry," he said with a sigh. "I'm sorry I tried to hit a cop. What else do you want me to apologize for?"

"That'll be quite sufficient." The judge initialed a half sheet of paper and handed it to Davison. "That was your release. You're free to go."

The policeman he swung at untied his hands warily. "Can I stay for the rest of this?" he spoke to the judge. "I want to see what happens to Esther."

The judge shook his head. "Whatever the decision of this court is toward Miss Cox is entirely none of your concern, sir. You are free to go. Please do so. Now."

Van Amburgh shrugged again and rubbed his wrists. He went over to Esther and kissed her lightly on the forehead. "Don't let the bastard wear you down," he whispered. Then he was escorted from the room.

Judge Bliss now looked at Esther, for the first time that morning. "Miss Cox, have you changed your mind about your plea of innocence?"

"Do you mean," she said in a small voice, "do I want to say I'm guilty?"

"That's correct," he nodded.

She shook her head. "I can't tell you I'm guilty when I *know* I'm innocent. I did not steal from the Davisons, and I did not set that barn afire. That is the truth."

"The truth as far as you see it," the judge replied. "That being the case"—he initialed two sheets of paper in front of him—"I have no other recourse but to find you guilty as charged. Based on the evidence before me and the evidence of your previous escapades. For the charge of thievery, I sentence you to one month in the county jail." Olive, in the back row, muffled a cry. "And for the crime of barn-burning—a most serious offense because a rural family's livelihood is centered about their barn—for that offense I sentence you to three months in the county jail." This time Olive let her cry escape. "That's a total of four months to be spent incarcerated."

Esther didn't flinch. She forced herself to remain calm.

"Now I did consider, because of your sex and your age, mandating you to serve this time in the kitchen of the county poorhouse, but I would be worrying for four months that you would set that place afire. That's all. You may take her," he motioned to the constable.

They led her out through a rear door so she didn't have a chance to talk with her sisters, both of whom sat close to each other, crying. She glanced at them and then shot a look of defiance at the judge. He ignored it and reached for a pitcher to pour himself some water.

There was the sound of breaking and then a yell from the judge. He sat there, the pitcher handle still in his hand, and the cool drinking water suddenly steaming hot as it ran over his desk and down into his lap.

Esther smiled as the door closed behind her.

* * *

The cell they put her in was bigger and cleaner than the last one. It had a bed, not a cot, with a clean-smelling mattress, sheets, pillow with a pillowslip, and two blankets. There was a table beside the bed, and against one wall a wooden wardrobe with several wire hangers. A dry sink and a bucket of fresh water stood near the door. A chamber pot could be seen under the bed. The floor had been painted black at one time but now was worn down to the bare wood in paths that led from the bed to the window, the window to the water, the water to the door. A gaslight burner stuck out of the wall near the bed. She supposed someone would come in and light it when the sun went down.

The room was cold. Not just because there was snow outside on the ground and the wind whined around the wall but because it was chilled from despair, poverty, and loneliness. Esther stretched out on the bed. She tried to think of nothing. If she kept thinking of nothing, then she wouldn't go mad. They had taken four months from her life. They had taken a Christmas and a New Year's and a springtime from her. They had put her in a cage, like an animal, and would keep her there because they thought four months would tame her. She couldn't picture four months. Four months was forever. In four months, she could be dead. If Bob Nickle and his gang had their way, in four months she *would* be dead. "How convenient," she said aloud, "you finally got me into a place where I can't get out. It shouldn't take you long to do what you want to do." She wondered why there were no tears; then she understood: She was empty. The emotions, the events of the past fourteen months had drained her. Nothing remained of her but the physical part, and Bob Nickle would soon have that as well.

She wasn't sure how long she had lain there, staring at the peeling paint on the ceiling, when the door opened and the policeman, her friend Sadie's brother, put two large paper-wrapped bundles on the floor. "They're from your family," he said. "Outside. Look out the window. They want to talk to you."

Esther almost fell over her own feet getting to the window. There, through the bars and the wire screen across the bars, stood Olive and Jennie. They had the two small boys with them. All four waved when they saw her. The ground looked to be some six feet from the windowsill, and her gaze quickly took in the downtown square, the trees and snow-covered bushes, and a little farther down, the stone walls of the Baptist church. She could hear the noises on Victoria Street but she couldn't see it.

"Oh, I'm so glad you came!" she said. "Isn't this just silly?" she tried to laugh. "I keep getting into the darnedest scrapes!" She smiled, not wanting her sisters to know how she ached to be out there with them.

"Did they give you the parcels?" Olive spoke up. Esther nodded. "We put some of your dresses and sweaters and things in one of them and your toilet articles and some foodstuffs in the other. Let us know what else you need. We'll try to come by every day."

"Every day," Jenny promised. "Esther, we're so sorry. It's all such a mistake. I'm sure Judge Bliss will see reason."

"He can't see past his nose," Esther said. "He doesn't want to see. I'm a menace, and this is his jail. It's that simple."

"Are you cold?" Olive asked. Esther nodded yes. "Well, put on some of those woolen things. It must be like an icebox in there. There's nothing over that window, is there? Shutters you can close?" Esther shook her head no. "So you get cold air all the time? Well, you ought to be able to do something about that. I'll fetch a quilt and you can get someone to nail it over the window for you. Would you like that?" The girl nodded. "It's a disgrace that they would subject a young girl to such indignities! A disgrace! I'm going to see the mayor myself about it."

"Olive," Esther replied calmly, "please don't stir things up. There's nothing you can do. The judge has the final say-so. Not you and not the mayor. The disgrace," she added, "is *me*. That I have come to this. And on your family that you have a common criminal in your midst. That's the disgrace, Olive, what I have done to you and your family."

"Now, don't be silly," Olive shouted, "and don't start crying! Tears don't help!"

"I'm not crying," she replied. "Look. My face is dry. There aren't any more tears inside me. I'm empty."

"Don't talk that way!" Olive said loudly above the wind. "That kind of talk is not beneficial!"

"It is if I am to remain sane," the girl responded. An icy blast came through the metal bars. "Anyway, you and Jennie and the children go on home now. It's too cold to be standing out there. Thank you for everything. I do appreciate it, but I'll be fine. I promise you. I'll be real fine." She waved and pulled back from the window. With her not looking out, she knew they would go. She sighed. It would be a long four months for the Teeds, too.

Lunch was brought in and she ate it. She was hungry, and if her body were to remain alive, it had to eat. She was surprised that the soup and the sandwich were so good. The policeman told her he got it from Lamy's Hotel. The jail didn't have a kitchen. It was rare that anyone stayed more than a night or two.

In the afternoon, she put away the things Olive had brought her and tried to organize them in such a way that it would seem like "home." Whatever that was. Supper was a pot of coffee and cream, a pile of salt crackers, and a hunk of yellow cheese. When the sun went down, nobody came in to turn on the gaslight. She got under the covers of the bed, fully clothed because of the cold, and forced herself to sleep.

"Hey! Esther! Esther Cox!"

She opened her eyes and tried to focus them in the darkness. It was coming from outside. She slipped from under the blankets and ran to the window. "Yes?" she called. "Yes?"

"Hey, witch-girl!" a youngish masculine voice shouted. "They gottcha in the clink, huh?"

"Who . . . ? Who is it?" She peered into the blackness below.

"About time they put your butt away!" another voice said loudly.

"Yeah," called a third voice, "hope they throw away the key!"

"Who is it?" she shouted. "Who are you?"

"Tell her your name," one of them laughed.

"And have her do her voodoo on me? Oh, no! You tell her yours!" and he laughed.

"If she's so smart, her ghosts will tell her our names," another said and they all laughed. "Yeah, Esther, ask your ghosts!"

She pulled away from the window and sat heavily on the bed.

"Ask your ghosts to blow up the jail, why don't ya?"

"Yeah! They ain't so tough now that your ass is in the clink!"

"Boo!" one shouted amid the laughter. "I'm a ghost and I'm gonna get ya!"

More laughter. "She ain't gonna walk down the street with her nose in the air after this!"

"You ain't gonna walk down these streets at all! No more. Bitch! Witch! Witch-bitch!"

She heard a dull thud against the outer wall. Then another, followed by a splatting sound as a snowball hit the screen and sprayed inside her cell. "Stones kill witches!" one of them called. "Now we got snowballs! When this stuff melts, we'll have stones."

"Yeah!"

"Remember, witch-bitch, when you get out we'll have stones!"

Another snowball hit the wire and splattered the cell with ice. Esther hurried under the covers and pulled them up around her ears. She didn't want to hear. She didn't want to know about those boys, about that town out there in the darkness. She vaguely heard their voices and the thuddings against the wall. Water ran down her cheek and for a second she thought one of their snowballs had somehow crawled in under the blankets. Then she realized that the water was tears. She was crying, and damn it, she didn't want to.

Friday, November 14, 1879

A full week had passed, and she had made the best of living in a one-room cell. As promised, Olive had sent around a heavy quilt that the guard had been nice enough to hang over the window for her. He put it on a drapery rod so she could slide it open for sunlight or pull it closed to keep out the wind. She also received permission for a box of safety matches to be in her cell so she could ignite the gas lamp on the wall whenever she wished.

Also, as promised, Olive appeared at the window every day. Not with the children because of the bitter winds, but almost always with a gift of some sort, be it an apple, a handkerchief, or a ladies' magazine. She had brought a framed engraving that had hung on Princess Street. Esther liked it. It was called "From Shore to Shore," and it showed a group of people crossing a turbulent river in a rowboat. She had often stared at the engraving, inventing stories about those people in that boat. They were such a diverse collection. How did they all happen to be in that same boat? Why did they leave the one shore, and what did they expect to find when they reached the other? Even though it was in black and white, it brightened up her small, confined world.

Olive had also brought her a needlepoint pillowslip to

work on. It was masses of small flowers, stems and leaves, and tiny butterflies. There was a great deal to do on it and, if she ever got it finished, it would look beautiful on the parlor sofa. She sat this morning with the quilt pulled slightly to one side, letting in just enough sunlight to sparkle on the needle as it went in and out of the small squares.

"Esther! Hey, Esther!" It was a strong masculine voice and she looked up warily, like a doe testing a sound in the forest. "Esther Cox!" the voice called again. "Get over to that window!"

She grinned and tossed the needlepoint onto the bed. She knew that voice! How wonderful of him to come.

John Van Amburgh stood on the ground below, his wife, Ruth, by his side, both of them stomping the snow from their boots. "Well, there you are, young lady!" the man called as her face appeared at the window. She grinned. "Just came by to see if you were still alive."

"I am," she said with a laugh. "It takes more than this to kill me off."

"Glad to hear it," he said. "Seen my friend, old Judge Bliss?"

"No. And don't want to."

"He doesn't want to see us, either," Ruth spoke up. "We've had words with him about you. He knows how we feel. Hey," she called, "do you want a surprise?"

"A surprise?"

"Yes," the old sailor said loudly, "we have a surprise but you have to close your eyes and wait till we tell you to open them."

"Okay." She shut her eyes tightly, wondering what it could be.

"Open," he called.

She opened her eyes and gasped. "Adam!" Her voice rose delightedly. "Adam Porter! What are *you* doing here?"

"Came to see you," the young man answered. "When I saw the story about you in the *Post* yesterday, I came to town. They wouldn't let me in the jail."

"No," she replied, "I can't have visitors in here."

"So I went to the Van Amburghs and they told me they'd come with me to the window. Here we are."

"I'm so glad to see you," she said. "But not like this. I didn't want you to see me like this. In here, and all."

"I've been thinking about you," he called.

"And I you."

"You've been thinking about me?" he asked.

She blushed. "Yes. Yes, I have."

"Been thinking about *us*?" he asked.

She blushed again. "Been trying not to," she replied. "It can't get nowhere."

"You won't be in there forever," Ruth said loudly. "Adam says he's willing to wait."

"Why, Mrs. Van Amburgh," said her husband, "let the young man do his own proposing."

Adam laughed. "But your wife does it so much better than I can."

"If that don't beat all!" The old sailor laughed and his warm breath came out in short bursts against the cold air. "The groom's on the sidewalk and the bride's in jail! Sounds like the start of a dirty story."

"There's no bride and groom, Mr. Van Amburgh," Esther said.

"Not yet," Adam replied.

"Not ever!" Esther replied.

"Isn't that sweet?" the old man said. "She loves you! Look how she's fighting it."

His wife punched him playfully on the shoulder. "You behave yourself. Remember, the judge placed you in my custody."

"Lordy, Esther, she doesn't let me forget that for one single day!" He laughed. "I do something she don't like and she threatens me with old man Bliss. She'll have me back in there with you in no time."

"I'd rather it be me," said Adam.

"You're all crazy!" Esther laughed. "Especially you, Adam Porter. You're the craziest one of all."

"For you. That's all."

"You stop talking like that," she admonished. "I'm in no position to listen to it."

"But it does feel kinda good, doesn't it?" Ruth asked. "To know you have people who love you?"

Now the girl felt the emotions welling up inside her. "Yes," she said, "it feels kinda good. It feels *real* good!"

Wednesday, November 19, 1879

The guard brought in her lunch tray. It was the usual mug of soup with a beef sandwich. "Letter there for you, too," he said. "Came this morning."

"A letter?" She picked it off the tray and stared at it. "Nobody ever sends me letters."

"Well, you got one now." He went out and locked the door behind him.

She examined the handwriting but didn't recognize it. It was postmarked "Port Philip, N.S." She held it to the light. "I don't know anybody up there," she said to herself. Then she opened it. It was one page of lined paper written on both sides in a large pencil scrawl. Her eyes quickly went to the signature; then her heart raced and she suddenly felt very warm. It was from Adam.

> My Dear Esther: I'm not so good at writing letters as you will see. I never got certificates for penmanship nor spelling when I was in school. But I wanted you to have this. I don't like freezing my bones, twisting my neck and making myself hoarse. That's what I have to do to talk to you while you are in that jail. Don't be sorry for me, nobody forced me to come see you and go through those contortions." *She warmed even more and smiled. He was silly but he was nice, too.* "I'll come to the point, I've always been very direct. I want to marry you. I've thought about it and talked about it with my mother and my two boys and they all want me to be happy. I told them you make me happy. I'm not happy when you are in that jail place. It makes me real unhappy." *She sighed. Strange, but having him unhappy made her unhappy, too.* "I know we really don't know each other all that good yet. We haven't had lots of time together but what I've seen in the couple times we've been together has been mighty pleasing. Lots of people know each other for years and then they get married and are unhappy so I guess maybe it's not how *long* a body knows another body but how they *feel* about them. When I think of you I get a flutter like a live bird is caged inside my stomach. I can make that

fluttering commence just by picturing your face. Yesterday I thought I saw your face when the wind swirled some snow across the backyard. I told my mother about it and she said it sounds like I am in love." *Esther felt the bird fluttering inside herself as well and marveled at the sensation.* "I didn't feel these things nor see these things with my first wife, the mother of my boys. She was a good woman, God rest her soul, but I didn't feel for her like I feel for you. I can't say these things standing outside your window and shouting so everyone on Victoria Street will hear. That's why I put them on paper. It's taken me all day to write this far. I hope it was worth it. To you. Your friend, Adam Porter.

She got up from the bed, where she had been sitting, and holding the letter close to her heart, stood staring out the window. The snow had piled higher, obliterating most of the footprints in the main square. The trees were like huge sticks of cotton candy, and the dark clouds coming up over the Baptist church roof promised an early-afternoon darkness. Yet she didn't see it. She saw green grass and flowers among the leaves and white clouds soaring against a radiant sky. She looked down at the letter pressed to her breast. The little bird inside fluttered against her rib cage. "Maybe it's not how long two people know each other," she said aloud, "but how they feel *inside* about one another. Maybe that's the secret. Maybe that's what everyone means when they talk about 'love.'"

She walked back to the bed and carefully, tenderly, put the letter on the table. She stood looking down at it, smiling at it, feeling so glad that she had it.

That's when it rose up, the page fluttering free of the envelope and bumping against the ceiling. It floated freely for a few seconds, teasing her, never coming close enough for her to grab it.

"No!" she called and her voice broke. "Please, don't! Oh, please, please don't!"

She jumped for it, but it eluded her one more time. Then she heard the hissing of the gaslight wall bracket. She drew in her breath and stood stock still. If they had decided to do it, she knew there was nothing she could do to stop them.

The gas jet burst into flame, a high blue flame tinged in

red. The sheet of paper glowed in the center for only a second until the flames spread through it from corner to corner. She watched, fists pressed in anguish against her face, as the pencil marks turned from black to white to ashes and floated lazily down onto the jail cell floor.

Monday, November 24, 1879

"Yes, she's the main reason we've come. We are the committee." The white-haired man with the large belly settled himself on a chair beside the judge's desk. "It was taken up for a vote after church yesterday and decided upon then and there."

"You have to get rid of her," a woman spoke up. "She's too dangerous to keep here in town."

The judge forced a smile. "Now, Mrs. Talbot, I think we can handle the young lady in question right here and without going to extremes."

"Well, I don't think you can, sir. It hasn't appeared so far as if you can. You have her there in that jail, with a window right onto the public square and where she can bother decent citizens any hour of the day and night." Mrs. Talbot's son had gone by with some friends, Esther had appeared at the window, and that very night he had come down with a high fever and severe headaches. "She's dangerous to the health of the community. A body's not safe."

"My little Lucille was hit by a snowball the other day," added Mrs. Gurnsey. "She and a group of her little school friends were outside the window when two grown men started throwing snowballs at it. One of them hit my Lucille. It's a terrible predicament when schoolchildren aren't safe in the public square!"

"Putting people in jail is supposed to change their attitude," Mrs. Talbot added. "It hasn't had any effect on Esther or her family. Before she burned down poor Mr. Davison's barn, I went to visit her on Princess Street and her sister, that Teed woman, treated me abominably. Like I was some sort of leper, or something. My own sister had come all the way from Halifax to meet the Cox girl, and Mrs. Teed practically threw her out of the house. And last week, when I saw that Teed woman in Chapman's store, she put up her nose and snubbed me as if I were trash. It would appear to me that *she*, with that sister of hers in jail, is the trashy one!"

"They've not learned from this," the man said. "The Teeds stand outside that window and shout things to her every day."

"So does that awful Van Amburgh person!" Mrs. Gurnsey said. "Him with his young wife and his foul mouth."

"What it is, Your Honor," the man broke in, "is that Amherst is becoming a laughingstock with that girl being on public display in the center of town."

Judge Bliss bristled: "She is hardly on public display, sir, she is incarcerated in the county jail. The jail happens to be right downtown. In the *center* of town. I really don't see what I can do about that. I can't have the jail moved."

"No," said Mrs. Talbot, "but you can have *her* moved. Far away. To another place."

"To Halifax. They have a bigger jail there. You could send her to Halifax."

"I can't send her out of the county," the judge replied. "She was arrested and tried for crimes inside Cumberland County. I can't send her to another county."

"Well, then, there must be other places inside the county she could go," Mrs. Gurnsey said. "After all, we voted at church yesterday, so that's what we want done."

"I can't do it," the judge replied. "Having any other location take care of her would cost the taxpayers money, more money than she's costing now."

"What's more important?" Mrs. Talbot stared at him. "A few tax dollars or the reputation of the entire town?"

"You have to make a decision," said the red-faced man. "You *are* an elected official."

"We *will* be having elections again." Mrs. Talbot wasn't smiling.

"And more discussions at more churches," Mrs. Gurnsey added. "The better informed the citizenry, the better the government. That's what I always say. Isn't that what you always say, Mrs. Talbot?"

"Oh, yes, certainly. That's what I *always* say!"

Saturday, November 29, 1879

"Right you are, missy! 'Ere's your supper. Look sharp now!"

Esther turned to stare at the policeman coming in with her tray. He was a new one. She hadn't turned on the gaslight, and his features were in shadow.

"'Ere you are! We'll just put it right 'ere on the table. Pretty as you please. There you go! Now, that's perfect!" He turned to her. "'Ow's about a kiss? Don't ya get a kiss when ya gets ya supper?" He reached for her.

She pulled back. "Sir! You get out of . . . ." She stopped as he pulled open the quilt over the window, letting the light of sunset into the cell. "Adam!" she gasped. "What are you doing here?"

"To see you." He was whispering now. "Came to see you. I had to." He embraced her.

"But"—she pulled away—"that uniform. Where did you get it?"

"From the guard. I only got it for thirty minutes. He wanted to see his girl, too. It *is* Saturday night, you know. Not a bad fit." He turned slowly so she could admire him.

"But what if you get caught? Suppose somebody comes in and catches you?"

"Who's to come? The guard is the only one in the building, except for you, of course. It's Saturday night. Everybody's home."

"Why would he do this?"

"For money. Why else? That and the fact that he can be with his girl for half an hour. I paid him two dollars. It was worth it." She started to say something else but he put his finger to her lips. "No more words. Please. Just let me hold you." She sank willingly into his arms and felt her legs shaking as he folded those arms around her. "Hey," he whispered into her ear, "relax. I'm here. We're together. That's the important thing."

She felt the warmth of his body, the strength of his arms and hands. Someone was touching her, holding her, after all the days and nights of being so alone, of being so lonely. Then he pulled back, slightly, and she saw his face up close. It was getting nearer as he closed his eyes and tilted his head. She shut her eyes and moved her mouth until it was next to his lips, then touching his lips. They stood like that and she felt the caged birds flutter up, settle back, and then relax.

"Adam," she sighed. "Oh, God, how I need you!" Their lips met again and stayed longer this time.

"I have something for you," he said. "I want you to wear it. It's important." He fumbled in the jacket pocket and bought out a polished stone. It was egg-shaped, but flat on one side and curved on the other. There was just enough light coming in through the window to see that the flat surface had some strange carvings on it. "I want you to wear this," he said.

"Why?"

"Just put it on." There was a hole in one end of the stone, and a large circle of black human hair hung through it, braided tightly for strength. Adam slipped it over her head. "Don't take it off from now on. Promise me."

Her fingers caressed the smooth face of the reddish stone. "Where'd you get it? What's it for?"

He took her hands and they both sat on the edge of the bed. "I have some friends who are Indians. Micmacs from up near Pugwash Point. I've known them for years, used to play with them when I was growing up, and then went hunting with them before I got married. I saw them yesterday. I went to see them about you."

"About me?"

"I went to ask them what they could do to help you."

"And they gave you this rock?" He nodded. "It's supposed to *help* me?"

"It will. The medicine man who gave it to me swore it would help you. He said it would keep evil spirits and things away from you. As long as you wear it, nothing bad can happen. And I don't want anything bad to happen, no more," he said. "No more bad things. You've had enough." He leaned forward and kissed her again. "You're gonna be okay now. You've got me. I'll make sure you're okay." Then it was her turn to lean over and kiss him.

"Thank you," she smiled. "There's so many other things that I thought I would say, but now the only thing that comes out is 'thank you.'"

"That's enough," he grinned. "Plenty enough. Now listen. We have a plan to get you out of here."

"We? Who's we?"

"Old man Van Amburgh and myself. We've come up with this idea—at least *he* has—and we've talked about it and we think it'll work."

"You and your Indians are going to go on the warpath and blow up the jail. Right?" She grinned.

"Wrong. There'll be no violence and no explosives. Old man Davison will be the one to explode, and then Judge Bliss will explode right afterward. At least that's what we hope."

"Aren't you going to tell me?"

"No. If you don't know about it, then you can't be implicated if it doesn't work. This is our doing, Van Amburgh's and mine. Here, let me give you one last kiss. I've got to get this uniform back to the guard."

"He must be cold without his coat and pants." She laughed.

"He's not going to freeze. He's got his girl." Esther turned beet red, and Adam put his hand on her cheek and grinned. "You just get all burned up when you get embarrassed. Here, let me have one last kiss. Until the next one, that is." They came forward, together, and their lips met. Adam put his hands on her face and held the kiss tenderly. "I've got to go," he whispered. "My half hour."

At the door she hugged him, brought him close to her, wanted to feel his body and his strength and his caring one more time before he left. Even after the door closed, she felt him pressed against her.

She heard the clatter of the coffee mug upon the tin tray. She whirled in time to see the coffee pot, spoon, and plate of cheese lift off and come at her. She screamed and jumped to one side. The objects hit the far wall and fell noisily to the floor. Then the tray came up off the table. It was thin and made of tin. With a crash, it swung against the bedstead. One corner broke off, leaving, jagged, sharp metal splinters. She backed against the quilted window as the tray, this weapon of theirs, hovered just inches from her throat. She tried to scream again but the sound wouldn't come. The tray shifted closer, moving in a zigzag pattern as if it had already started cutting through her flesh. Then her hand went to her breast and clutched the smooth stone that hung around her neck.

"Adam said it would protect me!" she yelled. "Do you hear me, Bob Nickle? I have something to protect me! At last!"

The tray made a sweeping motion and came to a quivering halt over her head. It was as if the invisible hand holding it was about ready to swing it down, bring it down, and let the jagged edge slide through the veins that throbbed in her throat.

"I have someone to protect me!" She shouted again. "He loves me! He wants me! I'm not afraid of you anymore, Bob Nickle! Do you hear me? For the first time, I'm not afraid of you!"

The tray flipped up and over, backward, away from her.

Then it started slashing at the walls, the ragged edge chopping at paint and plaster. Esther clutched at the stone, both hands grabbing it and holding on to it as she slid to the floor.

The tray spun through the air, bounced off the metal gas fixture, and landed on the bed. It raised itself and started cutting the blankets, slitting the pillow and sending feather ticking everywhere. Esther kept her hands on the stone. The tray spun crazily, then sped toward the window, chopping and ripping and gouging great holes in the hanging quilt. Then it fell onto the floor, unmoving, as if exhausted.

"I'm not afraid anymore!" She started to laugh and cry at the same time. "Oh, God, I'm not afraid anymore!"

Thursday, December 4, 1879

"It is important, James, or else we wouldn't be here, wouldn't have come all this way." The tall man in the heavy dark greatcoat stood in front of Judge Bliss's desk. "Thank heavens the train can get through this snow. A horse never would have made it up here from Halifax."

"It's good to see you again, Roy," said the judge. "I assume you've come on official business."

The police officer accompanying the man from Halifax nodded. "We came to see Mr. Arthur Davison as well. Your clerk of court."

"Davison?" Judge Bliss was surprised. "What do you want with him?"

"Will you call him, please." The first man said it as a statement, not a question.

The judge looked at them, one an old friend from the judicial system in Halifax and the other an officer he'd not met before. They were here, unannounced in his office, and wanting to talk to Davison. The judge hurried down the hallway, motioned for Davison to leave his office, and the two men returned together. "A drink of something to chase away the chill?" Bliss offered as he sat down at his desk. Both men shook their heads no. Davison leaned against the wall, waiting.

"Jim, I need your advice on this," the man called Roy said slowly. "It's mighty strange, but it concerns you."

"Me?" the judge's eyebrows raised.

"You and Mr. Davison over there," Roy replied. "On Monday of this week, we arrested a vagrant. He was in the dock area, sleeping off a lot of booze in the hold of a merchant ship. His name is Cyrus Rafferty." He paused. "That name mean anything to you?" The judge shook his head. "How about you, Mr. Davison? Name ring a bell with you?"

"No," Davison said after a moment of thinking, "don't believe I'm acquainted."

"Well," Roy continued, "after we got him into the jail and checked up on him, we found that he had been arrested in many places around the province and had been *in* jail more than out of them. Usually for drunkenness and vagrancy. We would have kept him a day or two and put him back on the street if it had not been for something he confessed as we were sobering him up."

"Confessed?" the judge repeated the word.

"Yes. It seems that he was up here, in Amherst, the beginning of last month and working with some scalawags who were smuggling tobacco and cigars into the province. The boats, he says, came up from the States into Fundy Bay and unloaded their stuff on that deserted point where Chignecto and Shepody bays divide. You know the place I mean?"

The judge and Davison said they did.

"Ah-hah. Well, from there this character, Rafferty, took the smuggled goods by horsecart and delivered them to a farmer in Amherst."

"In Amherst?" Davison was interested.

"Yes. Here in Amherst. The contraband was stored in the farmer's barn until another man took it out and sold it, distributed it, across Nova Scotia and New Brunswick. He even has contacts in Prince Edward Island, Rafferty says."

"So you want us to find where the goods are being stored and arrest these two men?" Judge Bliss always enjoyed a cops-and-robbers story.

"No, that won't be necessary. You see this man, Rafferty, after he had filled the man's hayloft with the smuggled stuff, opened one bottle of booze too many and fell asleep. Unfortunately for us, he fell asleep with one of those contraband cigars in his hand. A lighted cigar. That cigar set fire to the hayloft and the barn burned down. Destroying, of course, all the evidence." Roy looked at both the Amherst men.

"So?" the judge finally said after a long moment of silence on the part of his visitors. "So what?"

"We haven't had a barn burn down here," said Davison, "in a long time. The last one," and he laughed a little, "the last barn to burn down was *my* barn. But none other that I can think of. Not recently."

Both Roy and the officer stared at him.

Judge Bliss again broke the silence. "That's the only barn I can think of, too. Davison's barn."

Roy kept his gaze on the face of his friend Jim Bliss. "That's the barn that Rafferty said he burned."

A team of oxen could have been driven through the silence.

Davison finally was able to move his jaw. "That's impossible! He didn't burn down that barn! We know who did it. It was a demented girl from right here in Amherst. We have her in jail now!"

"Rafferty says he did it. He also says the name of the farmer who owned the barn was Davison."

The clerk of court wished he had been sitting down instead of leaning against the wall. "That's . . . that's impossible!" he repeated. "I don't know anyone named Rafferty!" His face grew redder. "I'm not in the business of smuggling!"

"Who better to handle it," said the police officer, "than someone working right inside the courthouse."

Davison now sought out an empty chair and sat in it. "Well, now," said the judge, "that is the biggest load of horse droppings I've heard in years! Arthur isn't a smuggler! He doesn't know anything about contraband! That sailor is a liar!"

"Are you sure?" said Roy.

"Of course I'm sure. Arthur Davison is my friend. I know all about him. Why, we've worked together for years."

"Interesting," said the policeman, "that's what Rafferty said."

Judge Bliss looked sharply at the man. "What do you mean?"

"Rafferty said you and Davison worked together. Davison used his barn to store the goods, and you used your contacts to sell it."

"Me?" The judge jumped up from his chair. "Me? That drunken stumblebum implicated *me*? He's . . . he's crazy! I'm . . . I'm the judge around here! I'm not some kind of criminal!"

Roy and the police officer sat and stared at both of them. Nobody said a word. The judge seemed to deflate, sinking back down into his chair. Suddenly the desk seemed awfully large for such a small man.

"Davison . . ." the judge said, "if you've been . . . and if you've implicated me . . . in your schemes . . ."

"My schemes! What in Hell are you talking about? I don't know anything about these charges! I haven't done anything wrong!" He stared at Bliss. A light seemed to go on behind his eyes. "Unless you . . . yeah, unless you have been bringing stuff in and have been telling people it's me—"

"Don't be an ass, man!" the judge shouted. "I'm not involved in this! I can't get involved in your outside dealings!"

"*My* outside dealings!" Davison shouted at him. "Now they're *mine*! Things heat up and the blame is dumped on me! Well, I won't have it! I won't sit here and be called a smuggler! You can be," he shouted in the judge's face, "you can be called a crook! Lots of people have been calling you that for years!" He stomped out of the room, slamming the door behind him.

"These are preposterous charges," the judge finally said. He pretended to straighten some of the papers on his desk. He looked up. "You have no proof."

"No," agreed Roy, "we have no proof. It's the ravings of a drunk against your word. Yours and Davison's."

Judge Bliss tried to stand up, but his knees were too weak. "What if this story . . . this drunkard's ridiculous story . . . gets out? What'll it do . . . I mean . . . do to me and my reputation as a . . . judge, I mean?" His gaze went from one to the other. "Who else knows about this? I mean . . . newspaper people? Who else?"

"Of course no one else knows about this," Roy answered. "Rafferty has no *proof* of what he's saying."

"Of course he doesn't." The judge relaxed a bit. "He has no proof at all that what he's telling is the truth."

"But you, on the other hand," Roy added, "have no proof at all that what he says *isn't* true." He paused to let this sink in. "It's your word against his."

"The man's a liar," the judge said loudly, "and a story like this could kill me!"

"That's true," Roy agreed, "it could kill you."

"But you're sure," the judge spoke quickly, "you're positive nobody else knows about this? Nobody from around here?"

"Well," said the officer, "there was one man from Amherst who was in the station when Rafferty made his confession. He just happened to be in there, on another matter, when Rafferty started to talk. You know how thin those partitions are, people can hear anything being said. In fact, this man told me he was acquainted with both you and your clerk and that he wasn't the least bit surprised at the allegations."

"From Amherst?" the judge's voice rose. "Who was he? Did you get his name?"

The officer reached for a note pad in his breast pocket. "I wrote it down at the time, just in case we needed to call him to testify on what he heard in the station." He thumbed through several pages. "Here it is. Unusual name. Van Amburgh. A Mr. John Van Amburgh."

* * *

Ruth came away from the front door and stood at the entrance of the parlor. "Mr. Van Amburgh," she said, "you have visitors. Two gentlemen visitors."

"Have them come in," the old sailor said.

After pounding their feet on the porch mat and apologizing for carrying snow into her house, they followed Ruth into the parlor.

"Afternoon, sir," Judge Bliss said softly.

"Yes, afternoon," Davison said just as meekly.

"Come in, gentlemen, come in. Nasty day for a ride in the country, isn't it?" He motioned them to the sofa. "Have something to drink? Some brandy, perhaps?"

Neither man sat. They stood there in their coats and mittens like schoolboys. "No, thank you, sir," the judge said. "We can't stay too long. County business never seems to let up, don't you know." He laughed dryly.

"I don't know how you two do it," Van Amburgh said as he poured himself a full glass of brandy, "all that work, all that concern about the community and the welfare of the people. Takes dedication. It surely does. Dedication and honesty. Honesty, so very important. Don't know how you do it." He raised his glass. "To your health," and he took a giant swig.

"Mr. Van Amburgh," the judge started, "we are here on a delicate matter. This morning, two representatives from the Halifax police department visited my office."

"Halifax? Police? Now, isn't that a coincidence. I was down there and in that very police station just this week." He took another swig.

"We heard," Judge Bliss tried to smile. "We also heard that you heard . . . or rather *overheard* an insane story being told by a drunken reprobate . . . that referred to Mr. Davison and myself."

"True," the old man replied. "Fascinating material it was, too."

"Of course, it's all a lie," Davison spoke up.

"Of course, I don't know that," Van Amburgh replied.

"The man has no proof." This from Judge Bliss.

"It's only hearsay." This from Davison.

"If it came to a court of law—" said the judge.

"If it came to a court of law, sir," Van Amburgh said, "*your* court of law, whether it was 'proof' or not would be immaterial."

"I don't follow you," the judge said.

"Well, sir, take what happened to me. I was accused of helping Esther Cox steal some of Davison's valuables. There was no proof that I helped her. Hell, there wasn't any proof that she stole them. Yet I got locked up overnight, had my face busted by one of your uniformed monkeys, and Esther, poor child, got sentenced to a month in the hoosegow. And with no *proof*!" He looked each of them in the face. "I can understand how you both must feel to be falsely accused of something you didn't do, but I wouldn't depend on lack of 'proof' to get you out of it. No, no," he said with a laugh, "not around here, anyway."

While Davison looked down at the floor, Judge Bliss said, "I probably was too quick in my assumption against you, sir. And for that I apologize. I did let you go, a free man. Remember?"

"Uh-huh, and I also remember having to spend a night in jail. And I remember the bruise I had on the side of my face because of it. Oh, yes, I remember."

"My husband has an excellent memory," Ruth said with a smile.

"I probably was harsher with you than I should have been," the judge declared. "I'm sorry."

"And about Esther?" Van Amburgh asked. "Are you sorry about her, too?"

"She burnt down my barn!" Davison said quickly.

"And you have 'proof'? Your precious 'proof'?" the old man asked. "I don't think you do. In fact, I know you don't. That girl is still in the clink because of hearsay. Hearsay can be very dangerous, gentlemen. Very." He poured himself another stiff shot of brandy.

"I think she got what she deserved," Davison said.

"Not according to Mr. Rafferty," Van Amburgh replied. "He's got a whole different story. Oh, sure," he said with a grin, "call it hearsay if you wish, but once it spreads around town, other good souls will have to make up their minds. Perhaps then, Mr. Davison, folks will think that you and the judge should get what *you* deserve. Two officials of the county court? Smuggling? Using your exalted positions to avoid paying Her Majesty's import taxes? I can just hear them." To his wife: "Can't you just hear them, my dear? All those pious taxpayers discussing hearsay about the judge and his top clerk? My, my. How the church halls will buzz with that one!" He grinned. "Gentlemen, are you positive you wouldn't like a drink?"

"Mr. Van Amburgh, sir," the judge said, stammering, "you're the only person in Amherst who knows this story. Certainly you wouldn't—"

"Oh, yes, sir, I would! Believe me, I would and with the greatest of pleasure. After all, I wouldn't be spreading hearsay, I'd be spreading the *truth* about what I heard in Halifax. Hearsay is one thing, but the truth is the truth. Can't change it. No, gentlemen, you can't change the truth. No matter how bad you want to." He walked to the parlor door. "Now if you'll both excuse me, I have to go into town."

Judge Bliss hurried over to him, putting his hand on Van Amburgh's shoulder. "What . . ." he said with a sigh, ". . . what can I do for you?"

The old man had a blank look on his face. "I don't understand. What is it you're trying to say?"

Judge Bliss took a deep breath. "Just this. What can I and Mr. Davison do for you?" Van Amburgh shrugged. "Do for you so you will *forget* the story of what you heard as 'truth' down in Halifax?"

"Well, Judge, coming from anybody else, I would say that sounded a lot like a bribe. But I know you and I know you are a man of integrity and you would never try to bribe an honest citizen."

"What do you *want*, man?" the judge was getting red in the face.

Van Amburgh took two steps forward and the judge took two steps backward, almost falling over Davison, who had been following right behind him. "What do I want?" he said loudly. "Just one thing: I want Esther Cox released from jail, and I want it done today! This afternoon! She has been illegally locked up because of *hearsay*. She must be released. This is supposed to be a democratic government. And if Esther can be thrown in jail because of hearsay, then so can you! So can *you*, your honorable sir! She's already served one month for a theft she didn't commit, and I'll be damned if I'll sit back and watch her serve another three months for a barn-burning she didn't do!" He stomped to the front door and held it open. "Now get your honorable asses out of here and get them back to town. I'll be at that jail in one hour and Esther had better be free to leave with me. If not, there's going to be *hearsay* piled in the gutters of this one-horse town!"

* * *

She linked her arm with his, pulling herself closer yet not interfering with his driving of the horse and sleigh. With her all bundled up in scarves and sweaters and coats it was difficult to see her face, but there was a light coming from it, a glow of surprise and happiness.

It had all happened so fast. One minute she was stitching up the rips in the quilt over the jail window and the next she was being hustled out of the cell by Judge Bliss himself. While the guard and Mr. Davison packed her belongings, the judge let her use the hot water, soap, and towel in his private washroom. He didn't say much, but it seemed that everyone was more than anxious to have her out of there.

Then the Van Amburghs came into the courthouse and Adam came in just a few minutes later. After the hugging and the crying, the Van Amburghs had loaded her things into their sleigh, had promised to stop by and tell Olive that Esther was free and where she had gone. She was then put into Adam's sleigh and was now sitting very close to him while the horse headed north, out of town.

She listened to the story he told her. There was a drunk named Rafferty in Halifax and because of him, she had been released from jail in Amherst. "I don't follow this," she said. "This man set fire to Mr. Davison's barn because he was asleep?"

"Drunk."

"Drunk, then, and he put smuggled cigars and tobacco up there?" She looked at the man beside her. "Mr. Davison used it as a receiving point for illegal merchandise?"

"That's what the man said."

"And Judge Bliss was selling this merchandise and he and Mr. Davison were making illegal money on it?" He nodded. She shook her head. "I've been up in that hayloft dozens of times. I used to take the children up there to bounce and jump in the hay. There never were any cigars up there! I don't believe that man. And I don't believe Mr. Davison would do such a thing. I never saw Judge Bliss at Mr. Davison's all the time I worked there. Not once. Adam, that man in the Halifax jail is a liar."

Adam smiled. "I know."

"You know?" She was shocked. "What do you mean by that?"

"Easy. It was old man Van Amburgh's plan," he laughed, "and it worked, too!"

She waited as the horse hurried on up the road. "Well," she said after a minute had gone by, "aren't you going to tell me?"

"Can you keep a secret?" he grinned at her.

"Adam Porter, are you going to tell me or not?" she demanded.

"Well, Van Amburgh decided he had to get you out of jail and he had to get back at Davison and Bliss at the same time. He knew that if he kicked them right where they would feel it worst—in their reputations—they'd do as he wanted; they'd let you go. So he went down to Halifax and looked up his old friend Cyrus Rafferty."

"His old *friend*?"

"Van Amburgh and Rafferty were seadogs together on many a voyage. Van Amburgh retired to Amherst, but Rafferty just kept bouncing around, with no money and getting into trouble. Van Amburgh went down there and convinced him to pretend he was drunk and make a fuss so they'd arrest him for trespassing and drunkenness." He laughed and it echoed across the frozen afternoon air. "Van Amburgh watched them arrest his pal and then hurried to the police station and pretended to be there for something else when they brought Rafferty in. The man acted like a drunk and when he saw Van Amburgh he began to loudly confess about the barn-burning. All the officers heard it, and Van Amburgh offered information that he knew Davison and Bliss and he wasn't at all surprised that they were crooks. The cops put Rafferty in jail, and Van Amburgh came on home. I didn't think it would work when he first told me about it, but it did. Damn! I wish I could have been there when those Halifax policemen came calling on the judge and Davison." Again the loud masculine laugh could be heard above the bells on the horse's reins. "Van Amburgh told me that they practically got down on their knees and begged him not to tell anyone in Amherst about it."

"Why . . ." Esther was speechless. "I think that's terrible! Two innocent men charged with something they didn't do. And you and Mr. Van Amburgh put yourself up to do it! Now what? The judge and Mr. Davison will go to jail? Because of *your* joke?"

"Wait a minute," he said quickly. "Hold on, we did this for you. Remember?"

"Well, I think it's a disgrace. Those men aren't smugglers. They shouldn't be punished."

"You're not a thief, either," he said, "nor did you burn down that barn. But you got punished for it."

She thought a moment. "Yes, I did, didn't I? But will they be put in jail?"

"I doubt it. It's their word against Rafferty's. Their standing in the community against Rafferty's. Someone would have to bring formal charges against them for there to even be a hearing let alone a jail sentence. No, Cumberland County has already found *you* guilty of burning down that barn. They won't open the case again, not on the word of a drunken bum against two respected citizens. You'll not hear another thing about it, ever."

She was silent again, but just for a bit. "Well, why would this Mr. Rafferty admit to doing something he didn't do? He doesn't know *me*. I mean nothing to him."

"That's true," Adam replied, letting the reins rest easily in his gloved hands, "he didn't do it for you. He did it for his old mate Van Amburgh and because the Halifax jail is one of the most comfortable in the whole province. The sheriff makes sure it's kept clean, that it's warm, and that the food's good. He's very proud of conditions in his jail. It's not like that awful place where they had you. So, of course, Rafferty was delighted to admit to doing something that would keep him warm and well fed for the rest of the winter. He knows everyone who works in the jail. He told Van Amburgh it would be nice to have Christmas surrounded by old friends."

She stared at him. "That Van Amburgh!" She sighed, then

started to grin. "What an old fox he is!" Then she laughed. "Thinking that up just so I could get out of jail."

"And also so his friend could get *into* jail," Adam grinned. He shifted the reins to his left hand and put his right arm around her. "I'm glad the old rascal is on our side," he said and kissed her lightly on the lips.

They rode without talking for the next few miles. Esther decided she didn't need any words. She needed the silence and the contentment and the promises. Those were all she wanted, and she had them. Her world was almost complete.

The sun had started toward the horizon by the time they came into view of the shacks. There were about a dozen of them, round on top and room size, made of bent saplings, mud, animal hides, newspaper, and tar. The horse turned off the road and bounced them along a side road—a path, actually—toward the cluster of dwellings. She could see smoke, a single strand of grey smoke, coming up and out the top of each hut. He hadn't told her they were coming here, yet she wasn't surprised. She reached up and felt for the magic stone around her throat. It was still there.

Adam turned the sleigh inward, running it now along the first row of huts. Esther's eyes darted from the view of the ice-blocked stretch of ocean to the faces that looked out from behind the hide doorflaps of the shacks. The ringing of the sleigh bells brought out a pack of dogs that barked and snapped and protested these strangers in their midst. Adam and the horse ignored them.

He pulled up in front of the last hut, the farthest one from the roadway. It wasn't round, like the others, but oval. Esther thought it looked like a loaf of bread. Adam didn't get down, just sat there and waited. Soon a young boy, an Indian boy wearing heavy winter clothes that had once belonged to white men, came out of the hut and said something to Adam that Esther didn't understand. Then he went back inside.

"It's okay," Adam said to her with a smile. "We can go in now."

She put out her hand, halting his descent for a moment. "Adam, what is this? What are we doing here?"

"We're going to get you taken care of," he said. "It'll be all right." He winked and jumped to the ground. "You'll see. Come on. Get down." He held out his arms and she slid across the seat and out into them. He kissed her again before he released her. "One thing I want you to know—to remember—I love you. No matter what happens in there, always remember that I love you and I'm with you. That's very important." She nodded. "We're going to be together for a long time after this is over. I want you to understand it's being done for both of us. Not just for you alone." She started to reply, to form a question, but he put his finger to her lips. "Don't ask. Just trust me. Promise?" She nodded. "Okay"—he exhaled deeply—"let's go in."

She brushed past the fur covering the doorway and stood erect on the inside. She didn't know what she had expected, but it was not this. The first thing she saw was a bonfire in the center of the room. It spread out about three feet, and the flames rose six feet toward the roof. The smoke from this blaze disappeared out a large opening that let in the sky. There were seashells around the fire, rimming the blaze as if to contain it. There was another row of seashells some ten feet from this first row and laid in an undulating, imperfect circle. They were like reflectors as they threw back the colors of the bonfire. Between these two borders of shells, on the hard, earthen floor, strange lines, designs, and symbols had been sketched out in what she guessed was yellow cornmeal. She thought one of them looked like an eye and another could have been a flying bird, yet not really like an eye or a bird.

She jumped as out of the shadows at one end of the hut a man appeared. He came closer, looking at her, examining her as he walked. She saw he was also an Indian, probably in his fifties or about, and wearing baggy woolen pants, at least three different sweaters that she could see, and soft moccasins. His long black and grey-flecked hair was twisted into two tight braids that hung down over his chest. She stared at the red stones that held the braids in place. They were almost like the red stone she was wearing.

"Tul Nac," Adam said, "this is Esther. This is the girl I was telling you about."

"Hmmm," the man muttered. He walked around her, taking in her size and her shape. "Take off the coats. You inside now."

Esther glanced at Adam, he nodded. She started removing her gloves, her heavy coat, and her woolen dress jacket. The Indian saw the stone was still there. He touched it and smiled. "Did you give me this?" she asked him. "Thank you."

"Not for thanks," he said. He walked to a packing crate that was standing on end near the wall and came back with a small bowl. He dipped his fingers into it and then drew a line across her face. She glanced at the purple stuff in the bowl and hoped it came off with soap and water. Then he drew another line from her forehead down to her chin. There was the taste of berries and rum as it passed her lips. "The hands," he said. She held them up and he drew a circle on the top of each hand, turned them over, and drew a couple of wavy lines in her palms. Then he put his hand gently but firmly in the small of her back and pushed her toward the fire and the outer circle of seashells. She stepped carefully over the line and tried to stand where she wouldn't smear any of the cornmeal drawings.

The medicine man walked back into the shadows, then returned with a large bowl of dried leaves and twigs. He took a fistful of them and passed them in the air around Esther, then threw them into the bonfire. There was a muffled explosion and the air was filled with an overpowering sweet perfume. Then he walked back into the shadows. She glanced at Adam. He was standing where she had left him, his hat in his hand. She smiled and shrugged. He just looked at her. The Indian returned; his sweaters were gone. His upper body was bare except for several necklaces around his neck. Some were of tiny shells, others were stones. One was made from bear teeth, another from chicken bones. In the center of them all hung a large red polished stone; she saw at a glance that it was exactly like hers. He drew out another handful of the dried herbs and after passing them around her, tossed them, too, onto the fire. Again the hut was filled with the sweet incense smell.

The boy who had welcomed them to the hut now came out of the far corner and sat cross-legged near the outer circle of shells. He carried a small round drum, and getting the signal from the man, began rapping a regular beat on the stretched top.

From behind a roof pole the man took a brown glass bottle. It looked like a whiskey bottle to Esther. He began a low chant, his voice droning to the beat of the drum. At first she strained to catch the words but soon realized he wasn't speaking English. It must be Micmac language, she thought, or whatever these Indians spoke. He shuffled his feet, still outside the rim of shells, sometimes turning, sometimes leaning, but always chanting in time with the monotonous drumbeat. He lifted the bottle to his lips and took a full swig. Then he leaned across the circle, right in front of Esther, and spat the liquid straight into her face.

"Adam!" she cried in surprise and indignation. Adam didn't move.

The man did another shuffle, took another swig, and again spat full in her face. This time she saw it coming and closed her eyes. "Ta!" he shouted and poked her sharply on the shoulder with his pointing finger. She almost lost her balance. "Ta!" Again the finger shoved at her, hurting her other shoulder. "Ta!" Back again to the first shoulder. "Ta!" the finger hurtfully drove into her other shoulder.

"Now, just a minute!" she yelled. "Adam!"

"Ah! Ah! Ah! Ah!" Four times he shouted and four times his fists hit her chest. She cried out, felt her feet beginning to wobble under her. She stepped onto one of the designs, smearing the outlines of the cornmeal symbol. Suddenly he grabbed both her hands and began jumping up and down. She, startled, tried to follow this new movement as he began to jog around her in tiny steps. She had to twist her body to keep up with him. At that moment he grabbed her hair, took a handful of it, and dragged her down onto her knees. She felt herself falling, felt the crunch of the cornmeal even through the material of her full skirt. He jumped in front of her, pulling her forward by her hair. Then he shouted something and jumped behind her, pulling her backward by her hair. She started to cry out, but he grabbed her head in both hands and pushed her across the width of the circle of the bonfire. She could feel the heat of the flames against her skin, could smell the scorch of the hair that had gotten too close. She tried twisting away from him. What was this madman trying to do? Why didn't Adam stop him? What kind of nonsense was she enduring? Hadn't she been through enough?

He grabbed the stone around her neck with his left hand. In his right, he held the other stone that was hanging around his own neck. He shouted something long and commanding; then he touched the two stones face to face.

Esther screamed and tried to rise. The pain tore through her body, twisting her fingers and doubling her over. She felt a terrible bitter fluid rise up inside her, burn up her chest and into the back of her throat. She wanted to gag, to throw up as this thick, foul stuff began to fill her mouth. The Indian twisted her jaw, forced her to open her lips. With a deep retching sound she began to spit out, to vomit out, this slimy, sea-green ooze that was welling up from inside her. She tasted the bitterness of it, felt the particles, clots and lumps of it, sensed its burning as it tumbled out of her mouth and ran down her chin. She opened her eyes and saw the stinking slime spilling thickly onto the cornmeal, watched in horror as it bubbled and fought against being absorbed by the meal and the earth of the floor. It kept oozing out of her, kept rising up from someplace so deep, someplace so dark and hidden that she never suspected it existed. Now her hands were in it; she could see the chunks and pieces flow up over her outstretched fingers. The skin on her hands burned as this stuff, almost a bucketful of green horror, slopped out of her mouth, down her chin, and onto the floor. She wanted to cry out, to call for Adam, to plead with him to help her, but her tongue wouldn't move under the weight of this vomit. Her vocal cords, thickly covered with the slime, refused even her most simple command to scream.

The Indian was beside her again, pulling her by her hair, twisting her around to face the flames. She kept up the steady flow of green vomit, and her dress was smeared in it as she was yanked through it.

He held her face close to the flames again. "You want her?" he cried in English. "Tell me. You want her?"

The voice came from her body, came up amid the slime and the stench, a rough, masculine voice: "You son-of-a-bitch! This girl is mine!"

"She not yours!" the man shouted.

"She is *mine*, you bastard! Leave her alone!"

"*You* leave!" the medicine man shouted. "You leave and you leave now!"

"Get out of my way!" the harsh voice gushed from Esther's throat. She whirled around, hands and knees sliding in the green thick liquid on the ground. She lunged for the man's leg. She caught it, pulled him off balance, and then jumped on top of him as he landed on his back. "You red son-of-a-bitch!" the voice yelled. Her hands, now clenched into fists, came down again and again on the medicine man's head.

"No!" Adam shouted and he jumped over the ring of seashells and grabbed Esther around the waist. He tried to tear her away from the man on the ground, but his feet kept slipping in the green vomit that squished under his shoes.

"Don't you touch her, you bastard!" The voice boomed out and she flailed out her arms, sending Adam sprawling.

The medicine man, blood trickling from the corner of his eye, scrambled to his feet. "You leave now!" he demanded.

"She's mine!" the voice screamed. "She's always been mine!"

Adam staggered to his feet, rushed at Esther, and still slipping in the slime, pulled her to the ground. "She is mine now!" Adam shouted. "She is mine and *I* claim her!"

"No!" the man's voice screamed. "Mine! Mine and Bob McNeal's!"

"Bob McNeal is dead!" Adam yelled. "He's dead! Dead and buried! He has no need for you anymore!"

"No! You're lying! This is for Bob!"

"There is no more Bob McNeal! I have taken his place. I have life and he is dead."

"He is not!" the voice broke.

"Dead! Dead! He is Dead!" the medicine man chanted. The boy on the drums began beating it again. "Dead! Dead! Dead!

"No!" The voice was weaker now. "I don't believe you!"

"Then go," said Adam, "go and see for yourself. He is dead, and his body has been buried. He has no need for you."

"No need for you anymore," the Indian added. "You have no worth now."

Esther's body went limp in Adam's grasp. "I don't believe you!" the masculine voice faltered. "I don't believe you."

"Then go," said the Indian. "Go see for yourself."

"I don't believe you." The voice was fainter. "Doing this for him. Don't believe you."

Adam picked up Esther in his arms; both of them were covered in the now-drying green vomit. "Go see for yourself," Adam said. "Go and leave *my* girl alone!"

Esther opened her eyes and looked into Adam's face. "No," she said in another voice, a feminine voice that was not her own, "Bob's not dead."

"Yes," Adam answered, "he is."

The girl inside gave one loud, high-pitched scream, and Esther fell unconscious. Adam carried her to a cot the medicine man had prepared before they had arrived. The

Indian motioned Adam to sit beside her. Then the Indian started to chant again, walking slowly around the cot, sprinkling a layer of salt around them, enclosing both of them in a blessing, the age-old blessing of pure white energy and protection.

* * *

Bob McNeal walked up the two flights of stairs and turned the skeleton key. He opened the door to the furnished room he had been living in for over a year. He struck a match and lit the oil lamp on the dresser. The room had only one window, and even in the summer he had to light the lamp when he came home from work. He hung his heavy coat and muffler on a door peg and unbuttoned his blue work shirt, pulling it off his sweating body. He sniffed at the shirt. It stank of armpits, but if he hung it up and opened the window a little, he'd be able to wear it tomorrow. He would probably have to wash it before the week was out.

He sat on the edge of the bed and untied his ankle-high boots. He watched his fingers pulling at the laces. They were dirty fingers, with grease imbedded in the wrinkles and impacted under the nails. Repairing ship engines was a dirty job. The parts were thick with grease and oil. They had to be soaked and scrubbed, then reassembled and then greased again. It was a helluva job, but it was the first one he got when he came to St. John, and it paid better than making shoes in Amherst.

He tossed his boots against the wall. He stood up and unbuttoned the fly of his work pants. They were filthy, too. It didn't do any good even to try to keep them clean. Nobody cared, anyway. He was just one more pair of hands in the shipyard.

He still had some water in the pitcher near the bed. It was yesterday's water, but at least he didn't have to walk down two flights into the freezing backyard and use the pump.

He poured some of the water into the grime-edged bowl and cupping his hands, brought up enough to smear across his face. He rubbed the warmish water into his skin, reached for the stained towel on the wall nail, and as he dried his face, he heard it.

Bam!

He stopped. The towel to his face, his breath cut off in his lungs.

Bam!

He shook his head. He didn't really hear that.

Bam! The pounding came from the wall right beside the washstand. Bam! There it was again. This time it rattled the pitcher against the basin.

He backed away. "No," he said aloud. "No."

Bam! The pounding was alongside him now. He reached for his shirt, in a hurry to put it back on, but the sensation was there. Already there on his bare chest. The fingers. The caressing, invisible fingers. The hand went down and tugged lightly at the wisps of hair that appeared above the line of his short B.V.D.'s. He tried to pull the hand away, but he knew it was no use.

"No!" he shouted and struck out wildly with both arms. "I don't want you! I don't want you back again!"

Bam! This time his lunch pail skittered across the room. He stood and watched it in dismay.

There was a rustling sound at the window and he saw the blind pull itself down and then snap suddenly back up, rolling and flapping noisily at the top. "Please," he said, "go away. I don't want you back."

The fingers moved along one side of his face; he twisted to get away from them and fell against the dresser. The oil lamp jiggled and fell over. He lunged for it but instead of catching it he knocked it sideways and it broke against the leg of the dresser. He jumped back as the flame from the wick fell into the pool of oil and blazed into life.

He staggered backward, brushing at the hands that were moving all over his body. He fell onto the bed.

Bam! The pounding was on the wall.

He tried to get off the bed, to make his legs get over to the door.

Bam! The pounding was on the ceiling.

"Please!" he cried. "I'm sorry! I'm sorry!"

Bam!

That was the noise other tenants said they heard above his screams. Everyone remarked on how the lamp had broken near the dresser but how only the bed was charred. Only the bed and the body of the young man who lived by himself on the second floor.

Epilogue

Things calmed down in Amherst after Esther's exorcism. Nobody knew why. Only a few people ever heard the ending to the story. In fact, the *Moncton Daily Times* of December 12, 1879, wondered in print:

"Esther Cox is out of jail now. The mystery this time is how she got out before her term of imprisonment."

None of the local newspapers ever published the true story of her release from jail and the ceremony with the Micmac medicine man.

Daniel and Olive Teed remained in Amherst for many years afterward but *not* in the house on Princess Street. Their baby, George, died suddenly after Esther left, but Olive had four more children—all girls. Willie, her first son, grew to manhood in Amherst and has descendents living in Nova Scotia today.

Jennie Cox corresponded with Walter Hubbell for a while until she met and married a man who took her to live in the United States. Nothing is known of her after that.

Dr. Carritte continued his practice in Amherst. He never really understood what had happened to Esther yet never denied what he had seen. In a letter just two years before his death, to a professor in Philadelphia, he wrote: "Honestly skeptical persons were on all occasions soon convinced that there was no fraud or deception in the case. Were I to publish the case in the medical journals, as you suggest, I doubt if it would be believed by physicians generally. I am certain I could not have believed such apparent miracles had I not witnessed them." In 1885 he died suddenly, while on a visit to Virginia. He was fifty-five years old.

John and Ruth Van Amburgh, never popular with the locals and vice versa, moved away from Amherst. Their names were not in the 1881 census.

Arthur Davison became a prosperous merchant. His business card read: "Arthur Davison (Successor to R. B. Huestis & Co.) Dealer in Dry Goods, Groceries, Boots and Shoes, Flour & Meal. Victoria Street, Amherst, N.S." His son, R.B.H. Davison, later became high sheriff of Amherst. The story about Rafferty and the smuggling was never told.

Judge Bliss remained a prominent figure in local politics and society. He moved into the Princess Street house after Daniel moved out. Judge Bliss died there in about 1893. His stepson, Robert Davis, inherited it and sold it. Princess Street deteriorated and became an area of run-down boardinghouses and garages. One day all the tumbledown houses were torn down. The space where the "haunted house" sat was empty for a while. Now it is the site of a two-story brick and glass box that is club headquarters for the Royal Canadian Legion, Branch No. 10.

Walter Hubbell never saw Esther again after that final visit on August 1, 1879. He did correspond with Olive and Jennie for a while. He published his book, *The Great Amherst Mystery*, a slim volume financed out of his own pocket, in 1879. In 1888, it was enlarged with new material and published by Brentano's of New York. In 1916, a tenth edition came out (also enlarged), and the publisher proudly claimed it had sold fifty-five thousand copies. The writer part of him went on to publish a book of poetry titled *Marcus Brutus and Other Verses*, another poetry book titled *Midnight Madness*, and a novel, *The Curse of Marriage*. The actor part of him kept him on the road most of his long life, doing *Macbeth* and *Hamlet* in the West, *Othello* and *Richard III* in Chicago. He blew his own genealogical horn in a self-published book called *History of the Hubbell Family*. He died sometime before 1920, an old man and alone. He never gained the fame he so very much desired.

Esther married Adam Porter in a simple ceremony in Springhill, Nova Scotia. She had one son. Adam died suddenly, and Esther moved out of Canada down to the United States. There, outside of Boston, she met and married a man named

Shanahan. She had one son by him. She got a job with the city of Brockton, Mass. An investigator for the American Society for Psychical Research received this report, dated 1907, about her: "Esther Cox is a very hard-working woman, but respectable, honest and reliable. In fact, the department officials consider her as one of their very best workers. They tell me during the four years she has been known to them they have found her square in all her dealings with them and perfectly truthful. . . . They say they would not hesitate to take her word as to this old experience of hers, as she is not at all of an imaginative turn of mind, and would not be likely to make up any such thing. In regard to that experience, however, she could not be induced to say a word; said it was something she 'dared not talk about' . . ."

Apparently the demons—Bob Nickle and the rest—never returned. Esther did not keep in contact with the rest of her family or with anyone in Amherst. She died, in Brockton, on November 8, 1912. She was fifty-two years old. It's almost as if the citizens of Nova Scotia wanted to forget their strange ghost girl. When she died, not one newspaper published her obituary.

Bibliography

The following publications were consulted in preparation for this text:

Carrington, Hereward. *Personal Experiences in Spiritualism*. London: Society for Psychical Research, 1913.

Hubbell, Walter. *History of the Hubbell Family*. New York: self-published, 1915.

———. *The Great Amherst Mystery*. New York: self-published, 1879; New York: Brentano's, 1888, 1916; Amherst, N.S.: Babineau Printing, 1982.

Johnson, Raynor C. *The Imprisoned Splendor*. New York: Harper & Brothers, 1953.

Prince, Dr. Walter F. "A Critical Study of 'The Great Amherst Mystery,'" *Proceedings of the American Society for Psychical Research* (1920).

Toole, J. Lewis. "The Possession of Esther Cox," *Fate*, Vol. 5, No. 1 (1952).

Underwood, Peter. *Hauntings*. London: J.M. Dent & Sons, 1977.

Wilson, Colin. *The Occult*. New York: Random House, 1971.

In addition, back issues of The *Amherst Gazette*, The *Amherst Sentinel*, The *Chignecto Post*, the *Moncton Daily Times*, and the *Halifax Morning Herald* were consulted.

ABOUT THE AUTHOR

This is DAVID ST. CLAIR's tenth book, the seventh to deal with "the mysteries of the psychic and occult." Born in Ohio in 1932 he has lived around the world, wherever his writings have taken him. He was a correspondent for TIME & LIFE magazines for six years in Brazil where he saw firsthand "the reality behind this idea of ghosts and curses." His book on Brazilian spiritism, *Drum & Candle*, is required reading in university metaphysics classes. He is past president of The Southern California Society of Psychical Research in Los Angeles and a member of the Society for Psychical Research in London as well as psychic research groups in New York, Brazil, South Africa, and India. He often appears on television talk shows firmly defending that "there really is an unseen world of energy and entities out there around us."